Why Vote?

For nearly 200 years, Americans have pinned the democratic character of their system on elections. In many ways, we have become an election-crazed nation, ever-hoping that the next grand contest or the next great candidate will save the day. But tectonic shifts abound – changes that are distorting the nature of the process. From the rise of fear-centered partisanship, new limits on voter access to the polls, the omnipotence of social media, declining standards of objectivity, Russian interference, the reemergence of the partisan press, the growing weight of elites and more, elections – our "grand democratic feasts" – are transforming before our eyes. We've reached a precarious intersection, and it is no stretch to say the future of the republic is at stake.

Written by one of the nation's leading parties and elections scholars, *Why Vote? Essential Questions About the Future of Elections in America* explores a range of topics. Each chapter is set by a guiding question, and concludes with a novel, often surprising argument. Who or what is to blame for the rise of rabid, hate-centered polarization? Can a third party really save our system? Should we even try to limit money in campaigns? Do elections stifle other, more potent forms of engagement? Who's to blame for the growing number of voter access restrictions? Might attitudes toward immigration and race form a "unified theory" of voter coalitions?

This lively, accessible book is sure to inspire robust discussion and debate. The election process in the United States is coming apart at the seams, and *Why Vote?* tees up a new way of thinking about the future. This book will be of particular interest to students and scholars of US politics and elections, and to general interest readers.

Daniel M. Shea is Professor of Government at Colby College. He received an MA in Campaign Management from the University of West Florida in 1988, and a doctorate from the University at Albany, State University of New York in 1993. He has written or edited nearly 20 academic books including *New Party Politics* with John White in 2005 (St. Martin's Press), *Campaign Craft* with Mike Burton in 2011 and 2015 (Praeger), *The Fountain of Youth* with John Green in 2007 (Rowman and Littlefield), and *Let's Vote!* in 2013 (Pearson), among others. His most recent volume is an edited work with Stanford University scholar Morris Fiorina: *Can We Talk? The Rise of Rude, Nasty, Stubborn Politics* (2013, Pearson). He is also lead author of a widely used American Government text, *Living Democracy* (Pearson).

Praise for *Why Vote?*

Why Vote? is an impressive book, thoughtfully delivering on its promise to address essential questions about the future of elections in America – as well as to cover the present and past of American elections comprehensively. It is well written and lively; both students and their teachers will find it appealing.

Paul A. Beck, Academy Professor of Political Science,
The Ohio State University

Shea provides a provocative look at elections and whether they can be reformed to sustain democracy for future generations of American citizens. Offering no quick fix, he encourages students to face current challenges to the electoral process head on as they seek their own solutions.

J. Cherie Strachan, Central Michigan University

Shea has assembled a rich, thoughtful and accessible volume that uses both historical and social science perspectives to evaluate recent developments in the US electoral arena. The book is eye-opening and thought-provoking.

Costas Panagopoulos, Professor, Department of Political
Science; Director, Big Data and Quantitative Methods
Initiatives, Northeastern University

In this book, Dan Shea provides a critical and lively assessment of many challenges facing electoral democracy in the United States.

David Kimball, University of Missouri–St. Louis

Why Vote?
Essential Questions About the Future of Elections in America

Daniel M. Shea

Routledge
Taylor & Francis Group

NEW YORK AND LONDON

First published 2019
by Routledge
52 Vanderbilt Avenue, New York, NY 10017

and by Routledge
2 Park Square, Milton Park, Abingdon, Oxon, OX14 4RN

Routledge is an imprint of the Taylor & Francis Group, an informa business

© 2019 Taylor & Francis

The right of Daniel M. Shea to be identified as author of this work has been asserted by him in accordance with sections 77 and 78 of the Copyright, Designs and Patents Act 1988.

Library of Congress Cataloging-in-Publication Data
A catalog record for this title has been requested

ISBN: 9781138617896 (hbk)
ISBN: 9781138617926 (pbk)
ISBN: 9780429461446 (ebk)

Typeset in Sabon
by Newgen Publishing UK

This book is dedicated to Professor Dennis M. Shea (1933–2017), a lifelong student of electoral politics.

Contents

Acknowledgments

I am grateful for the help of several students at Colby College, including Jackson Ward, Jeff Endler, Kate Blauer and Carlo Macomber. Carlo, a budding scholar of American politics and already an expert on Maine, provided a great deal of assistance with research, citations and editing during the final push to complete the manuscript. His support was particularly significant on topics related to the media and the Russian interference in the 2016 election – so much so that he is appropriately listed as a co-author on that chapter.

One of the best parts of writing this book was again having the chance to work with Jennifer Knerr, at Routledge, the iconic editor of academic publishing. I dare say no other politics editor has a sharper sense for tone, content and market trends than Jennifer. She is thoughtful, frank, and as they say in Maine, wicked smart!

As always, I received tremendous support from family during the development of this volume. As I struggled with an appropriate ending, one afternoon my darling wife strolled into the office with a book she had found in a used book shop: Howard Fast's *Freedom Road*, first published in 1944. "I think you'll want to take a look at this." I spent the next several hours glued to the pages and of course she was right. Once again, Christine to the rescue!

Finally, this book is dedicated to my father, Dennis M. Shea, who passed away in the spring of 2017. Dad was a professor of political science at the State University of New York at Oneonta for nearly 40 years, helping generations of students better understand our system and cultivating a passion for politics. I have never known anyone with a keener sense of the nuances of our system or a sharper understanding of the subtle forces that drive American politics. He was my go-to interpreter, and how I long for another chat or handwritten note stapled to an article from *The Atlantic* or *New York Times*, replete with underlines and comments in the margins. It is telling, however, that with all his wisdom and knowledge of American politics, Dad was baffled by the ascent of Donald Trump. "You're on your own with this one, Dan."

1 The 2016 Election and Aftermath
Did Donald Trump Break the Mold?

Right from the start, Donald Trump made it clear that his candidacy would be different – very different. His announcement at Trump Tower in New York City drew a great deal of attention not because he was expected to do particularly well in the race for the 2016 Republican presidential nomination, but because he seemed a novelty act. Trump was a character and his entry into the race would add a wild turn; the media was attracted to him like moths to a flame.

A few years earlier, in the wake of Mitt Romney's defeat to Barack Obama, the Republican National Committee produced a post-mortem analysis. Among much else, the report, dubbed the "Growth and Opportunity Project," said that going forward the Republican Party should be known for its tolerance and respect, and that it should "ensure that the tone of the message is always reflective of these core principles." This was a not-so-subtle nod to changing demographics of the electorate and the party's interest in cultivating support among minority groups, particularly Hispanic Americans. Trump's announcement threw cold water on the goals of tolerance and respect, however. He told his audience and the television cameras, "When Mexico sends its people, they're not sending their best ... They're sending people that have lots of problems, and they're bringing those problems with us [sic]. They're bringing drugs. They're bringing crime. They're rapists. And some, I assume, are good people."

As the race progressed, Trump continued to shatter all manner of rules and norms of modern electoral politics. For instance, a widely read book from a decade earlier, *The Party Decides*, documented the importance of early endorsements in presidential nomination contests. The backing of prominent party leaders and officials during the "invisible primary" was thought to be one of the most important determinants of success. Early money was believed to be critical – which is probably why former Florida Governor Jeb Bush had raised an unprecedented sum by the summer of 2016, a whopping $114 million. But Trump had very few establishment backers and little early money.

Republicans, particularly those who turn out for primaries and caucuses, were thought to be "values voters." Numerous studies found that while a set of economic and foreign policy matters were important to this group, an array of social and cultural concerns was paramount. As noted in an article in *The Atlantic*, "[Conservatives] clung to the idea that character counts."[1] A 2011 poll by the Public Religion Research Institute found that only 30 percent of white evangelicals believed "an elected official who commits an immoral act in their personal life can still behave ethically and fulfill their duties in their public and professional life." Many Grand Old Party (GOP) voters focused their attention on the candidates' positions on abortion, in particular. But Trump did not fit this mold. His position on abortion was muddled; he was pro-choice a decade earlier. Many considered themselves faithful Christians, yet Trump was the most secular Republican candidate in generations. In an awkward attempt to reach out to Evangelicals, Trump traveled to Liberty University in January 2016, where he tried to drop a line from the Bible: "I hear this is a major theme right here, but Two Corinthians, that's the whole ballgame." (The accurate term is "Second Corinthians.") Above all, Republican primary voters zeroed in on character. Is the candidate virtuous, a good role model for children? Here again Trump did not fit the mold: he has been divorced twice, was known for a flamboyant, playboy lifestyle, and was unabashed about using all manner of profanity. Following a lackluster debate performance, Trump suggested that the moderator might have been tough on him because she was menstruating, and at a rally he mocked the physical disability of a *New York Times* reporter.

While perhaps not always policy experts, successful presidential candidates for both parties have always had a basic knowledge of key issues. Being unprepared or even slow to respond to major policy points can be fatal. Nevertheless, Trump's inability to answer even the simplest policy query was exceptional. Not only did he not seem to understand rudimentary concepts and important parts of history, he seemed unrepentant in his ignorance. His style and approach would be more important than policy nuances. After all, his opponent was the policy geek.

Ronald Reagan, the star of the GOP in the 1980s, had popularized the so-called Eleventh Commandment for the Republican Party: thou shall not speak ill of fellow Republicans. Although robust disagreements on policy were fine, GOP candidates should not attack each other. At the very least, they should refrain from personal assaults that might cause problems in the general election. Trump quickly cast that rule aside, too. A small selection of insults he directed at fellow Republicans includes the following: regarding Carly Fiorina, former Chief Executive of Hewlett-Packard, he said, "Look at that face! Would anyone vote for that? Can you imagine that, the face of our next president?!" He said of former President George W. Bush, "Say what you want, the World Trade Center came down during his time." On Senator John McCain of Arizona, Trump commented, "He's not a war hero. He was a war hero because he was captured. I like people who weren't captured," and regarding physician Ben Carson, "You don't cure these people. You don't cure a child molester ... Pathological, there's no cure for that." Trump also used pejorative nicknames for his opponents, dubbing Texas Senator Ted Cruz "Lyin' Ted" and former Florida Governor Jeb Bush "Low Energy Jeb."

To be fair, insults were lobbed in the other direction as well. Texas Governor Rick Perry said Trump was "unfit to be president ... [he is] a barking carnival act, a cancer on conservatism." Louisiana Governor Bobby Jindal suggested Trump was "dangerous, a narcissist and an egomaniac," and Kentucky Senator Rand Paul called him a "delusional narcissist and an orange-faced windbag." He added for good measure, "A speck of dirt is way more qualified to be president." South Carolina Senator Lindsey Graham is quoted as saying, "You know how you make America great again? Tell Donald Trump to go to hell." And former Florida Governor Jeb Bush commented, "He's a bully. Punch him back in the nose."

Trump campaigned like a bull in a china shop stung by a swarm of hornets. He raised and spent money in unconventional ways, broke all the rules about overexposure on radio and television, and blundered from one fatal gaffe to another. He spent less money than most of the top-tier candidates, rarely used polling, flip-flopped on one issue after the next, salted his speeches with vulgarities and recurrent grammatical mistakes, and lobbed offences at women, Hispanics, Muslims, Iowans, and many other groups of voters. He even insulted the looks of his opponents' wives!

It is difficult to recount all of the exceptional elements of Donald Trump's drive for the Republican nomination in one volume, let alone a few pages. Flatly stated, in the history of American elections, no candidate has decimated as many norms and codes of conduct as Donald Trump. Scholar Frank Mackaman, a lifelong student of American politics, called the GOP nomination "virtually unprecedented" and "you would have to go back to the Bull Moose (Progressive) Party, Teddy Roosevelt's splinter from the Republican Party in the early 20th century, to get something that resembles [the race]."[2]

On the Democratic side, most assumed Hillary Clinton was the heir apparent. She had narrowly lost to Barack Obama in 2008 and then served five years as his Secretary of State. After leaving that post, she had assembled a state-of-the-art campaign operation and raised a ton of money. It was her time and she was ready. Yes, there might be some nipping at the edges from insurgent candidates, probably from the far left, but it was Clinton's nomination for the taking – or so it was thought.

To most party leaders, scholars and pundits, Vermont Senator Bernie Sanders' candidacy represented a typical protest from the progressive wing of the party. After all, he was not even a Democrat, but rather a Democratic-Socialist, and he came from the most liberal state in the union. Like Trump, few prominent leaders or officials had endorsed Sanders and his coffers in the early stages were shallow. Like an irritating bug at a summer picnic, Sanders would be brushed away as the nomination season unfolded.

That did not happen. In Iowa, the first of the nomination contests, Sanders stunned the establishment by battling Clinton to a draw. He then swamped Clinton in New Hampshire, which was not a surprise because Vermont is next door, but on the night of the victory he made a plea to the public: "I'm going to hold a fundraiser right here, right now, across America." Sanders urged anyone who would listen to visit his website and make a donation, "whether it's ten bucks, or 20 bucks, or 50 bucks." Money poured in and by the end of the next day the campaign had collected a staggering $8 million.[3]

In the next contest, Nevada, Sanders narrowly lost (47% to 52%) and on Super Tuesday, a few weeks later, Clinton won the lion's share of contests (and delegates), but Sanders beat her in several states. Perhaps even more significantly, his crowds were massive and his war chest was bursting at the seams – nearly all of it coming from small contributions (a sign of popular support). By early March, Sanders had gathered over four million contributions, with an average donation of $27. He had become a force, a threat to Clinton's nomination, and would not be brushed away easily.

When all was said and done, Sanders netted about 44 percent of primary and caucus votes, with 23 wins to Clinton's 34 victories (the US territories and DC have nomination contests). He raised a whopping $228 million. Sanders endorsed Clinton at the Democratic National Convention in late July, but to many his backing seemed rather tacit, more of a call to defeat Trump at any cost than a full-throttled validation of his former rival.

To say that the general election was also unconventional would be one of the grand understatements of our day. Trump drew large and energetic crowds, but continued to push a novel policy agenda; elements of his platform were plucked from the playbook of die-hard conservatives, but other components were snatched from the populist wing of the Democratic Party. In one breath, for instance, he pledged to rid the nation of both the Affordable Care Act ("Obamacare") and the North American Free Trade Agreement (NAFTA). Most expected Trump to moderate his hard-line positions that seemed to propel him through the nomination process, like his insistence on building a wall along the Mexican border and banning the entrance of Muslims into the nation, but he never tacked to the middle. His early debate performances were weak, rife with flubs and generalities, but his rallies were massive and supporters exuberant. Their candidate would surely "make America great again."

In the middle of the general election campaign, on October 7, the *Washington Post* released an audio recording of a conversation between Trump and *Access Hollywood* reporter Billy Bush. Perhaps unaware the microphone was on (it's not clear), Trump said he might start kissing the woman they were about to meet. "I don't even wait. And when you're a star, they let you do it, you can do anything ... grab them by the pussy." It was a bombshell, what many, including the author of this book, deemed the unequivocal end to Trump's candidacy. No candidate could come back from such a blow. Trump apologized, claiming it to be mere "locker room talk," and quickly turned attention toward his Democratic opponent and her husband: "Bill Clinton has said far worse to me on the golf course," Trump argued. He pushed forward, seemingly unfazed. His poll numbers dropped a bit, but huge crowds continued to show up at his rallies. The race moved on.

It was also the most expensive general election race in history. The Clinton campaign had raised a staggering $1.4 billion and the Trump campaign had pulled in $958 million.[4] Spending by outside groups (units not officially affiliated with the candidates) also grew to historic levels. Whereas these groups spent about $900 million in 2012, in the Clinton–Trump contest it mushroomed to $1.4 billion.

True to form, Clinton was perfectly polished and prepared at the debates, but on the campaign trail she seemed to go through the motions. And why not – there was no way the American electorate would send Donald Trump to the White House. A vast preponderance of the polling confirmed that she was way ahead. From Labor Day on, not a single mainstream poll suggested Trump would win. A "poll of polls" conducted by *USA Today* had Clinton up by four points on the weekend prior to the election. It was tighter than most had expected, but Clinton's win seemed certain.

Neither candidate was well-liked; both had historically higher unfavorable ratings than favorable ones. Gallup reported that by the end of the race, Trump had a 62 percent unfavorable rating (35 percent favorable), while Clinton was not much better, with a 57 percent unfavorable rating (40 percent favorable).[5]

On election night, signs that Clinton was in trouble came early. Exit polling from several East Coast states suggested a tighter-than-expected race, and the actual returns from Florida and Pennsylvania – thought to be good states for Clinton – pointed to problems. There were hopes that she might even snatch North Carolina, but that evaporated quickly, and even Virginia was neck-and-neck. Soon Pennsylvania and Florida were put on Trump's tally sheet, and with most of the western states a foregone conclusion, all eyes turned to the Midwest – particularly Ohio, Michigan, and Wisconsin. This was believed to be Clinton's firewall. Ohio was tough, but Michigan and Wisconsin should have been fine (she made very few trips to either, assuming they were in the bag). As the evening wore on and the results trickled in, the outcome crystallized. To the astonishment of pollsters, pundits, politicians and perhaps the candidate himself, Trump swept the entire Midwest. With these states in his pocket, the die was cast: Donald J. Trump would be the 45th president of the United States.

In the end, Trump scored a hefty electoral college victory: 304 to 227, but Clinton won the popular vote by more than 2.9 million. Trump won states (and one district in Maine) worth 306 electoral votes, but two electors from Texas did not cast their ballots for him. Clinton's state totals added up to 332, but five of her electors voted for someone else. Never before had a presidential election produced as many faithless electors. It would also be the fifth time in American history that the winner of the popular vote would not take up residence in the White House. Did we say that the 2016 election was exceptional?

The Aftermath

The hours and days after any election are always filled with divergent emotions, ranging from relief to regret, joy to despair. The aftermath of the 2016 race was different. Since the advent of sophisticated polling, colossal surprises have been rare. Races can be tight, sometimes too close to call, but true shockers have been few and far between. Even seasoned GOP operatives were astonished by Trump's easy win. His core supporters were euphoric; they had snatched the presidency away from "The Clintons" and "The Establishment" and their outspoken, unconventional hero would renew America. Clinton and her supporters were thunderstruck, despondent beyond measure. Clinton herself was badly shaken, unable to utter a concession speech until the next day.

For many Americans, the outcome of the 2016 presidential election was *not* disastrous. While his unfavorable ratings might have been a record high, Trump's victory was interpreted by many as a vivid, direct response to a growing list of unwelcome changes in the economy and society. Trump, a truly different sort of candidate, would usher in a new policy agenda and a new approach to governance. He would disrupt the status quo. The great slumbering mass of discouraged and dislocated working-class Americans had risen and pounded its chest. For them, Election Day delivered a long-awaited fundamental change. In states and communities across the country, many conservatives were emboldened by the election.

For those on the ideological left, Trump's victory was nothing short of catastrophic. Not only had they lost the presidency in what many thought was a slam dunk, but the House and Senate were captured by the GOP. Two-thirds of state legislatures would be controlled by Republicans – and a majority of governorships as well. All this had transpired during a time when more Americans considered themselves Democrats than Republicans. In fact, when it comes to self-identified partisanship, Democrats had been the majority for decades. Young citizens were also much more progressive and more likely to support Democratic candidates (Barack Obama had won a whopping 68 percent of those under 30 in 2008). None of this seemed to matter in 2016. It was a grand shellacking.

Monday morning quarterbacks on the left complained that the top of the ticket, Clinton, had failed to inspire. While Vermont Senator Bernie Sanders might have confronted a different set of problems in the general election, at least he stirred passions and represented a break from the status quo. What was the Democratic message, anyway? What did the party stand for? How could so many candidates miss the anguish of so many working-class voters?

But to others, larger questions came to the fore – questions about the viability of the *entire* election process and maybe even our democracy. Has the election–democracy nexus in the United States been strained, if not broken? All manners of critiques were offered in the weeks and months following the election. We select leaders based on their experience, character and intelligence, but also their policy positions, correct? This process, where elections are thought to direct the course of public policy, can work in different ways, but it centers on rationality – both the voters' and the elected officials'. Policy concerns should drive vote choice, and once in office, officials should respond to those issues. "[I]t is essential to liberty that government should have a common interest with the people," wrote James Madison in Federalist No. 52. "Frequent elections are unquestionably the only policy by which this dependence and sympathy can be effectually secured." But do voters pay enough attention to public policy questions to redirect the course of government? Did voters in 2016 really understand what Trump stood for, or was it simply a cult of personality?

A book written by political scientists Christopher Achen and Larry Bartels just prior to the election added fuel to the fire regarding voter rationality. *Democracy for Realists: Why Elections Do Not Produce Responsive Government* is aimed at understanding the fundamental elements of vote choice and party identification. With bushels of data to support their claim, Achen and Bartels find that "issue congruence [between voters and parties], in so far as it exists, is mostly a byproduct of other connections, most of them lacking policy content."[6] They argue voters align themselves with racial, ethnic, occupational, religious, recreational and other groups. And it is a group identity that determines vote choice, not a particular policy concern or array of policy preferences. People do not seem to like or even understand the policy choices they make.

Achen and Bartels further claim that in most elections the balance between Democrats and Republicans is close, and the outcome hinges on pure independents. This group is also not especially issue-oriented, basing their vote choice on familiarity, charisma, a fresh face, or a host of other non-policy cues. The outcome of the election becomes nothing more than "random choices among the available parties – musical chairs."[7] This may help explain the odd coalition that brought Donald Trump to power. On the one hand, many of his policies such as tax cuts for the wealthy, the easing of banking regulations, opposition to raising the minimum wage and scaled-back health insurance guarantees, would seem at odds with the concerns of blue-collar workers. On the other hand, the group identity of his supporters was well defined. The heart of the winning Trump coalition was the shifting support of working-class and middle-class white men. Jim Tankersley of the *Washington Post* put it this way: "Whites without a college degree – men and women – made up a third of the 2016 electorate. Trump won them by 39 percentage points … far surpassing 2012 Republican nominee Mitt Romney's 25 percent margin. They were the foundation of his victories across the Rust Belt."[8]

Then, many pointed to the potentially game-changing developments that emerged during the 2016 campaign and in the early months of the Trump Administration: fake news and alternative facts. Here the need for evidence is gone and emotion-rich information is used to draw in more viewers, readers and voters. If we add the continual drive for fresh news and the costs of traditional journalism, we are left with no consensus or authority. *New York Times* blogger Farhad Manjoo put it this way: "We are roiled by preconceptions and biases, and we usually do what feels easiest – we gorge on information that confirms our ideas, and we shun what does not."[9]

Citizens (voters) are called upon to judge those in power. If officials have done a good job, they are returned to office; if not, they are sent packing. Elections make the governors accountable to the governed. But there must be an objective standard for the assessment, which is why the constitutional framers were adamant about a free press. But with fake news and alternative facts your side has *always* done a good job and the other party has *always* failed. If the key ingredient in the accountability process, objectivity, has disappeared, has the core rationale for elections evaporated?

It is also held that as public policy veers from the concerns of citizens, new leaders are chosen to right the ship. Elections become a safety valve – or a tension-management device. But has this changed as well? With few exceptions, like the Depression, the pressure never got that intense because there were abundant natural resources and an expanding economy. Each generation assumed their kids would be a bit better off, and they generally were. But can any election resurrect the fading American Dream? Nicholas Eberstadt, in an essay shortly after the election, suggests not: "For whatever reasons, the Great American Escalator, which had lifted successive generations of Americans to ever higher standards of living and levels of social well-being, broke down around then – and broke down very badly."[10] While some elites may hold that the economy remains sound, "this is patent nonsense."

Given these new economic realities, perhaps Trump was the perfect candidate. Many thought that his behavior and personality were abhorrent, but in a desperate move to "make America great again," and in the privacy of the voting booth, they held their noses and voted him to power. Perhaps Trump's outrageousness and ideological ambiguity were perfect features in 2016 because they rekindled faith in elections – at least for some Americans. Elections could *still* make things better, but exceptional times call for exceptional candidates.

Social scientists have long-understood how self-interest in politics could yield a collective good. For example, in *Economic Theory of Democracy,* written in 1957, Anthony Downs argued that rational, vote-seeking candidates (and parties) will find the center of the partisan distribution of voters. The outcome of government would fit the preferences of the median voter. The selfish interest of the candidate would yield a common good. But things have changed since Downs' era. As part of his rationale for not seeking reelection in 2018, Arizona Senator Jeff Flake lamented the disappearance of policy moderation. "What is best for the country is for neither party's base to fully get what it wants, but rather for the factions that make up our parties to be compelled to talk until we have a policy solution to our problems."[11] The pages to follow will also chart the rise of geo-political sorting, where voters now cluster in ideologically homogenous communities. Can officials from such solidly red or blue districts seek compromise, middle-of-the-road solutions?

Do we even like or have faith in elections anymore? The *Washington Post* conducted a poll of 3,000 respondents during the waning days of the 2016 election on a range of issues.[12] Among much else, they found that 40 percent of respondents claimed to have "lost faith in American democracy." Asked if they would accept the results if their candidate lost the election, just 31 percent said they definitely would see the outcome as legitimate. According to the American National Election Study (ANES), in the 1960s about two-thirds of Americans believed elections made government pay attention "a good deal." In recent years, that figure has dropped to about 25 percent.

In the months and years after the election it was revealed that Russian actors (likely the Russian Government) made concerted moves to shape the outcome of the election and undermine the legitimacy of the process. As will be discussed in the pages to follow, this was done by hacking into the email accounts of Clinton campaign officials, stealing strategic data and publishing embarrassing information, and by broadly spreading a litany of false stories on an array of social media outlets. It is probably impossible to know if these acts shaped the outcome of the election, but we do know that for the first time in our nation's history a foreign power attacked the workings of our elections. Moreover, in summer of 2018 Trump's personal lawyer, Michael Cohen, confessed to campaign finance law violations, where he had secretly paid off two women so they would remain quiet about their affairs with the candidate. In this light, it is certainly no surprise that an increasing number of Americans have lost faith in the system.

A large poll (1,477 respondents) conducted by the Pew Research Center in 2018 found deep cynicism about the conduct of our politics. For instance, even though 80 percent agreed that corrupt elected officials should face serious consequences, just 30 percent said this is a reality in the United States. Fewer than 50 percent thought congressional districts are drawn fairly. Just 39 percent said "voters are knowledgeable about candidates and issues" and 56 percent said they have little or no confidence in the political wisdom of the American people. A whopping 61 percent said that "significant" changes are needed in the design and structure of American government to make it work in the 21st century. Only 18 percent said our democracy is working "very well" these days.[13]

Beyond the shortcomings of the election process, a number of thought-provoking works have set their guise on the very nature of our democratic experiment. In an article published in the midst of the 2016 election, scholar Roslyn Fuller offered a novel look at the elections–democracy nexus. "Americans," she writes, "made one fatal mistake in attributing the fruits of their labor solely to their own hard work, and another in believing that just because they were doing well economically, occasionally voting actually put them in control of the government."[14] America's success did not spring from Madison's novel scheme or participatory democracy, she argues, but instead the exploitation of groups (slaves, immigrants) and seemingly inexhaustible natural resources. That is to say, elections were an effective placebo so long as each generation had a higher standard of living. But that's gone. The masses are as "superfluous to the economy as they always were to the political system, required to act merely in a superficial capacity as consumers or as voters – roles that have increasingly come to coincide."[15]

A full-length work published after the election offers a similar perspective. In *How Democracies Die*, Steven Levitsky and Daniel Ziblatt zero-in on America's history of racial discrimination and its link to elections. They argue that throughout the 19th century, Americans confronted numerous challenges. We endured, where many other nations fell victim to fascism. But there was a catch:

> The norms sustaining our political system rested, to a considerable degree, on racial exclusion … Racial exclusion contributed directly to the partisan civility and cooperation that came to characterize twentieth-century American politics. [After Reconstruction in the

1880s,] the "solid South" emerged as a powerful conservative force within the Democratic Party, simultaneously vetoing civil rights and serving as a bridge to Republicans. Southern Democrats' ideological proximity to conservative Republicans reduced polarization and facilitated bipartisanship. But it did so at the great cost of keeping civil rights – and America's full democratization – off the political agenda.[16]

In other words, foundational changes came with the passage of the 1964 Civil Rights Act and 1965 Voting Rights Act. Shortly after, a vivid, fear-centered polarization began to spread. Members of each party began to see the other side as a threat, bringing an already cumbersome, difficult policy process to a grinding halt. Compromise and moderation seem impossible in Congress and state legislatures today. This is not evidence of a mere rough patch, but a harbinger of deep, systemic problems. As Levitsky and Ziblatt note, the process of racial inclusion that began after World War II today forms the core of recalcitrant polarization, thus posing the greatest challenge to established forms of mutual toleration and forbearance since Reconstruction.[17]

Writing nine months after the election, a team of scholars detailed what they believe to be the impact of the 2016 election and the advent of a Trump presidency on our democracy. "In the eyes of many citizens, activists, pundits, and scholars, American democracy appears under threat. Numerous indicators suggest growing popular anxiety and mistrust about American democracy and governing institutions." These authors note that in the annual ratings of 167 nations from around the globe, the *Economist* reclassified the United States as a "flawed democracy" (as opposed to a "full democracy") due to declining public confidence in American political institutions. Trump's election in 2016, they argue, "represents the intersection of three streams in American politics: polarized two-party presidentialism; a polity fundamentally divided over membership and status in the political community, in ways structured by race and economic inequality; and the erosion of democratic norms at the elite and mass levels."[18]

The Election–Democracy Nexus

What powerful critiques. Truth be told, however, the democratic character of American government – and the precise role of elections in our limited government – has been an ongoing debate since its inception. We know that democratic impulses played a role in the drive for independence, and the framers understood that the Constitution would only be ratified if it reflected populist principles. Some saw this as a pragmatic necessity, while others were true believers in Jefferson's lucid treatise on limited government, the so-called Spirit of '76. There was an explicit rejection of hereditary rule and the Bill of Rights codified essential liberties – the base ingredients of democratic engagement.

And yet, these men also worried mightily about the "excesses of democracy" and sought to create a governing framework that would check popular impulses. James Madison's rationale for a large, extended republic, the foremost issue during the ratification debate, was that it would curb popular factions and enlarge and refine the general will. Only one branch of the government, the House of Representatives, would be chosen by the people. Presidents would be selected by an Electoral College (originally picked by state legislatures) and Senators would be chosen by their states' legislatures (until the 17th Amendment in 1913). Six-year terms for the Senate, coupled with rotation (where only one-third of the chamber is replaced every two years), further reflect concerns about popular uprisings. Federal judges would serve for life, rather than face the pressures of public opinion.

Alexander Hamilton was rather direct in his concerns about the wisdom of average citizens. Speaking about the importance of keeping parts of the new government removed from public opinion, such as the Senate, he proclaimed at the Constitutional Convention:

> The voice of the people has been said to be the voice of God; and, however generally this maxim has been quoted and believed, it is not true to fact. The people are turbulent and changing; they seldom judge or determine right. Give therefore to the first class a distinct permanent share in the government. Can a democratic assembly who annually revolve in the mass of the people be supposed steadily to pursue the public good?

It is telling that neither the Constitution nor the Bill of Rights protected voting rights. States were left to define voter eligibility; most states used property clauses, others added literacy qualifications and others employed religious tests and poll taxes. All limited the franchise to men. Subsequent amendments to the Constitution defined categories of citizens who could not be barred from voting and outlawed the poll tax, but other qualifications, such as residency and identification requirements, are controlled by the states. As strange as it might seem, the Supreme Court affirmed in *Bush v. Gore* (2000) that individuals have no federal constitutional right to vote for presidential electors. Citing several previous cases, the five-member majority said that a state's ability to decide how to appoint electors is plenary. In fact, many states did not hold elections to determine presidential electors in early decades of our nation's history, and Colorado did not hold a presidential election as recently as 1876.[19]

Another part of the Constitution that reflects the concerns of the framers regarding public opinion and direct elections is the Electoral

College. The rationale for this rather odd institution is complex, and it will be discussed in subsequent chapters. Part of its justification, assuredly, was to limit the role of citizens in the selection of the chief executive. The voters would have a say in the process, but only indirectly: through their state legislatures. (By the 1840s most states changed their rules so that voters would be allowed to directly choose electors but, as noted above, it was not until 1876 that all states did the same.) Federal judges are not elected, nor are members of the federal bureaucracy. And, of course, the Constitution does not allow for ballot initiatives, referenda, or recall elections. Once again, the framers wanted to create a system where the governors considered the wishes of the governed, but mostly they wanted a stable system where change would be moderate and incremental.

American University professor Allan Lichtman recently penned an important volume about the ongoing struggles to codify voting rights in America. In his first chapter, entitled "The Founding Fathers' Mistake," he charts the ambivalence surrounding voting. On the one hand, the constitutional framers drew on lessons of ancient Athens: direct rule by a fickle and unreliable people would bring corruption and chaos. On the other hand, there was a strong belief that "popular consent anchored all constitutional powers."[20] They were pragmatic considerations, too, understanding that without explicit democratic mechanisms the Constitution would probably not be ratified by the states. Their solution was twofold: rest the system mostly on indirect voting and allow the qualifications for voting to be set at the state level. "In choosing not to decide on voting rights, the Philadelphia delegates made a choice, with profound, lasting consequences for American democracy.[21]

Beyond their uncertainties regarding the capacities of voters to act with good judgment, the framers were also unsure about the mechanics of elections. They were heading into new, uncharted territory. How would elections work? How many candidates would run for a particular office? Would candidates actively pursue office, or would others speak on their behalf? How should candidates or their advocates persuade voters? How long should election contests last? And perhaps most importantly, how would violence during heated contests be averted? All of these questions, and many others, were left unanswered.

Likely the single greatest misapprehension in the early years centered on the role of political parties. The framers worried that political parties would threaten their democratic experiment. Madison noted, "The friend of popular governments never finds himself so much alarmed for their character and fate, as when he contemplates their propensity of this dangerous vice."[22] The problem with parties (also called factions) was that they would foster self-interest and greed, rather than promote the long-term public interest. John Adams bemoaned the drift of the country's elites toward party politics in the 1790s: "There is nothing

I dread so much as a division of the Republic into two great parties, each arranged under its leader and converting measures in opposition to each other."[23]

Despite these warnings, elections soon became partisan contests. In 1800, Thomas Jefferson ran for the presidency as a Democratic-Republican and John Adams sought reelection as a Federalist. Many people at the time believed the nation was coming apart at the seams, given the intensity of the contest. It endured. There were a few minor disruptions and a bit of violence, but the election proved to be one of the highpoints in our nation's history. The Democratic-Republicans swept into power and one group of rulers was peacefully replaced by another. This was unprecedented in world history. Because of this, many, including Madison and other framers, had a change of heart about political parties. The term "legitimate opposition" emerged, which described an out-of-power group that vyed for public support, and checked the actions of the in-power group. Parties became another check on the ruling elite.

The party system, which burst onto the scene in the late 1790s, fueled a modest level of engagement, but it faded a bit after the raucous election of 1800 in a period scholars dubbed the Era of Good Feelings. Few working-class citizens were linked to the affairs of government; overt political action was limited to affluent white men. During the next three decades, turnout for *eligible* voters hovered around 25 percent. As a percentage of the population, turnout never got above 3 percent. If one were to look to our nation's formation period for either theoretical or pragmatic connections between elections and the democratic character of our system, you would be disappointed. These men envisioned the interplay of local groups as the most prevalent and potent form of political action. They structured a system to ensure that faction-centered politics would not overheat and cripple the new government.

And then things changed. It is difficult to overstate shifts ushered in with the arrival of Jacksonian Democracy, a period stretching from about 1830 to 1880. The so-called corrupt deal of 1824 brought John Quincy Adams to the presidency even though Andrew Jackson had won more popular and Electoral College votes. The backlash against the perceived elitism was immediate and gigantic. As noted by political historian Joel Silbey, "The entire texture and structure of the political world shifted markedly. A new political universe [had arrived]."[24]

The nucleus of the transformation was local political organizations. Like mushrooms after a summer rain, vibrant local party committees sprang up in every hamlet, town, and city. Propelled by these structures, voter turnout soared to astonishing levels – often above 80 percent. Rallies, demonstrations and parades were common. State and municipal contests were particularly raucous affairs. Electoral politics became integral to social life in America, and of course steadfast party loyalty, fueled by a dogmatic partisan press, became ubiquitous. Americans were partisan and engaged. Consider a quote from Charles Dickens, who traveled around America in the 1840s:

> Quiet people avoid the question of the Presidency, for there will be a new election in three years and a half, and party feelings run very high: the great constitutional feature of this institution being, that [as soon as] the acrimony of the last election is over, the acrimony of the next begins; which is an unspeakable comfort to all strong politicians and true lovers of their country; that is to say, to ninety-nine men and boys out of every ninety-nine and a quarter.[25]

So began our nation's obsession with elections. The voter became the protagonist of the American political drama. The simple act of raising a hand, checking a box, pushing a lever, hitting a button, or touching a video screen was thought to carry profound implications for citizens, government and society. Elections implied equality, the right to express preferences and to direct the course of policy. Characteristics that too often shaped one's standing in society, such as race, gender, affluence, education and social connections, seemed to evaporate in the voting booth. Everyone had a seat at the table of what H.G. Wells dubbed our "democratic feast." Wide segments of the population sometimes scorned the outcome of a particular election, but few challenged the legitimacy of these contests.

Americans placed such faith in elections that enfranchisement was viewed as a solution to the problems confronted by groups in society. The established American response to social discontent has been the extension of the ballot. "The protests of women led to their enfranchisement, but not to the end of sexual discrimination. Antiwar sentiments of the young facilitated the enfranchisement of 18-year-olds, even as fighting continued in Vietnam."[26] Elections became the panacea for economic, political and social problems.

Themes of the Book

Which perspective is right? How should we interpret the link between elections and democracy in the United States in light of our history and especially given all that transpired in the 2016 election? Did Donald Trump break the mold, or was 2016 a one-off? Was it a harbinger of a host of changes, building over the past few decades, or will we rebound quickly?

This book centers on several related assumptions. The first is that with all the flaws and shortcomings in the current system, voting matters. Elections are critically important events that determine who holds key leadership posts and at least partly shaping the outcomes of public policy disputes. It matters that Donald Trump was sent to the

White House and not Hillary Clinton. In fact, it is probably only fair to say that much of the post-election introspection about the viability of the system – particularly the outcry from scholarly quarters – might not have materialized if a few thousand votes in key states had shifted to Clinton. It also matters that Democrats were able to take back the House in the 2018 midterm elections, as well as flip seven governorships and nearly 350 state legislative seats. There are numerous routes for citizens to influence government, and a myopic focus on elections can sometimes stifle other modes of activism. Citizens should do more than vote. Yet, elections *do* make a difference. One might even argue that elections offer the single best opportunity for citizens to influence the course of government. For all that has changed in American politics, this basic truth remains.

In the wake of the horrific murder of 17 students and staff at Marjory Stoneman Douglas High School in Parkland, Florida, on Valentine's Day 2018, young citizens across the nation began to mobilize – desperate to compel public officials to do something about gun violence. There were demonstrations, sit-ins, and walk-outs. The editorial board of the *New York Times* made the following observation:

> This is a fragile moment for the nation. The integrity of democratic institutions is under assault from without and within, and basic standards of honesty and decency in public life are corroding. If you are horrified at what is happening in Washington and in many states, you can march in the streets, you can go to town halls and demand more from your representatives, you can share the latest outrageous news on your social media feed – all worthwhile activities. But none of it matters if you don't go out and vote.[27]

For all their failings, voting and elections continue to merge three elements of the American Creed: egalitarianism, which holds that all are created equal and have a right to participate in the conduct of government; populism, where average folks have wisdom (and conversely, that there is much to fear about elites); and majority will, where just outcomes can be reached through a simple tabulation of citizen preferences.

In the fall of 2018, former President Barack Obama hit the campaign trail for Democrats. Much of his appeal focused on particular policies and on Donald Trump's unconventional approach to governing. But the heart of his pitch underscored a core democratic tenet:

> When we don't vote, when we take our basic rights and freedoms for granted, when we turn away and stop paying attention and stop engaging and stop believing and look for the newest diversion, the electronic versions of bread and circuses, then other voices fill the

void ... [T]here is actually only one real check on bad policy and abuse of power. That's you. You and your vote.[28]

The second core supposition of the book is that many Americans, especially young Americans, doubt the utility of elections and tune out the process. By sitting on the sidelines, they buttress the probability that elections do *not* reflect the will of average citizens and that elections do *not* compel pubic officials to respond to the public's will. One estimate, for example, is that Clinton defeated Trump by 18 percentage points among those under 30, but turnout among this group was roughly 10 percent less than for those over 30.[29] Just 55 percent of eligible Americans turned out to vote in this incredibly high-profile, important election. In the critically important 2018 midterm election, just one in three citizens under the age of 30 came to the polls. Lackluster turnout in elections is a key indicator of this indifference, but there are many other measures – such as the willingness to help candidates, work for a political party, or even talk about campaigns with friends and family. There has been a modest upturn in some modes of participation in recent elections, but far too many Americans shun electoral politics. Disengagement is a collective-action problem. When individuals make the choice to tune out electoral politics, the entire system suffers – which, of course, leads more people to sit on the sidelines.

The third assumption of the book is that a better understanding of the complexity and controversies of the modern election process can help engage citizens. For many, the process is distant, confusing, and confounding. There have been dramatic transformations in the way elections are conducted, but the core of the process has remained the same. As more Americans, especially young Americans, better appreciate how the system works and precisely *why* certain components are important, the likelihood of their involvement increases. The broader the scope of citizen engagement in elections, the more democratic the final outcome.

Finally, it would be a mistake to assume there are not critically important developments that threaten the democratic character of elections. The electoral process has morphed over the centuries, and today we confront a set of unprecedented challenges. There are assaults on access to the voting booth, the rise of fear-centered, hyper-partisanship, a changing media landscape, new technologies that distort the accountability process, interference by domestic and foreign actors, and new avenues for big money to tip the scales. The foremost goal of this book is to confront these issues head on. Each chapter offers a guiding question, and moves from background information to a thought-provoking argument that aims to spur deeper investigations, conversations and perhaps even new modes of thinking.

Americans have had a love affair with elections for two centuries, but the relationship is under stress. Donald Trump is not the cause, but rather a symptom. He did not break the mold but instead was successful, in part, because of changes that were already underway. And it would be a mistake to assume that our democracy will continue as if on autopilot, immune to forces that have crippled younger democracies, or that it will rebound with the next election. No single reform will make things right, and no savior will redeem the system.

This book is not about solutions, per se, but rather awareness – a better understanding of how we got here and potential implications. A few vague reform ideas will be offered, but the pages to follow will not chart a list of prescriptions for the ailments. Our nation's history has shown that each generation has the potential to renew democracy, to move our system toward a more perfect union. But the wheels of change sometimes grind slowly. The choice is up to us. As with any failing relationship, the first step is a frank assessment of the problems.

Notes

1 McKay Coppins, "You Need to Think About It Like a War," *The Atlantic* website, December 7, 2017 (https://medium.com/the-atlantic/you-need-to-think-about-it-like-a-war-bf0b78287054).

2 Sharon Woods Harris, "Mackaman: Presidential Race 'Virtually Unprecedented,'" *Pekin Daily Times* website, January 26, 2016 (www.pekintimes.com/article/20160125/NEWS/160129564).

3 Clare Foran, "Bernie Sanders's Big Money," *The Atlantic* website, March 1, 2016 (www.theatlantic.com/politics/archive/2016/03/bernie-sanders-fundraising/471648/).

4 "How Much Money is Behind Each Campaign?," *Washington Post* website, December 31, 2016 (www.washingtonpost.com/graphics/politics/2016-election/campaign-finance/).

5 Gallup Polling, "2016 Presidential Election: Key Indicators" (http://news.gallup.com/poll/189299/presidential-election-2016-key-indicators.aspx?g_source=ELECTION_2016&g_medium=topic&g_campaign=tiles).

6 Christopher H. Achen and Larry Bartels, *Democracy for Realists: Why Elections Do Not Produce Responsive Government* (Princeton, NJ: Princeton University Press, 2018), 301.

7 Ibid., 312.

8 Jim Tankersley, "How Trump Won: The Revenge of Working-class Whites," *Washington Post* website, November 9, 2016 (www.washingtonpost.com/news/wonk/wp/2016/11/09/how-trump-won-the-revenge-of-working-class-whites/?noredirect=on&utm_term=.0c19ed6b1901).

9 Farhad Manjoo, "How the Internet Is Loosening Our Grip on the Truth," *New York Times* website, November 2, 2016 (www.nytimes.com/2016/11/03/technology/how-the-internet-is-loosening-our-grip-on-the-truth.html).

10 Nicholas Eberstadt, "Our Miserable 21st Century," *Commentary Magazine* website, February 15, 2017 (www.commentarymagazine.com/articles/our-miserable-21st-century/).

11 Jeff Flake, "Enough," *Washington Post* website, October 24, 2017 (www.washingtonpost.com/opinions/enough-it-is-time-to-stand-up-to-trump/2017/10/24/12488ee4-b908-11e7-a908-a3470754bbb9_story.html?hpid=hp_no-name_opinion-card-e%3Ahomepage%2Fstory&utm_term=.c844863b731c).

12 Nathaniel Persily and Jon Cohen, "Americans are Losing Faith in Democracy – and in Each Other," *Washington Post* website, October 14, 2016 (www.washingtonpost.com/opinions/americans-are-losing-faith-in-democracy-and-in-each-other/2016/10/14/b35234ea-90c6-11e6-9c52-0b10449e33c4_story.html?utm_term=.abcf24206820).

13 Pew Research Center, "The Public, the Political System and American Democracy," April 26, 2018. Accessed at: www.people-press.org/2018/04/26/the-public-the-political-system-and-american-democracy/.

14 Roslyn Fuller, "Why Is American Democracy So Broken, and Can It Be Fixed?," *The Nation* website, June 9, 2016 (www.thenation.com/article/why-is-american-democracy-so-broken-and-can-it-be-fixed/).

15 Ibid.

16 Steven Levitsky and Daniel Ziblatt, *How Democracies Die* (New York: Crown Publishing Group, 2018), 143.

17 Ibid.

18 Robert Lieberman, Suzanne Mettler, Thomas B. Pepinsky, Kenneth M. Roberts, and Richard Valelly, "Trumpism and American Democracy: History, Comparison, and the Predicament of Liberal Democracy in the United States," *Social Science Research Network*, August 29, 2017 (https://papers.ssrn.com/sol3/papers.cfm?abstract_id=3028990).

19 Joe McKeegan, "The Constitutional Right to Vote: *Bush v. Gore*, Ten Years Later, FairVote Website, December 4, 2010 (www.fairvote.org/the-constitutional-right-to-vote-blog-bush-v-gore-ten-years-later).

20 Allan Lichtman, *The Embattled Vote in America* (Cambridge: Harvard University Press, 2018), 13.

21 Ibid, 16.

22 "How Much Money is Behind Each Campaign?," *The Washington Post* website, December 31, 2016 (www.washingtonpost.com/graphics/politics/2016-election/campaign-finance/).

23 Quoted in David McCullough, *John Adams* (New York: Simon and Schuster, 2001), 422.

24 Joel Silby, "Beyond Realignment and Realignment Theory: American Political Ears, 1789–1989," in *The End of Realignment?*, Byron E. Shafer (Madison, WI: University of Wisconsin Press, 1991), 9.

25 Charles Dickens, *American Notes for General Circulation*, Chapter IV, 1842 (www.gutenberg.org/files/675/675-h/675-h.htm).

26 Gerald Pomper, *Elections in America*, 2nd Edition (New York: Longman, 1980).

27 *New York Times* Editorial Board, "Vote. That's Just What They Don't Want You to Do," *New York Times* website, March 10, 2018 (www.nytimes.com/2018/03/10/opinion/sunday/go-vote.html?action=click&pgtype=Homepage&clickSource=story-heading&module=opinion-c-col-left-region&region=opinion-c-col-left-region&WT.nav=opinion-c-col-left-region).

28 Isaac Saul, "Obama Says the Next Election is More Important than the One that Elected Him," APlus, September 7, 2018 (https://aplus.com/a/barack-obama-young-people-vote-november-elections?no_monetization=true).

29 William A. Galston and Clara Hendrickson, "How Millennials Voted this Election," *Brookings Institute* website, November 22, 2016 (www.brookings.edu/blog/fixgov/2016/11/21/how-millennials-voted/).

2 Voting and Elections in Theory

Do We Consent to a System that Limits Our Say in Government?

America is an election-crazed nation. We elect a president and members of the national legislature, of course, but also governors, thousands of state legislators, county officials, mayors and other city officials, town trustees, court justices in many states and counties, sheriffs and other law enforcement officials, assessors, attorneys general, comptrollers, auditors, and scores of other government posts. In some communities, even the choice of animal control officer (i.e., dog catcher) is put to a vote. In many places coroners are elected. All told, there are more than half a million elected posts in the United States. No other nation even comes close to this total.

Not only do we rely heavily on elections to fill government positions, the frequency of these events far outpaces what is found in other nations. Some Americans believe that elections occur only every four years, given that this is when we select our president, but elections are held every year. Most state legislators are selected every two years, and municipal posts are usually filled in odd-numbered years. Given that parties nominate candidates to run in the general election through primary elections, it is fair to say that Americans are called to the polls at least twice every year – once for the primary and once for the general election.

Americans use elections not only to select candidates but also to change government policy. Referenda and other ballot initiatives, common in 27 states and the District of Columbia, allow citizens to vote on policy matters, essentially sidestepping the legislative process. In some states, voters may even remove elected officials from office in a special election, called a recall. Interest in these sorts of opportunities is growing. Many Americans believe this process is a better reflection of the public will than candidate-centered elections, but others are quick to point out numerous downsides, especially the growing role of big money.

Our faith in the election process springs from numerous sources, not the least of which is childhood socialization – the way younger citizens learn about appropriate modes of political behavior. By a young age, perhaps just four or five, American children have discovered that voting is a good way to resolve disputes. Want to play kickball or dodgeball? Dress up or play house? Watch television or go on a sleigh ride? Let's put it to a vote! And when the powers that be establish unpopular public policies, such as mandatory vegetable-eating or limitations on video games, the "citizenry" often calls for a vote. How surprising and frustrating it must be for these future civic leaders to hear that they do not necessarily live in an election-based democracy – at least when it comes to eating broccoli!

As noted in the previous chapter, it is widely assumed that elections are the sole means of expressing the public will. One might argue that other mechanisms, such as group activism, direct lobbying, or the careful assessment of public opinion, might be a better way of directing public policy. And, as will be discussed in the pages to follow, there are many ways a government might yield to the will of its people without holding elections. But such possibilities would not get very far in America. We believe that elections are the lifeblood of a democracy.

This chapter explores some essential theoretical questions regarding the widespread use of elections in the United States. The core issue is whether elections provide citizens all we expect. Average Americans spend little time, save perhaps a few hours in high school or a lecture or two in college, thinking about the democratic underpinnings of their democracy. They can hardly imagine other ways of picking public officials. But is faith in the electoral process misplaced? Have we been sold a bill of goods? If so, would it be wise or even possible to shift away from elections – or at the very least put less stock in them as a means of expressing the public's will? There may be some mid-level reforms like stiffer campaign finance regulations or getting rid of the Electoral College, but if the foundation of choosing public leaders is irreparably broken, shouldn't we consider an entirely different approach?

The Theoretical Strengths of Elections

The United States boasts a republican form of government – a system where representatives act on behalf of citizens, who are also called constituents. Setting aside a few tiny communities mostly in New England and the ballot initiative process, very few have a *direct* say in what government does. We do not have a direct democracy, but instead a system where leaders are selected to run essential parts of government – and where it is incumbent upon these representatives to make decisions on our behalf. Thomas Paine, the revolutionary propagandist and political thinker, suggested in his famous 1776 pamphlet *Common Sense* that legislators must "act in the same manner as the whole body would act, were they present."

Republicanism was introduced in the United States for several reasons. The constitutional framers believed discussion and deliberation to be an essential part of the policy process, something impractical with too many people in the mix. It might be nice to have everyone in a community join the debate on a particular issue, but what if there are thousands of residents? Should they each be allowed a say? How would a large number of issues be tackled when everyone is given an equal say in the process? And what if these issues are complex, multi-faceted? How would you even bring large numbers of people together? In short, even if there was a preference for direct democracy, practical issues would seem to make it impossible.

Second, and more significantly, in the early stages of our nation's history, many believed that some citizens were better suited to serve in government than others. Many still believe this. Government and policy making are complicated, so it is prudent to let the educated and experienced, the ones with a greater understanding of the issues, lead the way. This idea has a long history in early philosophical thought. The precise origin of good leaders and qualities that they should possess shifted from one philosopher to the next, but most of the early thinkers held that governments that rely on the wisdom and virtue of enlightened citizens or small groups of citizens are more stable, more likely to flourish. For instance, in Plato's *Crito* we are told that one wise man may be better than the collective wisdom of the public.

Third, republicanism seemed to work well during the pre-constitutional period. Colonial assemblies, which relied on the periodic gathering of delegates from various parts of the colony, functioned rather well by most accounts. The problem, later on, was that the governors, usually appointed by the Crown, ignored their requests. Executives were the problem, not the assemblies. Also, the first and second Constitutional Conventions, which set the Revolution in motion, used a republican model. Again, a small group of leaders were charged with speaking and acting on behalf of citizens back home.

Finally, many of the framers of our system believed that mechanisms were necessary to curb the visceral, emotional impulses of the public. To quote James Madison, representatives would "enlarge and refine the public will." In other words, giving the public everything they want, whenever they want it, would not be a good idea, as suggested in the previous chapter. Many of the framers had a rather pessimistic view of the governing capacities of average citizens. Even if we were to overcome the practical issues of space and time, there are reasons to prefer a republic over a direct democracy, the framers would argue.

Interestingly, while republicanism was broadly accepted during the formation period, elections did not emerge as a bedrock component. Madison argued in the Federalist Papers that the surest way to create a "dependency on the people" would be frequent elections, but only one branch of the new government, the House of Representatives, would be chosen directly by the voters. The conduct of elections – including the when and how often they would be held, and who would be allowed to participate – was left to the states. There is no mention of voting rights or privileges in the Bill of Rights or any other piece of the Constitution until after the Civil War. One could argue that while representation was thought essential in the new system, the direct election by popular vote for *all* the leaders was considered excessive – and perhaps even dangerous. Even the Anti-Federalists did not push for inclusive voting rights.

The rage for popular elections did not occur in the United States until 1830, in a period called Jacksonian Democracy. The evolution of our faith in elections is complex and will be reviewed in subsequent chapters. For now, it is enough to know that while our system was founded on the republican principle, popular elections were not a fundamental piece of that concept.

It is also true that not everyone would agree that the core function of elections is to select representatives. Another possibility is that elections serve as a periodic expression of popular will – a means of informing leaders about the concerns of citizens. We select leaders based on their experience, character and intelligence, but also their positions on important issues and their approach to governance. "Politicians are far more often mirrors of public sentiment than they are molders; that is the nature of things in a popular government," noted a prominent historian.[1] This process, where elections are thought to direct the course of public policy, can work in different ways. A landslide, mandate, or wave election occurs when the winners are brought to office with the overwhelming support of the public. These events signal that the policies advanced by the winning candidates during the election are strongly favored. Halfway through his first term in 2010, for example, Barack Obama was not up for reelection, but Republican gains in the House and Senate signaled the public's dissatisfaction with the President's policies. The public was seeking a different kind of "change."

The same can be said about the 2018 midterm election. There was a surge of Democratic enthusiasm, leading to a 40-seat gain in the House of Representatives, the flipping of seven governorships and upwards of 350 state legislative seats. Republicans were able to add two seats in the US Senate, but most pundits agreed that the so-called "blue wave" was real and was a direct response to Donald Trump's policies and his exceptional, often bombastic style.

Similarly, some political scientists believe that throughout our history big elections regularly signal a dramatic change in the course of government. Much more will be said about these events – called realigning elections – in a later chapter. In short, some believe that at surprisingly regular intervals, around every 30 to 40 years, the outcome of intensely contested elections re-direct the course of public policy. These events snap the system back to what most citizens want. One party will become dominant at all levels of government for an extended period. For example, the election of Franklin D. Roosevelt in 1932 not only ushered in a very different public policy agenda, but secured the dominance of the Democratic Party for decades. In short, many believe the core rationale of elections is to redirect public policy.

Another key aspect of federal elections, particularly in recent years, has been control of federal court nominations. By controlling the presidency and the Senate, a party can fill the federal judiciary with men and women who share their broad outlook about government. In the 2016 election, for example, many Republican voters balked at supporting Donald Trump, but they also knew that a Republican in the White House would lead to at least one more conservative on the Supreme Court, which it did, as well as in many other lower court appointments, which also happened. In the summer of 2018, Supreme Court Justice Anthony Kennedy, known as a swing vote on many big cases, announced his retirement, spurring activists on both sides to remind voters of the consequences. As hyper-polarization grinds the legislative process to a halt, a topic discussed in subsequent chapters, the courts have become important vehicles for policy change.

But do voters pay enough attention to public policy questions to redirect the course of government? Much more will be said about this later in the book. For now, we might note that one perspective holds that while voters might not know a lot about the specifics of policy questions, they have a keen sense of how their world is going. They might not know too much about supply-side economics, for instance, but they want their taxes lowered. One of the most influential arguments along these lines was advanced by the late V.O. Key Jr., a pioneer political scientist during the mid-20th century. In his book *The Responsible Electorate*, Key argues that, contrary to what most scholars believe, American voters pay close attention to the goings-on of government – and structure their vote choices accordingly. "Voters," he writes, "or at least a large number of them, are moved by their perceptions and appraisals of policy performance."[2] In other words, voters know when things are headed in the right direction and when they are not. Elections serve as a powerful policy barometer, telling officials when the public is upset.

Sometimes the expression of public sentiment is voiced through a third-party candidate. In 1992, independent presidential candidate Ross Perot spent a good deal of time talking about the growing federal budget deficit. The major party candidates, Democrat Bill Clinton and Republican George H.W. Bush, paid little attention to the issue – possibly because it meant difficult choices would have to be made, given that many programs would have to be cut or taxes would have to be raised to lower the deficit. Perot's hour-long "infomercials," filled with graphs, charts, data, and statistics seemed out of place and somewhat quirky. But on Election Day, Perot netted 19 percent of the popular vote, the second highest third-party vote total in nearly a century (the first being Theodore Roosevelt of the Bull Moose Party in 1912). Perot did not win, of course, but a message was sent: the public cared about deficit reduction. By the next election, candidates in both major parties were telling voters about their budget deficit reduction plans.

Still another related possibility deals less with which candidates win than with how many people turn out to vote. Realigning elections and other high-profile contests can signal the need for change but so too can low turnout events. The presidential elections of 2000 and 2004 had historic low turnout, perhaps suggesting general dissatisfaction with the system. Not surprisingly, Barack Obama's campaign theme in 2008 was a call for change. Turnout in that election was the highest in decades. As noted above, there was also a surge of interest the 2018 midterms, with many Republicans coming to the polls to support Donald Trump and his conservative plans, and a historic number of Democrats and independents flooding polling places in an attempt to thwart the president and his agenda. By taking back the House, the Democrats were put in the position to modify, if not thwart, many of Trump's policies and to effect more vigorous oversight of his administration.

Another important consideration is system legitimacy. This term implies a process that is perceived to be proper and just; legitimacy suggests that the mode of selecting leaders is both legal and, in the eyes of citizens, appropriate. In the American setting, elections serve that end – and the constitutional framers understood this. According to Madison, the denial of electoral power would stigmatize most leaders as "suspicious characters, and unworthy to be trusted with the common rights of their fellow citizens."[3] Closely related, when citizens accept the need for representation and feel that the selection of these leaders is legitimate, the policies that follow are more likely to be accepted. We may not like the direction of government, but we recognize the process as lawful.

As Americans, we often take systemic stability for granted, but merely holding an election does not guarantee that the outcome will be accepted by either the candidates or the voters. For example, Iran's June 2009 election pitted incumbent President Mahmoud Ahmadinejad against Mir-Hossein Mousavi, a progressive, reform candidate. The Iranian government quickly published results showing an unrealistic landslide victory for Ahmadinejad, prompting charges of fraud from many people familiar with the elections. Prolonged, violent protests followed in which both the legitimacy and stability of the Iranian political system were called into question. *New York Times* columnist David Brooks wrote about the effects of the election on Iranian society, saying, "Recently, many people thought it was clever to say that elections on their own don't make democracies. But election campaigns stoke the mind, and fraudulent elections outrage the soul. The Iranian elections have stirred a whirlwind that will lead, someday, to the regime's collapse."[4]

The outcome of the 2000 US presidential election was worrisome for precisely the same reason. Americans usually accept the legitimacy of winners; candidates slug it out in the battle of ideas and character, with the winner simply having persuaded more voters. But what happens when an election proves to be a virtual tie? Worse yet, what happens when a candidate who receives fewer popular votes than his opponent is sent to office? The 2000 presidential election came down to a handful of states with very tight outcomes, most notably Florida. After a drawn-out recount process and a controversial Supreme Court decision, Republican George W. Bush defeated Democrat Al Gore in that state by 527 votes (out of nearly six million votes cast!). Nationwide, Gore netted over half a million *more* votes than Bush, but because of the nuances of the Electoral College (discussed in subsequent chapters), Bush was given the keys to the White House. Would Bush have legitimacy, the backing of the public? The question became moot with the terrorist attack of September 11, 2001, as Americans rallied around their new president. Regardless of the election's outcome, support for the country during crisis helped solidify Bush's standing as our nation's leader.

Of course, a similar issue arose again 16 years later in the contest between Donald Trump and Hillary Clinton. Throughout the campaign, likely suspecting he would lose, Trump told his supporters that there would be fraudulent voting. At one point he told reporters millions of illegal votes were cast in the 2008 election (the race that Barack Obama won), but he was unable to point to any evidence.[5] Asked if he would accept the results if he lost his race to Clinton, Trump said, "We'll see." Many considered this a dangerous statement, as it strikes at the heart of systemic legitimacy. Throughout our history, losing candidates took their defeats with grace, buttressing this key election function. Gore certainly had reasons to gripe, but he was quite gracious in his concession speech.

A similar possibility can arise when more than two candidates run for the same office. With only two candidates, the winner, by definition, has the support of a majority of voters. But when a third or fourth party candidate enters the fray, the winner often receives a plurality of votes cast – but not a majority. A good example would be Bill Clinton's first election to the presidency in 1992. That year Ross Perot captured some 19 percent of the vote, as noted above, and the contest between Clinton and George H.W. Bush was somewhat close. In the end, Clinton netted just 43 percent of the popular vote. Given that election turnout was slightly over 50 percent, the most important political figure in the nation – perhaps the world – was brought to office with support from roughly 25 percent of possible voters.

Abraham Lincoln was elected with just 39.8 percent of the popular vote in 1860. Is it possible that this "minority election" affected Lincoln's legitimacy enough to play a role in the Civil War? Because third-party candidates have been fairly common in presidential contests, and because the two major parties have often been more or less balanced through the years, plurality winners, as opposed to majority winners, have been sent to the presidency 17 times since 1824.

One might expect that the Electoral College/popular vote snafu and plurality victories can be destabilizing – and to some extent they are. But the overall electoral process seems to maintain widespread public support, at least so far. There are two likely reasons for this: First, faith in elections runs so deep in the American psyche that eventual winners are seen as legitimate, regardless of the potholes in the road. Second, a powerful political culture – a credo – dictates a code of conduct for losing candidates. That is, ever since the election of 1800, when Thomas Jefferson and his followers defeated John Adams and his followers, losing candidates have accepted election results regardless of how close or how many turned out to vote. Losing candidates, from the presidency down to town council, are gracious in our system. After the exceptionally contentious, heated campaign of 1860, Senator Stephen Douglas told Abraham Lincoln, who had just defeated him for the presidency, "Partisan feeling must yield to patriotism. I'm with you, Mr. President, and God bless you."

We will never know how Donald Trump would have reacted to a loss. Would he have accepted defeat gracefully, or challenged the legitimacy of the system? Would his supporters, urged on by Trump, have taken to the streets? We do know that the glitch of the Electoral College reared its head again, allowing Trump to become president even though Clinton netted some 2.9 million more popular votes. Trump charged that he would have won the popular vote if not for illegal voting and forged a commission to investigate the issue – even though there was scant evidence to suggest any problems. The commission was disbanded about a year later without finding any evidence, but Trump continued to claim there was widespread fraud in the election.

We know that as recounts were being conducted in Florida and Georgia in the wake of the 2018 midterm elections, President Trump once again charged there was widespread corruption – without citing evidence. In response to Democratic gains in the House in that election, he made a rather novel claim: "When people get in line that have absolutely no right to vote and they go around in circles. Sometimes they go to their car, put on a different hat, put on a different shirt, come in and vote again."[6] No evidence was produced. While such charges *might* have some sort of short-term strategic value with his base voters, undermining the legitimacy of elections in the United States is a dangerous move – certainly something historically not done by the president.

Another grave concern emerged after the Trump–Clinton contest. Americans came to learn that the Russian Government made a concerted, extensive effort to impact the process and the outcome. This was done by an array of tactics, including the hacking of campaign computers and the creation and sharing of false, incendiary "news" stories about Clinton on social media. There is some evidence that they also attempted to hack into the voter tally systems in several key states. Will the public maintain their faith in elections when the prospect of illegal hacking looms? About a year after the election, *Time* ran a cover story on the Russian plot to disrupt the election and American efforts to thwart those moves. Its author, Massimo Calabresi, made the following point:

> In the days leading up to the election, the top federal cyber-security officials realized that, for the efforts they had taken throughout the election, our voting system was still vulnerable, not to interference with the actual vote count, but to undermining the credibility of the vote, the integrity of the vote, which is, of course, the purpose of voting to begin with, to reach a consensus that the democratic will of the people has been expressed.[7]

We find, then, that a foundational goal of elections is to afford legitimacy to leaders and, as a result, add a potent dose of stability to the system. We may sometimes grumble in disappointment as one party or the other shifts in or out of power, but these transitions are not met with riots or rancor. Quite often, as was even the case with many of Hillary Clinton's supporters, attention is turned quickly to the next election: "Okay, you've won this time, but we'll get it back in the next election!" In fact, some would suggest our deference to election outcomes helps explain why alternative modes of political action are used less often in the United States than in other political systems. More will be said of this placebo effect below.

Elections can sometimes spur dramatic changes in public policy. Upward of 25 percent of Americans were out of work during the Great Depression, and another 25 percent were underemployed (meaning they had less work than they wanted). It was the greatest economic crisis in US history, and citizens were anxious for a dramatic change. Herbert Hoover and his Republicans in Congress believed that it was not the place for the federal government to assist, and they rejected appeals for intervention. Mr. Hoover was sent to early retirement in the election of 1932, however, as over 60 percent of all voters backed Franklin D. Roosevelt and his "New Deal" platform. Similarly, in 2006 and 2008, Americans came to the polls dissatisfied with the Iraq War, health care problems, and a widespread financial crisis. The Republicans, who had controlled the Congress and the White House, felt the brunt of this dissatisfaction; widespread Democratic victories occurred in both elections. As noted above, things turned in the other direction in the next few elections.

This is not to say that fear of losing the next election drives all politicians, under all circumstances, to heed the desires of voters. At times an independence from public opinion is admirable. Early in 1948, Harry Truman issued an executive order ending racial discrimination in federal government employment and desegregating the armed forces. He made this move knowing that a majority of Americans would disagree and that his reelection might be in jeopardy. Coupled with other controversial moves, Truman saw his 75 percent approval rating plummet into the 40s. Ironically, we often worship leaders who dare to stand up in the face of public opinion and do the right thing. John F. Kennedy's Pulitzer Prize-winning book, *Profiles in Courage*, is an account of numerous politicians who did what was right and not simply what was popular. But this is not to say that the voters see things the same way. Harry Truman barely kept his job in 1948, netting a slim 49.6 percent of the vote, but many other heroic politicians have been sent packing for disregarding the interests of their constituents.

Elections also help to control political elites by punishing corruption. Many in the earliest days of our republic worried that elected officials would too easily succumb to greed, self-interest, and personal ambition – and that our system would afford few checks against such transgressions. The framers realized that greedy legislators might use the trappings of office and the policy arena to their private advantage. They believed that there was a natural tendency for people to become corrupt once in office. Elections afford voters the opportunity to throw corrupt politicians out – something we have seen numerous times.

One of the most oft-cited examples of how this process can work is the case of John Quincy Adams' reelection defeat in 1828. Four years earlier, Adams had run for the presidency in a four-candidate contest. He came in second, behind Democrat Andrew Jackson, but because neither netted a majority of the Electoral College votes, the process was sent to the House of Representatives. Adams, it seems, made a deal with the Speaker of the House, Henry Clay. The House vote would be rigged to make Adams president, so long as Adams would appoint Clay Secretary of State (considered the second most crucial post in the federal govern-ment). The so-called Corrupt Bargain enraged Jackson supporters and many others, and four years later Adams was sent packing.

A contemporary example might be the election of Democrat Doug Jones in Alabama's 2017 special election to fill a vacant US Senate seat. The early frontrunner was the conservative firebrand Roy Moore. It should have been a low-interest, almost sleepy affair. Because Trump defeated Clinton in Alabama by a two-to-one margin (63 percent to 34 percent), most expected the Senate race to be a blowout. But about one month before the election, in early November, the *Washington Post* published a detailed account of how Moore had allegedly sexually assaulted three teenage girls when he was in his 30s. One of the girls was 14 at the time. The story caused a national uproar, and soon other women leveled similar accusations. Given how credible these women appeared, most Republican congressional leaders withdrew their endorsement from Moore and even suggested that if he were to win they might try to expel him from the Senate. But Donald Trump took a different route, arguing that the accusers lacked credibility and that Moore's character has been tested over time. On Election Day, Doug Jones defeated Moore by a whisker – due in no small measure to a massive turnout among woman and African Americans, and because many Republicans simply could not support Moore. It was a stunning turnaround for the Democrats. Elections, it seems, can check the corruption of elites even when it means backing someone from the other political party.

The framers even argued that elections would bestow fame on a person – and that the love of fame would help curb self-interest. Alexander Hamilton explains, in *Federalist* No. 72, that even a person prone to vice and corruption can be led to consider the public's welfare for his own pride and vanity or for the "marks of honor, of favor, of esteem" that come about through election. The fame and esteem bestowed through elections could even be more important than material gain acquired through greed, Hamilton reasoned.

Many believe that elections serve an educational role, too. In a relative sense, Americans pay only a limited amount of attention to public affairs. In a series of polls by numerous organizations, the overall finding seems to be that Americans lack understanding of many of the specifics of public affairs. For instance, even though he had been in the headlines a great deal during Donald Trump's first year in office, less than half of Americans could identify Robert Mueller, the person leading the Justice Department's investigation into Russian involvement in the 2016 election. Only about one-third of those under 30 could identify him. What is surprising about this is that levels of knowledge and interest are waning at precisely the same time there are more media outlets devoted to public affairs.[8]

Things might be much worse if not for the frequency of elections, however. Many would balk at the notion that elections educate citizens, given the growing number of 30-second television commercials and the craze for negative campaigning. But many studies suggest that voters learn a good deal from elections even when campaigns are negative.[9] One experimental study found that the more campaign ads a citizen sees, the more informed that person is. This team of scholars writes, "The brevity of the advertising message may strengthen its educational value. The typical person's attention span for political information is notoriously short-lived … [and] the great majority of voters bypass or ignore information that entails more than minimal costs … Campaign advertising meets the demand for both simplicity and access."[10]

Related, elections serve to introduce many Americans to their role as citizens. "Civic duty" is an amorphous term, but it implies, at the very least, helping to choose who will run the government. By providing citizens this opportunity, additional acts of civic participation may follow. Put a bit differently, many presume that elections serve to prime the pump of public life in a democracy.

Finally, elections serve as a safety-valve. Americans take it for granted that change in the control of government will be peaceful. We move from one administration to another, and from control by one party to the other, without violence. Losing candidates and their supporters may not like the outcome, but accept the will of the voters, peacefully, as noted above. But this was not a settled matter during the early days of our republic. Elections at the state and local level occasionally spilled over into violence. As the electorate organized into opposing camps (the first political parties) for the heated rematch between Thomas Jefferson and John Adams in 1800, many worried that the outcome would be violence. George Washington's fatherly charisma had created stability and calm in the previous contests, even as the nation was undergoing rapid transformation and developing a national identity. But in the 1800 contest Washington was absent. Indeed, many historians and political scientists believe this was the most important election in US history. Adams and Jefferson differed sharply on a range of issues and fundamental questions about the meaning of the separation from England (was it a war for independence or a true revolution?). In the end, the electorate selected Jefferson and handed the legislature to his like-minded colleagues, switching control of government to a new party. According to historian William Nisbet Chambers, the election of 1800 marked a high point in the nation's history – and perhaps even in the development of governments. He writes:

> It was the first such grand, democratic, peaceful transfer of power in modern politics. It was an example of a procedure which many old as well as many new nations have yet to experience, which many defeated factions or parties have found it difficult or intolerable to accept, but one which 1801 did much to "fix" on the American scene.[11]

Jefferson's victory signaled that the new system would indeed be very different, that the war had ushered in a bold democratic experiment. It also marked one of the few times in world history that a government (Adams and the Federalists) would be replaced by another government (Jefferson and the Democratic-Republicans) *peacefully*. Adams lost the election and was devastated. His humiliation would linger until his death. But he did not dispute the results. He did not call out the army or put guards in the windows of the White House. In the middle of the night, Adams departed the capital and headed home to his farm in Massachusetts.

Fast forward to the 1992 presidential election. Early in the race the incumbent Republican George H.W. Bush was way ahead in the polls. By the end of the Persian Gulf War in 1991 his approval rating stood at a staggering 91 percent. He seemed on his way to keeping his residency at the White House. But then a young, dynamic candidate from Arkansas named Bill Clinton burst on the scene. By pounding one issue over and over – "It's the economy, stupid!" – Clinton was able to nudge past Bush. And there was little love between the candidates; they did not like each other. But shortly after the election (and before Clinton was sworn into office) the president and Barbara Bush invited Bill and Hillary Clinton to the White House for tea. As the Clintons arrived, they were met with handshakes and smiles. As they walked into the White House, Barbara Bush reached down to hold Hillary Clinton's hand. The nasty, rough election was over – and a new leader would take over. As a noteworthy postscript, the two men became good friends after Clinton's presidency. In the summer of 2018, as Mr. Bush's health was fading, Bill Clinton once again traveled to the Bush summer home in Maine to visit and share memories.

Transitions of power in the United States have been peaceful, due in large measure to the legitimacy of elections. We may not like the outcome, but we accept the process. Without this mechanism, one can certainly imagine strife and maybe even violence. Frustrations are vented through campaigns and at the ballot box. Violence is checked by the opportunity to change the government through the ballot.

And Then … The Shortcomings of Elections

As we pull back the curtain, the limits of elections come into view. One real possibility is that our over-reliance on these events short-circuits our involvement in other, more effective modes of political action. They may not reflect the policy preferences of citizens and may maintain a system that is biased toward elites. Instead of offering a democratic check on the government, it is conceivable that elections stifle our involvement in the political process, distort the public will, and bolster the position of elites.

While we might all agree that republicanism is necessary for a nation as big and complex as the United States, what is the best way to select representatives? To suggest that the democratic governing process is enhanced when a smaller group speaks and acts on behalf of the larger public begs the question of how these leaders might be picked. Does the republican principle compel elections? Perhaps not. Consider a few other possibilities:

Random Selection. Why not randomly select members of the community, perhaps through a lottery? While many would think this an odd suggestion, something very similar to this occurs in every community in the United States when picking a jury for court proceedings. Those accused of a crime are judged by a jury of their peers. A process like this would not guarantee a government run by experts, per se, but as long as every citizen has the same chance of being selected it would be a fair, open system. It would likely bring to office leaders who reflect the overall population. We use polls to measure what the public wants, so why not employ a similar process for selecting leaders? And of course, under this model we could jettison the long, expensive, often nasty election process. Random selection would be quick, painless and representative.

A Review of Qualifications. If a random selection process would not fly, how about a board or computer program to review the qualifications of members of the community and select the "best" to serve? The philosopher Plato had something similar in mind. In his ideal state or utopia, rulers would be selected based on their superior wisdom. To win acceptance of this person, Plato suggested a novel scheme: "We shall tell our people in this fable, that all of you are brothers; but the god who fashioned you mixed gold in the composition of those among you who are fit to rule, so that they are of the most precious quality; and he put silver in the Auxiliaries, and iron and brass in the farmers and craftsmen." That is to say, why shouldn't the best and brightest be called to serve? Are elections the best mechanism to pick these men and women?

An Examination. Another possibility would be to give a test to those citizens anxious to serve and fill government posts, with those receiving the highest scores being sent to office. This approach would be similar to a merit-based or civil service system now used to fill many government posts. Why not give the best qualified and the most intelligent the opportunity to serve? Surely we could come up with an instrument to figure out the most qualified. Perhaps the criteria could shift given the circumstances of the day. Might there also be some sort of character assessment – a kind of political Rorschach test?

Hand-Picked Successors. As odd as it might seem, historically in some systems officials were allowed to hand-pick their successors. Wanting to preserve their standing with the public, these officials would choose citizens who would do a good job. Having been in office, they would know the strengths and limitations of many would-be officials and the skills necessary for the job.

In short, there are many ways to select representatives – elections being just one option. If you are interested in selecting leaders who will reflect the will of the people, then a jury-like system might be a better mechanism than elections. It would surely be less time-consuming and less expensive, and it would break any real or perceived link between big money contributors and elected officials. It would also immediately diversify halls of government; with a random system, we could expect, for instance, about half of the posts to be held by women, and members of other demographic groups that have historically been limited in politics would have a chance to govern. Again, if we rely on pollsters to tell us what people think, why not use the same types of techniques to select representatives?

When we look at the avenues for modifying the outcome of the policy – the heart of governance – elections emerge as a rather ineffectual choice. Elections may not ensure any redirection in policy. They merely guarantee the possibility that the people running parts of the government could change. In systems that have a two-party model, such as the United States, candidates usually merge toward the center of the ideological spectrum. In recent years, the polarization of American parties has grown and there are widening differences between the parties, but compared to other political systems across the globe the two parties remain quite similar, quite moderate. So even bringing officials of a different party to power does not necessarily translate into big policy changes. That is to say, the major parties in the United States hug the middle of the ideological spectrum.

Furthermore, many aspects of government are beyond the reach of elected officials. Most regulations that guide everyday life in America are set by bureaucrats, only tangentially linked to elected officials. Many of the most critical factors that impact daily lives spring from the acts of corporations and the acts of other nations. Then there is the issue of "constitutional obstruction." The framers of our system were so concerned about the potential for corruption and tyranny that they introduced an intricate system of checks, balances and shared powers. An election or even a set of elections that ushers in dramatic new policies – policies that change the lives of everyday citizens – have been rare.

Many political scientists and pundits have begun to speculate that the distrust many Americans feel toward government is due to frustration over the election–policy disconnect. "He told us that he would make big changes if he won the election. Well, he won, so why haven't things changed?" In other words, to win, candidates make big promises, but once in office, making changes becomes difficult. The break between what candidates promise and what elected officials can deliver leaves the public frustrated and at times angry.

Have we not seen big changes in our system ushered in by elections? The answer is yes, and in some ways no. On the one hand, there is no doubt that elections matter; that there are things that successful candidates can do to shift the government regardless of the limits discussed above. While Donald Trump had modest success on some of his big policy plans in the first two years in office, changes did happen. For instance, an article published in the *Washington Post* in December of 2017, entitled "How Scott Pruitt Turned the EPA into One of Trump's Most Powerful Tools," charts how environmental policy in the United States shifted dramatically.[12] There are many examples of big policy shifts brought in by new government personnel. Yes, elections have consequences.

On the other hand, were these really big changes or merely incremental shifts designed to stave-off large-scale revolts? During the middle of the Trump–Clinton election, scholar Roslyn Fuller penned a provocative piece in *The Nation*, where she raised an interesting point:

> If the people of a nation held political power, one would expect them to pass laws in the interests of the majority consistently, and that the political landscape would reflect this. But it was hard to see why the majority of citizens would ever agree, for example, to allow wealth to play such a dramatic role in elections (congressional candidates that outspend their opponents win 78 percent of their races), given that the vast majority of people are, per definition, not rich.[13]

She goes on to write that Americans only believed they had power because the standard of living seemed to go up for each generation. Their affluence was due to an abundance of free or cheap labor (slaves at first and immigrants later) and with abundant natural resources. The collapse of the middle and working class in America, she argues, springs from an end of these forces. And there's not a thing voters can do about it.

Another concern is that elections lead many citizens to believe that voting is their best or only opportunity to become involved in politics. They may be frustrated with the way things are going, but feel their only course of action is to vote or to help a candidate. This is called episodic participation, rather than ongoing involvement with multiple modes of engagement. Voting becomes a placebo – an act that has a limited effect but allows us to feel as though it does more. If Americans did not hold elections in such high esteem, it is likely that other modes of political participation that are equally or more effective might become more popular. Fuller hits on this point as well:

> Under the present constitutional system, there simply isn't much that the masses can threaten [the elite] with. They are as superfluous to the economy as they always were to the political system, required to act merely in a superficial capacity as consumers or as voters – roles that have increasingly come to coincide.[14]

American history has shown that significant change can occur when average citizens mobilize, lobby elites, take matters to the courts or seek changes in political culture. Writing of the civil rights movement during the 1960s, scholar Howard Reiter noted, "From organizing voter-registration campaigns under threats of violence in the South to massive rallies in the North, the civil rights movement resorted to almost every form of political participation besides voting in order to overthrow the old system in the South."[15] A more contemporary example might be the drive for LGBTQ rights. Incredible changes have been ushered in over the last decade, very few of them by elected officials. By putting all our eggs in only one engagement basket, the will of the people may go unnoticed.

Some might argue that if one were to envision a governing system where a large number of citizens were given a chance to play a role that they *believed* to be significant, but in reality had only a minimal impact, the current election-centered approach in the United States might rise to the top. This would be especially true if large pools of citizens with the most to gain from dramatic changes refrained from involvement. Even a cursory examination of the demographics of non-voters reveals that the citizens most in need of policy change are likely also the ones *least* likely to participate.

We believe elections push officials toward a particular policy course, but that may not be what occurs. Instead, voters select a given candidate for any number of reasons, a particular policy position being just one option. Each voter has a slightly different motivation or a mix of motives for choosing one candidate over another. Assuming that the results of an election mean a particular thing can be a mistake. An oft-cited example would be the election of 1980, which matched incumbent president Jimmy Carter against Ronald Reagan. Reagan prevailed by a rather large margin, suggesting that the American electorate had shifted toward his brand of conservatism. Reagan and his followers proclaimed a mandate and proceeded to make sweeping changes. Many Democrats, too, believed the election signified a turn to the political right, and were quite willing to go along. The so-called "Reagan Revolution" became the justification for a broad swath of changes. The only problem, however, was that public opinion polls suggested that the root of Reagan's win was dissatisfaction with Jimmy Carter – and much less to do with a growing conservative tide. If anything, the public was voting against Carter's failed economic policies and not necessarily for Reagan's plans. Reagan benefited from the perception that he was strong, stately and trustworthy. Voters simply liked Ronald Reagan – and disliked Carter.

In fairness, many Democratic victories have also been misinterpreted as an expression of a desire to radically change governmental policy. Some might point to the 2008 election. On the one hand, many, especially Democrats and supporters of Barack Obama, held that the thumping of the Republicans implied the public's interest in dramatic change. After all, Obama's campaign theme was "Change we can believe in," and his party won the White House and control of both chambers in Congress. But within one year after the election Obama's change agenda had stalled, if not collapsed. Republicans were winning governorships and state legislative contests across the country, and even Democrats seemed to be backing off from significant policy adjustments.

One of the early interpretations of Donald Trump's victory in 2016 centered on economic policies. Many voters, particularly in the Midwestern industrial states, sided with Trump because they thought he would reshape the nation's economy and bring back good jobs. His business background seemed well-suited to usher in a new approach, and it was the working-class voters who rallied behind Trump. And yet, a growing pool of studies suggests attitudes toward immigration, blacks, and social welfare were much more critical to Trump voters than the state of the economy.[16] It is likely that Trump's comments about immigrants and his steadfast promise to build a wall between the United States and Mexico were more persuasive to his backers than his economic plans. It is illustrative that as the 2018 midterm elections approached, and it appeared that Trump's GOP colleagues in Congress were poised for a rough election, the president repeatedly raised the specter of hordes of immigrants "infesting" America and seemed to pick what many saw as unnecessary fights with prominent black people, including Congresswomen Maxine Waters, CNN news anchor Don Lemon, and basketball star LeBron James. Many analysts thought these moves were a not-so-subtle push to fire up his base of supporters.

Related, the outcome of an election is as much a function of who comes to the polls as it is the policy preference of citizens. How could voters overwhelmingly send Barack Obama back to the White House in 2012, but two years later solidify Republican control of Congress? Can't the voters make up their minds? How could they send Trump to the White House, but turn around and give Democrats huge gains in 2018? Some voters change their minds, but much of the flip-flopping between elections is due to variations in turnout; some voters turn out for certain elections, while others stay on the sidelines. In this light, does it really make sense to interpret the outcome of a midterm election as a call to redirect public policy – or is it merely a reflection of the preferences of a *particular group* of citizens? Was the blue wave in 2018 a recalibration of the system, but the Republican tide in 2014 just an aberration? Even in high-turnout presidential elections, upward of half of citizens fail to cast a ballot.

Maybe it is not policy issues that drive vote choice, but vague, nebulous views of candidate traits and other idiosyncratic factors. There is a great deal of literature on voter information-processing, much of it unflattering.[17] It is not at all clear that voters have ever absorbed a broad range of information or sifted through competing evidence. It is likely elites have always been able to manipulate mass opinion, to some degree. Heuristics, especially party identification, are used to sort and filter information. In 2018, Vanderbilt University political scientist Larry Bartels commented,

> So much of politics, not surprisingly, turns out to be about expressive behavior rather than instrumental behavior – in other words,

people making decisions based on momentary feeling and not on some sound understanding of how those decisions will improve or hurt their life. And so if you think about people using the democratic levers that they have available to them to express themselves, rather than to make instrumental choices, you're probably more often than not going to be closer to the actual psychology of what they're up to.[18]

Democracy, in its purest form, is a process that brings citizens together to resolve issues and disputes. This implies face-to-face deliberation – airing your views and listening to the concerns of others. It is an interpersonal brainstorming process of give-and-take. Many clubs and organizations operate in this fashion; issues are debated and resolved with a show of hands. Through discussion and extended deliberation, citizens become not only better informed about their view on a particular matter, but also more sensitive to the opinions of others in the community. As noted by the philosopher John Stuart Mill, "He is called upon, when so engaged, to weigh interests not his own; to be guided in causes of conflicting claims, by another rule than his private partialities."[19]

But participation in elections is, in many ways, an isolated, individualized act. We discuss candidates and platforms before the election with friends and family, but when it comes to our behavior (casting a vote), it is a private matter, done in the concealment of the polling booth. Why is it considered impolite to ask someone how they voted? By turning elections into an individual act, private interests are more likely to displace the public spirit. In other words, is it possible that the current model discourages thinking about the collective? The long-term stability of a system is predicated on citizens looking beyond their short-term interest to the general welfare. The privation of politics makes that less likely.

Campaigning these days requires a tremendous amount of time, huge sums of money, and often unsavory mudslinging and negative campaign commercials. Running for statewide positions, and to some extent, congressional posts has become a full-time job for a year or more before the election. A trend in the press coverage of candidates is to disclose ever-more intimate, private information. Who would want to go through this process? Many outstanding citizens, thoroughly anxious to serve their community, state, or nation, will never run because elections have become personally invasive.

Along similar lines, it seems that the outcome of an election might hinge on small-scale campaign factors. During the 2012 race for the Republican presidential nomination, for example, Texas Governor Rick Perry seemed to be riding high in the early polls. He had a strong record and many endorsements from prominent members of his party. But in early November 2011, at a televised debate, Perry failed to remember the name of one of the federal agencies that he would eliminate if elected president. He had spoken of this issue on many occasions, but during the debate he simply could not remember the name. Perry's "oops moment" set his campaign on a downward spiral; he was never able to recover. He was out because of a momentary loss of memory.

Perry is not alone. The author of this book co-authored another volume on the "crisis points" of presidential campaigns since 1952. They write, "In most presidential elections there are critical moments, key events during the campaigns that weigh heavily on the outcome." Elections can be won or lost by tiny events, they argue. But how much impact should small gaffes have on the outcome of an election? Should a slipped word or phrase, an off-hand remark, or a one-time transgression trump other considerations? If elections allow voters to consider a broad range of character and policy matters, why would small transgressions matter? Part of the answer is that news coverage of modern presidential campaigns can relentlessly rehash even the slightest misstep. The former governor of Vermont, Howard Dean, was overly exuberant at a campaign rally during his run for the White House in 2004, leaning too close to the microphone and yelling to his supporters. An unflattering clip of the event, a mere 15 seconds from this long campaign, was shared widely, and mocked online and on late-night television. It marked the end of his campaign.

Finally, perhaps the most significant limitation of elections might be their vulnerability to corruption. The heart of the election–democracy nexus is that citizens should have an equal opportunity to select leaders and that they would do so based on the character of candidates and the positions they take. Each candidate would stand on equal footing – that is, no candidate would have an unfair advantage – and the ultimate decision is made by all of the citizens of the community.

But what happens when some candidates have a huge advantage, such as massive financial resources to get their message out? Is it possible that the media can distort the election process by giving some candidates better coverage than others? What about very well-funded "outside groups" that flood the airways with misleading commercials? What if laws limit which adults can vote? Should we care if most incumbent candidates – that is, those already in office – have no serious opposition? What if legal barriers aid certain political parties and their candidates, while at the same time limiting the potency of others? And of course the specter of computer hacking and the spreading of false stories on social media jumped to the fore in 2018.

Conclusion: Do We Consent to a System that Limits Our Say in Government?

If we were to ask what defines a democratic system, most Americans would mention, among other things, the ability of average citizens to select public officials. If we are allowed to select the personnel of government, then the system itself will respond to our needs and interests, it is assumed. Historians and students of government would likely note that our dependence on elections has contributed to our nation's stability and its democratic character. It is one of many elements of our body politic that has set us apart – and it has been a model for fledgling democracies across the globe.

At the same time, while we might suggest that elections can serve democratic ends, there is no guarantee that these events reflect the will of the people. In fact, one of the most destabilizing, discouraging developments can be an over-reliance on elections. This is especially true when there is an expectation of rapid, dramatic change in a system designed for slow, incremental adjustments – as is the case in the United States. While elections might be necessary for a democracy, they are not sufficient.

In the 1920s Italian political theorist Antonio Gramsci introduced the concept of cultural hegemony. There are two ways that the ruling elite seeks to control the public, he argued, control and consent. The problem with control is that it can be difficult to achieve and expensive, usually entailing the military. Brute force works, but it is costly. Consent, on the other hand, can be secured by the careful, deliberate construction of beliefs, expectations, norms, and perceptions. People will consent to their misery, Gramsci reasoned, if they unknowingly buy into a system they see as normal and inevitable.

After reviewing the limits of an election-centered system, perhaps we should consider Gramsci's cultural hegemony. Do we consent to a system that limits our say in the government? Has the belief that elections can solve our problems become so ingrained in our consciousness that we rarely think of their shortcomings? Do small-scale reforms dealing with, for instance, campaign finance, voter registration, redistricting and the Electoral College divert our attention from the big picture? Do those in power really want mass engagement in politics? Levitsky and Ziblatt argued that the death of modern democracies does not spring from violent uprisings and the rapid ascent of an authoritarian leader, but instead through the ballot box. "The tragic route to authoritarianism is that democracy's assassins use the very institutions of democracy – gradually, and even legally – to kill it."[20]

Effective political activism in a democracy can move along an array of pathways. Many important changes in our government and society occurred *in spite* of majority will, often reflected in election returns. Wise activists know the power of the courts to thwart recalcitrant, poll-driven elected officials, for example. Demonstrations, sit-ins, protests, boycotts, lobbying and an endless variety of civic actions have helped pave the road toward a more perfect union. Does trusting that the next election will redeem our faith in government pose a grave risk? Legitimacy is critical in any system but foundational in a democracy. Will disappointment and cynicism morph into outrage?

Elections have consequences. Again, it matters that Donald Trump was sent to the White House and not Hillary Clinton. Which party controls Congress is a big deal, and we should care about who is sent to the governor's mansion, the state legislature and the city council. We learn from elections and they can pull us from our private lives into the civic realm, which is a good thing. We will continue to pay close attention to these events if for no other reason than they are spectacles that drive ratings, viewers and hits. Americans will never completely break their love affair with elections, nor should they.

But Americans should appreciate that by narrowly focusing on these episodic contests, other, perhaps more viable, avenues of change are neglected. Is it possible that our fixation on elections is a mode of control – a nice, tidy way to allow the public to *believe* they are in charge? In real ways, elections have become the show pony when what we need is a work horse. In the next chapter we will question the judgment of James Madison and his colleagues for not codifying the right to vote and explicitly charting the conduct of elections in the Constitution. Leaving much of this up to the states has caused real problems. Yet, maybe they were in some ways right in arguing that and the true spirit of our democracy will be the clash of numerous, diverse groups, and the struggle will be ongoing rather than on a Tuesday in early November.

Notes

1 Jon Meacham, *The Soul of America: The Battle for Our Better Angels* (New York: Random House, 2018), 266.
2 V.O. Key Jr., *The Responsible Electorate: Rationality in Presidential Voting, 1936–1960* (New York: Vintage, 1968), 11.
3 As cited in Gerald M. Pomper, *Elections in America: Control and Influence in Democratic Politics* (New York: Longman, 1980), 20.
4 David Brooks, "Fragile at the Core," *New York Times* website, June 18, 2009 (www.nytimes.com/2009/06/19/opinion/19brooks.html).
5 Ainsley Earheardt, "Claim That up to 5.7 Million Non-citizens Voted is Wrong," *Politifact*, June 22, 2017 (www.politifact.com/florida/statements/2017/jun/22/ainsley-earhardt/following-trump-voter-fraud-allegations-claim-57-m/).
6 Philip Bump, "Trump Claims an ID is Needed to Buy Cereal and that Fraudulent Voters Simply Switch Hats," *Washington Post*, November 14, 2018.
7 Massimo Calabresi, "Inside the Secret Plan to Stop Vladimir Putin's US Election Plot," *Time*, July 20, 2017.
8 Pew Research Center, "From Brexit to Zika: What Do Americans Know?," July 25, 2017 (www.people-press.org/2017/07/25/from-brexit-to-zika-what-do-americans-know/).
9 John G. Geer, *In Defense of Negativity: Attack Ads in Presidential Campaigns* (Chicago, IL: University of Chicago Press, 2016).

10 Stephen Ansolabehere and Shanot Iyengar, *Going Negative: How Political Advertisements Shrink and Polarize the Electorate* (New York: Free Press, 1997), 60.

11 William Nisbet Chambers, *Political Parties in a New Nation: The American Experience, 1776–1809* (New York: Oxford University Press, 1963), 169.

12 Brady Dennis and Juliet Eilperin, "How Scott Pruitt Turned the EPA into One of Trump's Most Powerful Tools," *The Washington Post* website, December 31, 2017 (www.washingtonpost.com/national/health-science/under-scott-pruitt-a-year-of-tumult-and-transformation-at-epa/2017/12/26/f93d1262-e017-11e7-8679-a9728984779c_story.html?utm_term=.7f19345de714).

13 Rosalyn Fuller, "Why is American Democracy So Broken, and Can It be Fixed?," *The Nation* website, June 9, 2016 (www.thenation.com/article/why-is-american-democracy-so-broken-and-can-it-be-fixed/).

14 Ibid.

15 Howard L. Reiter, *Parties and Elections in Corporate America,* 2nd Edition (New York: Longman, 1993), 4–6.

16 Matthew Akers, "Voters and the 2016 Election," lecture presented at State of the Parties: 2016 and Beyond in University of Akron, November 9, 2017.

17 Phillip Converse, "The Nature of Belief Systems in Mass Publics," in D.E. Apter, ed., *Ideology and Discontent* (New York: Free Press of Glencoe, 1964); Bryan Caplan, *The Myth of the Rational Voter: Why Democracies Choose Bad Policies* (Princeton, NJ: Princeton University Press, 2007); Richard Niemi, Herbert F. Wiesberg, and David Kimball, *Controversies in Voting Behavior*, 5th Edition (Washington: Congressional Quarterly, 2010).

18 Sean Illing, "Two Eminent Political Scientists: The Problem with Democracy is Voters," *Vox*, June 24, 2017 (www.vox.com/policy-and-politics/2017/6/1/15515820/donald-trump-democracy-brexit-2016-election-europe).

19 John Stuart Mill, *Considerations on Representative Government* (New York: Liberal Arts Press, 1958), 114.

20 Steven Levitsky and Daniel Ziblatt, *How Democracies Die* (New York: Crown Publishing Group, 2018), 8.

3 Give Us the Ballot
Why Has the Right to Vote Been So Contentious?

Americans hold voting and elections as the cornerstone of their democracy, but throughout much of the nation's history vast numbers of citizens have been barred from entering the polling booth. We cling to the notion that Jefferson articulated in the Declaration of Independence, that the acts of our government should spring from the will of the people, but one of the clearest ways to instruct those in power – the ballot – historically has been the prerogative of white affluent men. It was not until 1828, for example, that the last state removed religious qualifications for voting. Most states kept property qualifications until halfway through the 1800s, and for nearly 100 years Native Americans were barred from the polling booth. In 1887, the Chinese Exclusion Act restricted the naturalization of hundreds of thousands of residents, mostly living in California, as a tool to limit their role in elections.

Constitutional amendments enfranchised African Americans in 1869, but southern states engineered all possible methods to deny blacks access to the polls. These constraints on African Americans lasted for nearly a century, and while the Voting Rights Act of 1965 ushered in monumental changes, the journey of its passage was long and very controversial, and a recent court decision has gutted key provisions. It was not until 1961 that residents of Washington, DC received the right to vote for the president, and even though they were being drafted and dying on the battlefields of Southeast Asia by the thousands, 18-year-olds were not granted the right to vote in all states until 1971. It took until 1920 for women to be granted the right to vote across the nation. Today, more than half of the states restrict voting for felons and a dizzying array of laws curb voting through residency, registration and identification requirements. The history of the United States is filled with examples of rules and requirements designed to keep people from voting.

Why would this be true? Harvard scholar Thomas Patterson explored this issue in his oft-cited book *The Vanishing Voter*. He writes, "Although there are many things to celebrate about the American political system, its handling of the vote is not among them. It is not simply that voting rates here are substantially lower than in nearly every other democracy.

America's electoral history is replete with examples of public policies designed to deny or suppress the vote."[1]

Over the course of our nation's history, legal changes have expanded opportunities to participate in elections, and the system is more open now than at any other point in the past. These changes have lessened the historic blight, but many limits and barriers remain.[2] There have also been moves at the state level to tighten the parameters of who can vote, as well as changes in the mechanics of the process. In some ways, it seems the electorate is expanding, but in others it appears to be shrinking. Voting, notes Patterson, is today too often "treated as a privilege rather than inalienable right, something to be earned (or, in some cases, arbitrarily withheld) rather than something so intrinsic to citizenship that government makes every reasonable effort to promote its exercise."[3]

This chapter will explore the institutional and legal dynamics that have shaped the right to vote in the United States. The core question guiding our inquiry is why access to the voting booth has been so restricted given our belief that elections are a foundational ingredient of any democracy. Why has America denied so many the right to vote for so long?

Voting and the Constitution

As we have said, the framers of the Constitution wanted to preserve the democratic ideals espoused during the Revolution, but also create a secure, stable political system. Under the Articles of Confederation, widespread elections, mostly at the state legislative level, fueled a turbulent process – at least in the minds of the men gathered at the Constitutional Convention. As one delegate suggested, "The evils we experience flow from the excesses of democracy."[4] A number of mechanisms were used to accomplish the goal of crafting a more stable democratic system, including a limited electoral system. Elections would be used heavily at the state level, but for the national government direct popular elections would be used to fill only one branch of government: the House of Representatives. But who should be allowed to vote for members of the House? Qualifications for voting were considered at length at the Constitutional Convention. A key issue was whether there should be property qualifications. Rather than yet another mechanism to deepen the elitist nature of the government, the concern was that those without property might be inclined to sell their votes. "Very few men who have no property," noted John Adams, "have any judgment of their own."[5] James Madison agreed. Conversely, those with property would be less susceptible to corruption. At the time, every state imposed property qualifications; it was not a controversial issue. (Interestingly, many states allowed non-citizens and even former slaves to vote, so long as they owned property.) But this and other qualifications were rejected at the Convention because, as noted by one delegate, "the right of suffrage was a tender point, and strongly guarded by most of the [state] constitutions."[6] In other words, why step on toes when the ratification of the entire scheme was tenuous?

The result of their deliberation is Article I, Section 2 of the Constitution: Voters for the US House of Representatives "shall have the qualifications requisite for Electors of the most numerous branch of the state legislature." In other words, if the state you reside in allows you to vote in state house contests, then you must be allowed to vote for the US House of Representatives. There is no record of any constitutional delegate suggesting a right to vote be codified in the Constitution – not even for white, propertied men. Similarly, the Anti-Federalists did not raise the issue during the debate over ratification.

The Constitution grants states the power to oversee most election rules and to set voter qualifications. Article I, Section 4 of the Constitution notes that the "times, places, and manner of holding elections" is to be "prescribed in each state by the legislature thereof." Congress, nevertheless, is given the opportunity to change these laws. "Congress may at any time by law make or alter such regulations." The intent was to allow states to regulate the election process – so long as the Congress remained silent. This clause would become critical for the Voting Rights Act of 1965, for example.

In order to help secure state ratification of the Constitution, the Federalists offered to add amendments designed to protect citizens from infringements by the federal government; they would create a Bill of Rights. A vast number of rights were considered, but none addressed voting or elections.

Given the wording and intent of the original Constitution and the absence of early amendments related to voting, it seems clear that the framers wanted the states to handle most election-related issues. The end result, as noted by Lichtman, was that the Constitution severed voting rights from citizenship. "Most US citizens in the early republic could not vote, because of gender, age, residency, race or economic restrictions. Yet in many states non-citizens could vote if they met other suffrage requirements."[7] What is more, "under the Constitution, any American-born citizen, boy or girl, black or while, could grow up to be president, even if they could not vote."[8] Then, as now, the right to vote is very much dependent on one's place of residence.[9]

The first constitutional changes to broaden the scope of the electorate were the 14th and 15th Amendments. These changes, plus the 13th Amendment banning slavery, are commonly referred to as the Reconstruction or Civil War Amendments. They represent the desire of the northerners to confer the rights of citizenship for black Americans. These amendments represent the first attempt to write a broader level of suffrage into the Constitution.

The 14th Amendment deals with voting rights indirectly. The first clause defines citizenship, and confers the rights of citizenship to all persons born or naturalized in the United States.[10] The authors of the amendment clearly hoped this clause would force states to broaden the franchise, given this inclusive definition of "citizen," but they were soon proved wrong. While the southern states were forced by the Federal Reconstruction Acts to give the vote to African Americans,[11] voters in several northern states refused to do the same. After eleven referenda (public votes on policy questions) in eight northern states, only two states approved black suffrage.[12] Seeking to guarantee the vote for African Americans, and to gain an electoral advantage from a wave of presumably Republican-voting blacks, the Republican Congress passed the 15th Amendment, which says that "race, color, or previous condition of servitude" could not be used to deny a person the right to vote. Representing the first clear broadening of suffrage in the Constitution, this amendment seemed to move our nation closer to the democratic ideal called for in the Declaration of Independence.[13]

But it did not last long. The presidential election of 1876 was extremely close. On the day after the election, Republican Rutherford B. Hayes held a one-vote margin in the Electoral College despite losing the popular vote to Democrat Samuel J. Tilden by 264,000 votes. There were contested results in three southern states, and because neither candidate could garner a majority in the Electoral College without the electors of those states, a deadlock ensued. A commission was set up by Congress to settle the matter, and after three months of partisan haggling, a compromise was reached. Congress would validate the electors necessary to make Hayes president, but in exchange he was to name one southerner to his cabinet and, most significantly, end Reconstruction. It would mean "home rule" for the South – the withdrawal of the federal troops that had been instrumental in enforcing the Civil War Amendments and protecting the rights of the newly freed slaves. In other words, Hayes would become president if he and his fellow Republicans in Congress agreed to withdraw the Union from the South, leaving the enforcement of civil rights for African Americans to the states. It was agreed, and in short order the curtain was drawn. The Compromise of 1877, often dubbed the Second Corrupt Deal, is yet another ugly chapter in our nation's long march toward racial equality.

Southern states quickly used their power to regulate federal and state elections to keep African Americans from the polls. Collectively called Jim Crow laws, they employed a variety of restrictions – literacy tests, poll taxes, complicated registration requirements, residency requirements and the infamous grandfather clause (which exempted a voter from the complicated requirements if his grandfather had voted before 1860). Using these restrictions, southern states managed to disenfranchise most blacks and even poor whites who would threaten the dominance of the conservative wing of the Democratic Party. Many other insidious tricks were used, such as locating a community's polling place in a remote area or near the site of recent lynchings of African Americans. Outright intimidation and threats of violence were commonplace.

It is hard to overstate the significance of the Compromise of 1877. It was a bold, egregious capitulation of the rights of millions of citizens. During Reconstruction, African Americans constituted a majority of the population in several southern states. There were waves of registration, and nationwide the percentage of black men that were eligible to vote rose from 0.5 percent to 80 percent by 1868.[14] One hundred years later and in front of a joint session of Congress to push for the 1965 Voting Rights Act, President Lyndon Johnson, himself a southerner, spelled out the barriers to voting for African Americans:

> Every device of which human ingenuity is capable has been used to deny this right. The Negro citizen may go to register only to be told that the day is wrong, or the hour is late, or the official in charge is absent. And if he persists and if he manages to present himself to the registrar, he may be disqualified because he did not spell out his middle name or because he abbreviated a word on the application. And if he manages to fill out an application he is given a test. The registrar is the sole judge of whether he passes this test. He may be asked to recite the entire Constitution, or explain the more complex provisions of State law. And even a college degree cannot be used to prove that he can read and write. For the fact is that the only way to pass these barriers is to show a white skin ...[15]

A favorite exclusionary tool was the white primary. The Democratic Party dominated the South after the 1870s, so the winner of the Democratic nomination contest was the de facto winner of the election. Southern election laws held political parties to be "private organizations" with the right to decide their own membership, and state Democratic parties took advantage of that by excluding blacks from their primaries. Thus, while blacks might have enjoyed the right to vote in the general election, as stipulated in the 15th Amendment, they could not vote in the only election that counted – the Democratic primary.[16] This practice remained in effect until the court decision in *Smith v. Allwright* (1944)[17] where the court said that primaries were part of the electoral system and therefore the exclusion of blacks from this process violated the 15th Amendment.

More will be said of the Progressive Era in subsequent chapters. Briefly stated, it was a period around the turn of the 20th century that included a series of reforms aimed at reducing corruption in business and politics. Several changes expanded the size of the electorate as a means of chipping away at the role of elites. The 17th Amendment, ratified in 1913, required the direct election of US Senators. Prior to this, Senators were selected by state legislatures, which were often controlled by corrupt party bosses and their fat cat financial contributors.

It is worth noting that the 19th Amendment, granting women the right to vote, was the product of a long grassroots movement. We can date the beginning of organized agitation for the vote to 1848, when the feminist Declaration of Sentiments was issued. This document, ratified by the first women's rights convention at Seneca Falls, New York, was modeled on the Declaration of Independence. Throughout the second half of the 19th century, the women's rights movement gained steam, propelled by knowledge and experience gained in the fight to abolish slavery and mandate broad-based public education. Frontier life helped fuel the movement for women's voting rights, too, as women stood side-by-side men to build communities in western states. The first state to grant women the right to vote was Wyoming in 1890, followed by Utah and Idaho in 1896. Conversely, urbanization also helped the feminist movement, as education, lower birthrates and the need for many women to work outside the home combined to break down traditional gender roles.[18] Opposition to the change came mainly from the South and from eastern conservatives who feared that women would support other progressive causes, such as child labor restrictions.[19]

Throughout much of American history, many states and many local jurisdictions also used a poll tax – a fee for voting. The 24th Amendment to the Constitution outlawed this practice for federal office candidates in 1962. When the amendment was proposed, the tax was used in five states, and generally only amounted to a dollar or two. Many believe the tax was aimed at limiting voting by African Americans, although the US Commission on Civil Rights found that its use was not generally discriminatory.[20] Nevertheless, the poll tax had symbolic value, and aroused heated emotions among many liberals. While its effect on the size of the electorate may have been negligible, especially since the poll tax is still allowed in state and local elections, the Amendment struck down one of the last symbols of American Democracy's elitist and racist past.

The 26th Amendment guarantees 18-year-olds the right to vote, and was the last change to the Constitution to expand the franchise. It was the product of the massive social movements of the 1960s and the baby-boom, post-World War II period. Images of young men going off to die in the Vietnam War but not being able to vote in elections were a key part of the movement. The slogan "old enough to fight, old enough to vote" was often heard during the late 1960s and early 1970s.[21]

Initially, Congress attempted to lower the voting age through the Voting Rights Act of 1970. The Supreme Court partially thwarted this attempt by ruling that while Congress could lower the voting age in federal elections, it had no jurisdiction over state or local contests. Thus, a curious situation emerged, where 18-year-olds could be allowed to vote for president but not for governor or mayor. To remedy this, Congress passed the 26th Amendment on July 1, 1971. It passed with little objection and was ratified in three and a half months.[22]

Redistricting and Suffrage

The Great Compromise at the Constitutional Convention stipulated that the Congress be divided into two chambers, one with an identical number of officials from each state (the Senate) and the other based on the population of each state (the House of Representatives). To know the number of citizens in each state – the population – the Constitution mandates that a census be conducted every ten years and that the apportionment of seats to each state be dependent on this count. This chore of creating precise districts was left to the states – and has been the source of controversy throughout American history.

In the earliest days of the republic, many states simply made at-large districts. That is, if it were granted three seats in the House, then they would simply elect three members from the entire state. There were no districts, per se. Other states chose to divide their state into the number of congressional districts equal to the seats they had in the legislature. A state granted five seats in the House would have five congressional districts. The idea of changing legislative districts in response to population shifts stems from the American idea of geographic representation – the notion that legislators should be responsible and responsive to a group of people living in a specific geographic location.

The tricky and controversial part of the process has been drawing the exact boundaries for the districts every ten years based on a state's overall population and the movement of citizens throughout the state. This process of redrawing the boundaries of legislative districts is called redistricting. Historically, state legislatures have been given this responsibility, and because these bodies have nearly always been divided by partisanship, the process has been rife with bias.

The practice of drawing districts for political advantage is called gerrymandering, named after founding father Elbridge Gerry who, as governor of Massachusetts, drew an odd shaped district in order to elect a political ally.[23] An observer commented that the new district looked like a salamander, and another responded by saying it was not a salamander, but rather a "gerrymander." The idea behind gerrymandering is to create districts that will support a certain type of candidate – commonly either of the majority party or white – and is generally done by either "packing" or "cracking." Packing is where the opposition is lumped into one area. For instance, if the state has five districts, the strategy would be to create one district filled with supporters of the other party, so that the majority party could win in the other four districts. Cracking is when the opposition is broken into pieces so that they do not have a majority in any district.

As one might have guessed, the redistricting process was also used to minimize the electoral weight of African Americans and other minority groups. A state might boast, for example, a 20 percent black population, but through cracking, African American candidates could not win office without the help of white voters. For over 100 years after the end of Reconstruction, the number of African American members of Congress from the South was minuscule even though many states boasted large numbers of black residents.

While it is fair to say that partisan-centered gerrymandering has been used by both of the major parties for more than a century, what occurred in 2010 was exceptional. The Republican turnout was heavy that year, leading to huge gains in Congress and in state houses across the country. Powered by a fuming, engaged base and a network of conservative financial groups and advisors, packing and cracking moved into high gear. Two states are illustrative. In 2012, the first race after the Pennsylvania lines were drawn, the spread between Democratic and Republican House candidates in the 18 districts across the state (the aggregate) was nearly dead even – about 50 percent for each party. One could imagine, all things being equal, that each party would get about nine seats, more or less. But Democrats wound up with just five of the 18 seats. In other words, 50 percent of the popular vote led to just 28 percent of the seats in the House of Representatives.

The story in North Carolina is even more egregious. After the election, Republicans engineered a redistricting plan that was widely seen as radical.[24] African American votes were packed into a small number of districts, leading to what one observer called apartheid voting districts.[25] Statewide, Democratic House candidates netted *more* votes than their GOP counterparts, but ended up with just four of the 13 seats. One of the architects of the plan was David Lewis, a Republican in the General Assembly. He was rather candid in his motivations: "I think electing Republicans is better than electing Democrats. So I drew this map to help foster what I think is better for the country." He added: "I propose that we draw the maps to give a partisan advantage to ten Republicans and three Democrats because I do not believe it's possible to draw a map with 11 Republicans and two Democrats."[26]

Related to the contentious issue of drawing district lines is the issue of the number of residents per district. Oddly enough, the Constitution is silent on this matter, so for most of our nation's history many states did not ensure parity between districts. And yet, American political culture holds a nebulous idea that each citizen should have the same weight in the political process – that all men and women should have an equal role in the political process. Malapportioned districts violate this goal. (Interestingly, few seem ready to challenge the legitimacy of the US Senate, where states like Vermont and California, with dramatically different populations, boast the same number of legislators.)

The issue came to a head in a suit brought by a group of Tennessee residents who claimed that the state had denied them equal protection under the law by refusing to draw state legislative districts of the same population. The court had previously found similar cases to be beyond its jurisdiction, but a new and more liberal court decided that the Tennessee districts were so malapportioned that they constituted a violation of the Constitutional rights of the plaintiffs.[27] The case, *Baker v. Carr* (1961), established the "one person, one vote" principle, and while it applied only to state house districts, the court extended this logic to the upper chamber of state legislatures in *Reynolds v. Sims* and to US Representatives' districts in *Wesberry v. Sanders*, both in 1964.[28]

Three related controversies have arisen in recent years. First, while the idea of each citizen having an equal role in government makes theoretical sense, one has to wonder if the exact criterion goes too far. Originally, the ratio of residents to House member was set at 1 to 30,000, leading to 65 House members in the first session of Congress. Today, there are roughly 750,000 residents for each House district. (This varies a bit for smaller states – the ones with only one or two legislators.) Some believe it would make better sense to focus on broader economic, demographic and cultural issues instead of a precise balance in the number of citizens. One rather controversial book even makes an argument that ideologically homogenous districts, where there is little electoral competition, might be preferable because the residents will be more satisfied with their representation.[29]

Second, who, exactly, should be counted when it comes to reapportionment? Historically, residents have been tabulated, but a few years ago this standard was challenged in the courts. Should states count voters or residents? After all, prisoners, undocumented immigrants and children all count as residents when drawing district lines, but they cannot vote. Does the resident-centered approach violate the "one-person, one-vote" standard? As noted by the editors of one newspaper, "Is it more important that every voter have the same potential effect at that ballot box or is it more important that all people in America, no matter their age, have the same representation?"[30] The Supreme Court wrestled with this issue in the case of *Evenwel v. Abbott* (2016). In a unanimous decision, it ruled that apportioning legislative districts by population, rather than voters, is permissible under the Equal Protection Clause of the 14th Amendment. The decision was based on the wording of the Amendment, the debates surrounding its adoption, and especially the long history of resident-based reapportionment. The Court did, however, leave open the door to voter-centered schemes in the coming years.

Finally, the redistricting process has been contentious because the allotment of seats per state shifts with each new census – a process known as reapportionment. The fastest growing states net seats each census, and states that are growing at a slower speed lose seats (few states are actually losing population). After the 2010 Census, for example, eight states gained at least one additional House seat: Arizona, Florida, Georgia, Nevada, South Carolina, Texas, Utah, and Washington. Texas gained an additional four seats. Ohio lost two seats, and Illinois, Iowa, Louisiana, Massachusetts, Michigan, Missouri, New Jersey, New York, and Pennsylvania each lost one seat.[31] Losing seats in the national legislature can be devastating for a state, as it results in a loss of federal funds and less representation in Congress. Also, when states lose seats it often forces some of the state's existing representatives – the incumbents – to run against one another. There is nothing an incumbent loathes more than running against another incumbent.

Believe it or not, here too we find controversy. The Constitution mandates that a census be taken every ten years in an effort to tabulate all those living in the United States – both citizens and non-citizens alike. The cornerstone of this process in the last few decades has been mail-in forms and community-based enumerators to fill in gaps for those living in shelters, nursing homes, prisons, and so forth.[32] The process is less than perfect, leading to undercounting of large pools of residents. By one estimate, the 1990 Census missed about eight million people – mostly immigrants, the poor, and inner-city residents – and over-counted some four million white Americans.[33] Democrats argued that missing residents represent a problem, and that the current process leads to an undercount of residents in areas more likely to support their candidates. The Clinton Administration offered a solution for the 2000 Census: instead of relying on an imprecise head count, computer-generated statistical models could be used, leading to a more accurate count. Many statisticians agreed that this would be a more precise approach. Republicans, however, balked at the idea, arguing the term "enumeration" in the Constitution refers to counting, not some sort of statistical estimates. In 1999, the Supreme Court agreed with Republicans, ruling statistical models could not be used for reapportioning congressional seats, but they may be used to redraw district lines.

Another controversy emerged during Donald Trump's first year in office. The Justice Department suggested several questions regarding citizenship be added to the 2020 Census mail-in form. By doing so, they argued, the Census would garner improved data, which could also be used to enforce the Voting Rights Act and protect against racial discrimination in voting. Many Democrats feared that within the broader context of Trump's immigration policies and enhanced deportation steps, adding questions of this sort would lower the response rate in certain areas of the country – again, in areas generally favorable to Democrats. The law governing the census gives the Commerce Secretary the power to decide on questions. In the spring of 2018, Wilber Mills decided the question would be included in the 2020 Census.

In short order at least 13 states, including California, had filed law suits against the Trump Administration with the aim of dropping the question. "The census is supposed to count everyone," said Attorney General Maura Healey of Massachusetts. "This is a blatant and illegal attempt by the Trump administration to undermine that goal, which will result in an undercount of the population and threaten federal funding for our state and cities."[34] Beyond the law suits, a number of grassroots and online organizations were created, and #SaveTheCensus picked up steam. By the summer of 2018, several measures were introduced in the House of Representatives by Democrats to bar the question. But the Trump team was steadfast behind the move. The White House press secretary, Sarah Huckabee Sanders, said the question was necessary to protect voters. "I think that it is going to determine the individuals in our country, and provide information that allows us to comply with our own laws and with our own procedures," she said.[35]

Acts of Congress

Consistent with the intent of the constitutional framers, a preponderance of laws related to voter eligibility have been at the state level, but Congress has not remained completely silent on voting rights. Beyond constitutional amendments, there have been moves by the national legislature to constrict voting rights, but more often to broaden the pool of eligible voters. Many of these changes centered around race. In 1876, for instance, the Supreme Court ruled that Native Americans could be barred from voting because they were not citizens. A decade later, the Dawes Act of 1887 granted Native Americans citizenship, and thus the right to vote, but only if they agreed to abandon their traditional tribal lands. About two-thirds did so. An act of Congress in 1924 allowed all Native peoples the right to vote regardless of their tribe.

After World War II, a growing number of federal measures were advanced to better secure basic rights for all citizens. The Civil Rights Act of 1957, for example, created a Civil Rights Commission with the power to investigate voting rights violations and to suggest changes.[36] The most significant change came with the passage of the Voting Rights Act in 1965. This act stipulated that in any state or municipality where fewer than 50 percent of adults went to the polls, a five-year "emergency state" was triggered. Affected areas could only change their election regulations with the approval of the Civil Rights Division of the Justice Department, and the emergency could only be ended by an appeal to a federal court with evidence that no discriminatory devices had been used in the previous five years. Although the Voting Rights Act did not end discrimination, it became the most important tool protecting the right to vote.[37] Election data underscore the act's importance: when the measure was first passed, black voter registration stood at 6.4 percent in Mississippi, and the gap between black and white registration rates was more than 60 percentage points.[38] Black voter registration in 11 southern states in 1960 was a meager 29.7 percent. By the end of the decade this figure had more than doubled to 63.4 percent.[39]

An important provision in the Voting Rights Act called for periodic renewal, which Congress did several times. Generally speaking, these measures garnered broad bipartisan support, but in 2006, when it was last reauthorized, a group of 80 legislators supported an amendment to strip the requirements for interpreters or multilingual ballots for US citizens who do not speak English. The challenge was not successful, but the rather bold move caught many off guard and was a harbinger of growing partisan divide in American politics.

There were also several controversial parts of the Act – especially Sections 4 and 5. Section 4 laid out a coverage formula used to designate a list of state and local jurisdictions that had engaged in voter discrimination. The formula was changed by Congress a few times and by 2013 the list included Alabama, Alaska, Arizona, Georgia, Louisiana, Mississippi, South Carolina, Texas, and Virginia, as well as parts of California, Florida, Michigan, New York, North Carolina, and South Dakota.[40] Section 5 stipulated that any state or jurisdiction that was on this list could not change its voting rules or laws until they receive preclearance by the US Attorney General and a three-judge DC Circuit court. It also allowed the Attorney General to send federal officers into those jurisdictions to check for violations. Put a bit differently, if the Voting Rights Act formula found a particular state, county or municipality to engage in voter suppression tactics, the federal government would take control. In 2012, for example, preclearance was used to block a voter ID law in Texas and delay the implementation of other changes in South Carolina.[41]

Many welcomed the watchful eye of the federal government, but others saw it as a usurpation of state prerogative. The debate intensified as many states sought to change their election laws and as partisan divisions in state legislatures increased. The formula and preclearance process came to a head in the 2013 Supreme Court case of *Shelby County v. Holder*. In a five–four decision, the court found the coverage formula outdated and unresponsive to current conditions and therefore unconstitutional. "Our country has changed, and while any racial discrimination in voting is too much, Congress must ensure that the legislation it passes to remedy that problem speaks to current conditions," wrote Chief Justice John Roberts for the majority.[42] The court did not strike down Section 5 (the preclearance provision), but without a formula there could be no list of violators. Section 5 became unenforceable. The decision was applauded by most conservatives but assailed by progressives as a grievous step backward.

The Court recognized that Congress could reauthorize the act and revamp the formula. Less than a decade earlier, Congress reauthorized the law by a vote of 390 to 33 in the House and a unanimous vote in the Senate. The grim reality of partisan divisions since *Shelby* suggests reauthorization will be unlikely, nevertheless. Since the court's decision, many states have shifted voting laws. Several states passed laws to allow online registration, but others moved to restrict voter access, such as by limiting early voting and voter registration periods and mandating strict voter-ID requirements.

Over the last several decades a number of moves by Congress allowed for greater access to the ballot box. The Voter Accessibility for the Elderly and Handicapped Act of 1984, for example, required polling places to be accessible to people with disabilities. The Uniform and Overseas Citizens Absentee Voting Act, passed two years later, made it easier for Americans abroad and those in the military to register and vote. This law was amended and updated in 2009 with the Military and Overseas Voting Empowerment Act. Among other changes, this law requires states to provide electronic access to election materials and to provide mail-in ballots at least 45 days prior to an election.

In 1993, Congress passed what is known as the Motor Voter Act. It directed the states to (1) allow all eligible citizens to register to vote when they apply for or renew a driver's license; (2) provide for voter registration by mail; and (3) make registration forms available at the local offices of state employment, welfare, and other social service agencies. It seemed to work; the Federal Election Commission reported that by the year 2000, approximately eight million persons had registered to vote as a direct result of the Motor Voter Law. The law also requires every state to mail a questionnaire to each of its registered voters every four years, so that the poll books can be purged for deaths and changes of residence. It also forbids the states to purge for any other reason, including failure to vote.

The Help America Vote Act (HAVA) was signed into law in 2002 by President George W. Bush as a result of problems in the 2000 presidential election. Its goals were to update the voting systems by replacing punch cards with computerized systems, to create a commission to manage federal elections (called Election Assistance Commission), and to establish Federal election standards for states. In the 2004 presidential election, HAVA withstood the test, proving to increase voter turnout and decrease fraud.

State-Level Regulations

The presidential election of 1824 was a very important event in the evolution of voting rights in the United States. Many historians believe that John Quincy Adams made a deal with House Speaker Henry Clay to make Adams president even though he had garnered fewer popular and electoral votes than Andrew Jackson. In response to the so-called Corrupt Deal of 1824, pro-Jackson forces ushered in a host of changes designed to help their candidate win the rematch in 1828. These shifts also opened up the election process. During this period – dubbed by historians Jacksonian Democracy – religious, property and literacy qualifications for voting melted away and soon all white male citizens had access to the ballot. By 1836, all states – with the exception of South Carolina – had moved to the direct election of presidential electors. The number of state and municipal elected posts skyrocketed. Citizens were called upon to select governors, judges, auditors, attorneys general, school boards, coroners and officials to all manners of offices and posts.

In the following decades, fueled by the partisan press and die-hard party loyalty among voters, many of the organizations morphed into corrupt party machines. These powerful organizations controlled public policy because they controlled the election process. Bribes, kickbacks, voting irregularities, and a broad array of illicit practices were common-place. In response, a cry for reform grew louder and louder – culminating in a series of Progressive Era changes, as noted above.

One of the most significant of these shifts was the use of the direct primary. Previously, party leaders would simply hand-pick candidates based on loyalty to the party machine. One of the most flamboyant party leaders of the day, Boss Tweed of New York City, commented, "I don't care who does the electin', so long as I do the nominatin'."[43] Minor party or write-in candidates stood little chance of victory. The direct primary is where the average members of a party, sometimes called the rank-and-file, vote for candidates in their party to run in the general election. The winner becomes the party's nominee and faces the other parties' nominees. From about 1904 to 1914, the direct primary craze swept across the nation and today most local, state, and federal office candidates are nominated through a primary. The precise means of conducting primaries has become quite varied, and will be discussed in a later chapter.

Another set of reforms from this period were designed to limit fraudu-lent voting. Party bosses would sometimes pay people to travel around the city voting in numerous polling places. Residency and registration requirements were thought to be the remedy. Residency laws stipulate that a person can only vote where he or she has resided for a proscribed period of time. The length of time varies from state to state, but the 1970 Voting Rights Act established a maximum of 30 days prior to the election. Registration means signing up to vote before casting a ballot.

Today, 49 states – all except North Dakota – require that most, and usually all, voters be registered in order to cast ballots. Typically, a pro-spective voter must register his or her name, age, place of birth, present address, length of residence, and similar facts. The information is logged by a local official, usually a registrar of elections or the county clerk. A voter typically remains registered unless or until he or she moves, dies, is convicted of a serious crime, or is committed to a mental institution. State law directs local election officials to review the lists of registered voters and to remove the names of those who are no longer eligible to vote. This process, known as purging, should be done every two or four years but is often ignored. When it is, the poll books (the official lists of qualified voters in each precinct) soon become clogged with the names of many people who, for one reason or another, are no longer eligible to vote.

Many believe registration requirements should be abolished because they act as a barrier to voting, especially among the young, poor and less educated. College students, for example, are often barred from voting because they fail to register in advance of the election. Those critics buttress their case by noting that voter turnout began to decline in the early 1900s, just after most states adopted a registration requirement. They also point to the fact that voter turnout is much higher in European democracies that do not have this requirement. In those countries, voter registration is not a matter of individual choice but the law. Public officials must enter the names of all eligible citizens on registration lists. The United States is the only democratic country where citizens decide whether or not to register to vote; citizens must "opt in" to vote whereas in other countries they are automatically registered.

Given modest levels of turnout and the increasingly transient nature of American life, another idea to make voting easier is same-day registration. Citizens simply register to vote when they go to the polls; it's a one-shot-deal. As of the 2018, 13 states and the District of Columbia allowed residents to register on Election Day. Two additional states – Maryland and North Carolina – let citizens register during a portion of the early voting period, but not on the actual Election Day. The backers of same-day registration point to higher levels of turnout as the biggest benefit. It is hard to know the precise impact, but most observers suggest it boosts turnout by about 8 to 10 percent.[44] The gain seems particularly sharp among low income and younger residents. We do know that North Carolina vaulted from 37th to 11th place in presidential election turnout from 2000 to 2012, an increase of 14 percentage points. "The elections in 2008 saw historic turnout levels across the state. Black voters outpaced white voters for the first time in the state's history, and then did so again in 2012."[45]

As one might guess, same-day registration has recently become a partisan issue. A full 11 of the 13 states that have some form of same-day registration lean Democratic. Setting aside North Carolina, not a single southern state has this law. The North Carolina case is revealing. The initial change to same-day registration came in 2007, but a Republican-dominated legislature eliminated the law in 2013. The Fourth Circuit US Court of Appeals reinstated the law in a blistering decision that accused lawmakers of targeting African American voters "with almost surgical precision."[46] It was back on the books throughout the 2016 election, but was challenged in the courts by a group called the Civitas Institute. According to Civitas president Francis De Luca, "Somebody who cannot make the effort to register to vote prior to the start of voting probably isn't giving the election a lot of thought. That doesn't mean you're not eligible to vote, but it makes the administration of elections much more difficult."[47] Those on the other side argue challenges to the law are a blatant move to curtail voting among particular groups of citizens – the same types of voters who tend to vote for Democrats. They point to a host of other moves by the state GOP aimed at the same outcome, including passage of a strict voter identification law (see below), reduced opportunities for early voting, ending pre-registration for 16-year-olds, and slashing the number of polling places in particular counties. As one Democratic member of Congress said of these so-called reforms, "American Democracy might be more fragile than we realized."[48]

The Controversy Surrounding Voter ID Laws

Several states, including Wisconsin, Texas, Tennessee, South Carolina, Pennsylvania, North Dakota and Kansas, have recently instituted new laws requiring voters to bring state-approved identification cards (such as a driver's license) to voting booths. Indiana already had a similar law on the books. Supporters of these measures argue that IDs are required for many public events, so it simply makes sense that they should be required for voting. These laws will limit corruption and add legitimacy to the process, they argue. Shortly after South Carolina moved to require voter ID cards for all voters, then-governor Nikki Haley commented, "We continue to improve the levels of South Carolina in terms of integrity, accountability, and transparency. I have heard from people out of state how impressed they are that we took it upon ourselves to say, 'We are going to make sure we maintain the integrity of our voters.' "[49]

Those who oppose voter ID measures argue that upward of 10 percent of citizens currently do not have state-recognized ID cards, and that requiring people to show IDs at the polls will disenfranchise large groups of voters. They suggest voter fraud is a tiny issue – certainly less significant than low voter turnout. Moreover, opponents argue that the real intent of the law is not to limit voter fraud, but to keep a particular type of voter from the polls. They point to studies that suggest citizens without state-issued ID cards are disproportionately poor, members of minority groups and more likely to be Democratic voters. "A number of state legislatures have taken up these bills and I think that it's a growing concern nationally that the effect is going to be the suppressions of the vote," said Victoria Middleton, executive director for the South Carolina American Civil Liberties Union.[50] In a stirring 2014 editorial, the *New York Times* made the following point:

In Texas [where one of the most restrictive voter ID laws was passed], ... there were two convictions for in-person voter impersonation in one 10-year period. During that time, 20 million votes were cast. Nor is there any evidence that these laws encourage more voters to come to the polls. Instead, in at least two states – Kansas and Tennessee – they appear to have reduced turnout by 2 percent to 3 percent, according to a report released last week by the Government Accountability Office.[51]

In 2004, North Dakota passed a voter identification law enabling citizens to cast a ballot if the poll worker that vouched for his or her identity or if the voter signed a voucher under penalty of perjury that he or she was qualified to vote. Without citing any evidence of fraud, the Republican-controlled legislature narrowed the path to voting in 2016 to only those residents able to produce a particular form of identification and eliminating the voucher process. Under the new law, residents are required to submit one of four forms of ID which must contain name, residential address, and date of birth. The problem is that a large number of Native Americans do not have a street mailing address because post office boxes are used on many reservations.[52] By one estimate, more than 72,000 voting-eligible North Dakota citizens lack a qualifying ID – out of a total state population around 750,000.[53] Native Americans, who tend to vote Democratic, are more than twice as likely as non-Native Americans to lack a qualifying ID. "Those that argue that people must present ID to buy alcohol or cigarettes miss a crucial point. Voting is a fundamental, constitutionally protected right," noted a lawyer fighting against the North Dakota law.[54] As of 2018, several legal challenges to the law remained unresolved.[55]

Historically, the courts have been reluctant to prohibit states from imposing stricter voter ID laws. In 2015, for example, the Supreme Court refused to hear a case challenging Wisconsin's law, thereby allowing it to stand. But in 2016, this pattern began to change when the Fourth Circuit Court ruled that North Carolina's 2013 voting reform package, which included the establishment of a strict voter-ID requirement and restrictions on early voting and same-day registration, "were enacted with racially discriminatory intent."[56] In the spring of 2017, the Supreme Court decided not to hear the case on appeal, letting the Circuit Court decision stand.

It is worth noting that the legislature in every state that created voter ID laws since 2010 was controlled by Republicans.

Other Restrictions

Many find it curious that we hold elections during the middle of the week and for a brief period of time. The tradition of holding elections on a Tuesday in early November has a seemingly benign, even quaint, history. In the first few elections for Congress and the president, states were allowed to hold their own contests so long as presidential electors were selected by the first Wednesday in November (when they meet in their state capitals). A uniform date, the first Tuesday after the first Monday in November, was set in 1845. The United States was primarily an agrarian society at the time, and early November made sense because crops would be harvested and the weather would still be reasonable. Tuesday was picked because travel to the polling places could take time and most were unwilling to depart on Sunday, the Sabbath. Wednesday was "market day." States could choose to hold state and local elections on other days, but most found it convenient and cost-effective to hold all of them on the same day.

Today, only about 2 percent of Americans work on farms or ranches, and they are able to travel to polling places in a snap – making the historic rationale for a Tuesday in early November moot.

But does it really matter when an election is held and for how long? According to the Pew Research Center, until the 2016 election (when "disliked the candidates" topped the list) the number one reason for *not* voting in the United States was "too busy."[57] Many find it difficult to take time out of their work or school day to vote. In another study, researchers found that the number one reason young Americans skipped voting was because of conflicting work.[58] In many communities, voters also confront long lines – upwards of an hour or more. In the 2016 election, for instance, there were long lines in North Carolina, Texas, Ohio, Pennsylvania and Arizona. The longest wait was reported to be in Maricopa County, which contains Phoenix. With a population of about four million, Maricopa is the most populous county in Arizona and fourth largest in the United States. The culprit was reported to be a dramatic cut in the number of polling places since 2012.[59]

In many democracies across the globe, elections are held on the weekend or are a holiday. As noted by one observer, "Election Day needn't be such an ordeal. Austria, Belgium, France, Germany, India, New Zealand, and a number of other countries, for example, facilitate voting with an extremely simple, low-cost innovation: they hold elections on either weekends or holidays."[60]

There have been some moves to make voting easier. As of the spring of 2018, some 34 states and the District of Columbia allowed early voting, either through the mail or in-person. Three other states – Colorado, Washington and Oregon – use mail-in balloting, eliminating the need for early voting. In all of these states the official results are tabulated on Election Day. In 2016, roughly 40 percent of the general election ballots were cast early. The goal of these changes would be to lower the costs of voting (i.e., make it easier), and by doing so draw more citizens into the process.

The evidence of the effectiveness of early voting is mixed. Several studies suggest overall turnout may actually decrease. It seems that early voting methods may detract from the excitement and energy of Election Day. As noted by a team of scholars from the University of Wisconsin–Madison, "Early voting dilutes the concentrated activities of Election Day itself that would likely stimulate turnout, an effect not counterbalanced by the increased convenience of voting prior to the election (which, as we have noted, may only provide an alternative outlet for voters who would have voted in any case)."[61]

But here again, the issue has become contentious and partisan, as several states have decided to pull back on early voting. North Carolina stands out, again. Upon retaking the legislature and the governor's mansion, Republicans in the Tar Heel State passed a number of changes, including reducing the number of polling places and curtailing early voting options. By July of 2016, federal courts had struck down the law, but local jurisdictions took matters into their own hands. The targeting of particular counties and communities seemed strategic; all of the new restrictions were in Democratic-leaning areas. In Charlotte's Mecklenburg County, for instance, there were 22 locations for the first day of early voting in 2012. For the 2016 contest there were ten. Voters in these precincts, predominantly non-white, reported waiting for more than three hours to cast a ballot.[62] Mark Joseph Stern, a columnist for *Slate Magazine*, put the matter this way:

> Millions of Americans eager to cast a ballot before the Election Day rush have stood in gallingly long lines … In a way, the lines were a nice symbol of democratic engagement, proof that citizens remain engaged after a miserable election season. But they also represented something much darker: voter suppression. Contrary to the suggestion of some election boards, these endless lines were not a fluke or a surprise. They were a direct result of the Republican Party's recent, coordinated assault on voting rights.[63]

Finally, 48 states and the District of Columbia prohibit prison inmates who are serving time for felony convictions from voting. The two states that allow them to vote are Vermont and Maine. In 37 states, felons on parole or probation cannot vote for a proscribed period of time (it varies by the state) and in ten states, felons are barred from the voting booth permanently unless the governor steps in, which rarely happens. By one estimate, some 6.1 million citizens are currently barred from voting because of these laws.[64] This comes out to roughly 2.5 percent of the voting age population. About three-quarters of those disenfranchised are not currently in prison.[65]

According to the Sentencing Project, several of the highest percentage of barred citizens are in the South.[66] For instance, in Florida a stunning 10.1 percent of the voting age population was barred from the polls, followed by Mississippi (9.1%), Kentucky (9.0%), Tennessee (8.3%), Virginia (7.8%), and Alabama (7.6%). States with the lowest rates of felon disenfranchisement tend to be in the Northeast and on the West Coast. In California and New York, for example, less than 1 percent of felons are disenfranchised. It seems that the regions of the country that have a history of barring African Americans from the polls are also more likely to use strict felon disenfranchisement laws. Because of these laws, one in 13 African American men are not able to vote.[67]

While one might assume that prison inmates and former felons might give up their rights as citizens, this is not the case. Many of the civil liberties in the Bill of Rights speak to those accused of a crime and those incarcerated. Former inmates reserve the right to free speech and much else. As noted by columnist Steve Chapman of the *Chicago Tribune*, "We let ex-convicts marry, reproduce, buy beer, own property and drive. They don't lose their freedom of religion [or] their right against self-incrimination … But in many places the assumption is that they can't be trusted to help choose our leaders."[68] It might also be noted that only a handful of European nations ban prisoners from voting and an even smaller number prohibit released inmates from casting a vote – most notably Russia.[69]

The issue of felon disenfranchisement has become heated and once again grounded in partisan differences. Take, for example, the case of Virginia. Shortly after being elected Governor of Virginia in 2015, Democrat Terry McAuliffe proposed a plan to restore the voting rights of felons who had served their sentences and were no longer on probation. According to his calculations, some 200,600 Virginians were being denied their right to vote – the majority of whom were African Americans. The disenfranchisement law was a vestige of race-based discrimination, said the governor. State law allowed the governor to restore felon voting right clemency on a case-by-case basis – meaning one at a time. In an unprecedented move, McAuliffe issued an executive order granting *all* former convicts the right to vote.[70] Republicans cried foul, arguing that the governor's move was aimed at enhancing Hillary Clinton's prospects of winning Virginia in the 2016 presidential race. The Virginia Supreme Court sided with the Republicans, saying the governor had overstepped his bounds with the en masse move; he had unilaterally changed state law, the court ruled. The governor responded by pardoning some 155,221 convicts *on an individual basis* by the summer of 2017.[71] "Expanding democracy in Virginia has been my proudest achievement during my time as Governor," said McAuliffe."[72]

It is also worth noting that voters in Florida passed a constitutional amendment in 2018 to allow most felons to vote once they have served their sentence. That will mean an additional 1.5 million potential voters in coming elections. Other states, including New Jersey, are considering similar moves.

Conclusion: Why Has the Right to Vote Been so Contentious?

In a nation that prides itself as one of the grand democratic experiments, a system grounded on the premise of open and fair elections, why has universal suffrage been elusive? Why has the struggle to vote been so long and difficult, and why are there vivid signs of backsliding?

While the framers of our system believed in the democratic process, their understanding of the best mechanism for turning the will of the citizenry into public policy was nebulous. Their ambivalence about elections was reflected in the Constitution, where there was only one part of the national government that was directly elected by the voters. As our nation began to mature, however, faith in the electoral process thrived. Average Americans began to see elections as *the* tool to popular control. Election fever swept across the nation by the middle of the 19th century during the age of Jacksonian Democracy.

Elections did not become a means of empowerment for *all* Americans, as we know. Barring women, African Americans, Native Americans, newly arrived immigrants, and other groups of citizens from the voting booth ensured the dominance of wealthy white men. With cries for broader suffrage, change occurred – but grudgingly and incrementally. By the dawn of the 21st century, suffrage had been expanded to most citizens over 18.

But the struggle for universal access to the polls is far from over. Regimes will sometimes tighten their control by creating electoral disadvantages for the opposition – often in the name of a public good. Rather than throw the opposition in jail, stacking the electoral deck against them can be more effective and can last for years.[73] A striking example of rewriting the rules to lock in an advantage happened in the United States – at the end of Reconstruction in the 1870s. Mass enfranchisement of African Americans posed a threat to southern white political control, so they changed the rules. "Give us a [constitutional] convention, and I will fit it so that ... the Negro shall never be heard from," said Georgia Senator Robert Toombs as Reconstruction was coming to an end.[74] Shortly after, all 11 post-Confederate states "reformed" their constitutions to disenfranchise blacks. In South Carolina, the 1882 "Eight Box Law" made it nearly impossible for blacks to vote, and a few years later, a new poll tax sealed the deal. Black turnout, which had been above 90 percent during Reconstruction, dropped to 11 percent in 1898. Similar moves were made throughout the region. "These 'reforms' effectively killed democracy in the American South."[75]

Several years ago, scholars Frances Piven and Richard Cloward offered a similar answer to our questions in, *Why Americans Still Don't Vote: And Why Politicians Want it that Way*. Non-voting, they suggest, is a means of elite control. But disenfranchisement is not an easy trick where the political culture is grounded in the celebration of elections. "When whole categories of people are denied the vote as a matter of acknowledged state policy – as southern blacks were – their exclusion may well strengthen their collective identity, provoke their indignation, and legitimate defiant forms of political action."[76] The solution is to maintain the *idea* of voting as a way to air grievances, but to also make the means of casting a vote difficult. "One of greatest ironies of how democracies die is that the very defense of democracy is often used as a pretext for its subversion," write Levitsky and Ziblatt.[77]

To be sure, there is scant evidence to suggest voting fraud is a real problem in the United States. A large study conducted by law scholar Justin Levitt and published in the *Washington Post* found just 31 instances of fraud from 2000 to 2014, out of more than one billion ballots cast.[78] In a decision that found a Texas voter ID law racially discriminatory, the Fifth Circuit Court noted there were only "two convictions for in-person voter impersonation fraud out of 20 million votes cast in the decade" before the law was passed.[79]

We might ask, sarcastically, why election fraud seems so egregious only in the states controlled by Republicans. Don't Democrats care about the integrity of elections? It is only honest to admit that strict registration and residency requirements, voter ID laws, reducing the opportunity for early voting, and many other changes to the rules of the game are designed to curtail the voting of particular types of residents. "The demobilization of large sectors [is] secured at less cost to the legitimacy of the electoral process."[80] In advance of a US Senate run-off election in Mississippi in the fall of 2018, incumbent Republican Cindy Hyde-Smith was caught on video telling supporters, "There's a lot of liberal folks in those other schools who that maybe [sic] we don't want to vote. Maybe we want to make it just a little more difficult. So, I think that's a great idea."

Over the last decade, Georgia's population has grown at a fast pace, but the number of registered voters has actually declined. How could that be true? Since taking office in 2010, Georgia's Secretary of State, Brian Kemp, has made voter fraud and "cleaning the voter rolls" a priority. He launched aggressive investigations, including into one group that registered upwards of 200,000 Asian Americans and African Americans just prior to the 2016 election. Not a single violation was found; there were no indictments, no charges. But the intimidation was palpable. One of the lawyers working with the group Asian American Legal Advocacy Center (AALAC), Helen Ho, wrote a letter to Kemp, asking why so many of the citizens registered did not show up on the rolls. The response from Kemp's office was that her group was now under investigation. "I'm not going to lie: I was shocked, I was scared."[81] One press account, titled "Register Minority Voters in Georgia, Go to Jail," noted the following:

> The investigation targeted her group not for any voter fraud, per se, but for more technical issues, such as whether canvassers had people's explicit, written consent to photocopy their registration forms before mailing the originals to the elections office. Kemp's investigation … lasted nearly two-and-a-half years … [I]t ended with no finding of violations.[82]

Caught on tape talking to fellow Republicans, Kemp hinted at his actual motivations: "Democrats are working hard, registering all these minority voters that are out there and others that are sitting on the sidelines. If they can do that, they can win these elections in November."[83] In the summer of 2018, Kemp became Georgia's Republican nominee for governor, due in no small measure to the backing from Donald Trump.

Not long after Kemp received the nomination, another potentially nefarious move was reported in the press. It seemed that the officials of Randolph County had pulled together a plan to close 75 percent of the polling places shortly before the 2018 election. It was a move to consolidate voting sites across the state. The rationale for the closures was that bathrooms at these locations were not accessible to voters in wheelchairs, but given that 60 percent of the residents in the county are black, that it would entail long drives for many residents who did not own cars, and that the county commissioner in charge of the plan was recommended for the job by Brian Kemp, many expressed suspicions regarding the real motivations. As noted by one observer, "[M]aybe this isn't about toilets. Maybe this is a flagrant example of the expansion of voter suppression nationwide, aggravated by the Supreme Court's 2013 weakening of the Voting Rights Act."[84]

Brian Kemp was elected Georgia's Governor in 2018 – by a paper-thin margin.

As a final note, it is also worth brief mention that in the summer of 2018, 12 residents of one county in North Carolina were arrested and taken away in handcuffs for illegal voting. All were on probation or parole for felony convictions and had assumed that they could vote. Each had reregistered and voted at their polling place. A mere book-keeping mistake was made, but this did not seem to hold water with the Alamance County District Attorney, Pat Nadolski: "That's the law. You can't do it. If we have clear cases, we're going to prosecute."[85] According to an account, titled "Arrested, Jailed and Charged with a Felony. For Voting,"

The cases are rare compared with the tens of millions of votes cast in state and national elections. In 2017, at least 11 people nationwide were convicted of illegal voting because they were felons or noncitizens ... The case against the 12 voters in Alamance County – a patchwork of small towns about an hour west of the state's booming Research Triangle – is unusual for the sheer number of people charged at once. And because nine of the defendants are black, the case has touched a nerve in a state with a history of suppressing African-American votes.[86]

One of the defendants, Keith Sellars, was driving home from dinner at a Mexican restaurant with his daughters when he was pulled over for running a red light. The officer ran a background check and came back with bad news for Mr. Sellars. There was a warrant out for his arrest. "As his girls cried in the back seat, Mr. Sellars was handcuffed and taken to jail."[87]

Notes

1 Thomas Patterson, *The Vanishing Voter* (New York: Knopf, 2003), 144.
2 Ibid.
3 Ibid.
4 As quoted in James MacGregor Burns, *Cobblestone Leadership: Majority Rule, Minority Power* (Normal, OK: University of Oklahoma Press, 1990), 5.
5 As noted in Lichtman, *The Embattled Vote in America*, 14.
6 Ibid., 15.
7 Ibid., 16.
8 Ibid., 26.
9 Ibid., 17.
10 Alan P. Grimes, *Democracy and the Amendments to the Constitution* (Lexington: Lexington Books, 1978), 43.
11 Ibid., 51.
12 Ibid., 53. Iowa and Minnesota approved African American suffrage, while Wisconsin, Connecticut, Kansas, Ohio, Michigan, New York, Missouri, and the Nebraska Territory rejected it.
13 Ibid., 58.
14 Steven Levitsky and Daniel Ziblatt, *How Democracies Die* (New York: Crown Publishing Group, 2018), 89.
15 Excerpt from a speech delivered by President Lyndon Johnson to a joint Session of Congress, March 15, 1965.
16 Ibid., 111.
17 321 U.S. 649 (1944).
18 George Anastaplo, *The Amendments to the Constitution: A Commentary* (Baltimore: The Johns Hopkins University Press, 1995), 131.

19 Alan P. Grimes, *Democracy and the Amendments to the Constitution* (Lexington: Lexington Books, 1978), 94–95.

20 Ibid., 131–132.

21 Ibid., 146.

22 Ibid., 142–147.

23 Gary W. Cox and Jonathan N. Katz, *Elbridge Gerry's Salamander* (Cambridge: Cambridge University Press, 2002), 3.

24 Steven Levitsky and Daniel Ziblatt, *How Democracies Die* (New York: Crown Publishing Group, 2018), 209.

25 Ibid.

26 Robert Barnes, "The Supreme Court Shows it is in No Rush to Decide Controversial Cases," *Washington Post* website, June 25, 2018 (www.washingtonpost.com/politics/the-supreme-court-shows-it-is-in-no-rush-to-decide-controversial-cases/2018/06/25/36b1c9ac-788a-11e8-93cc-6d3beccdd7a3_story.html?noredirect=on&utm_term=.d144cc2 d1b85).

27 Gary W. Cox and Jonathan N. Katz, *Elbridge Gerry's Salamander* (Cambridge: Cambridge University Press, 2002), 12.

28 Ibid., 13.

29 US Census, "Apportionment Data," 2010 (http://2010.census.gov/2010census/data/apportionment-data-text.php).

30 *St. Louis Post-Dispatch* Editorial Board, "Redistricting Should Count Residents, Not Voters," *St. Louis Post-Dispatch* website, December 14, 2015 (www.stltoday.com/opinion/editorial/editorial-redistricting-should-count-residents-not-voters/article_564738d4-1bea-599a-a6c9-7403f5102beb.html).

31 US Census, "Apportionment Data," 2010 (http://2010.census.gov/2010 census/data/apportionment-data-text.php).

32 Amy Sullivan, "Why the 2010 Census Stirs Up Partisan Politics," *Time* website, February 15, 2009 (http://content.time.com/time/nation/article/0,8599,1879667,00.html).

33 Ibid.

34 Michael Wines and Emily Baumgaertner, "At Least Twelve States to Sue Trump Administration Over Census Citizenship Question," *New York Times*, March 27, 2018.

35 Ibid.

36 L. Sandy Maisel, *Parties and Elections in America: The Electoral Process,* 3rd Edition (Lanham, MD: Rowman and Littlefield, 1995), 95.

37 Alexander Keyssar, *The Right to Vote: The Contested History of Democracy in the United States* (New York: Basic Books, 2000), 264–265.

38 Adam Liptak, "Supreme Court Invalidates Key Part of Voting Rights Act," *New York Times* website, June 25, 2013 (www.nytimes.com/2013/06/26/us/supreme-court-ruling.html).

39 L. Sandy Maisel, *Parties and Elections in America: The Electoral Process,* 3rd Edition (Lanham, MD: Rowman and Littlefield, 1995), 97.

40 Jenée Desmond-Harris, "Why is Section 4 of the Voting Rights Act Such a Big Part of the Fight over Voting Rights?," *Vox*, October 20, 2014 (www.vox.com/cards/voting-rights-fight-explained/what-are-the-key-sections-of-the-voting-rights-act).

41 Ryan J. Reilly, Mike Sacks and Sabrina Siddiqui, "Voting Rights Act Section 4 Struck Down by Supreme Court," *The Huffington Post,* June 25, 2013

(www.huffingtonpost.com/2013/06/25/voting-rights-act-supreme-court_n_3429810.html).

42 Ibid.

43 William L. Riordon and George W. Plunkitt, *Plunkitt of Tammany Hall: A Series of Very Plain Talks on Very Practical Politics* (New York: Penguin Group, Penguin Books USA, 1991).

44 Demos, "What Is Same Day Registration? Where Is It Available?," 2011 (www.demos.org/publication/what-same-day-registration-where-it-available).

45 Vann R. Newkirk II, "The Battle for North Carolina," *The Atlantic* website, October 27, 2016 (www.theatlantic.com/politics/archive/2016/10/the-battle-for-north-carolina/501257/).

46 Patricia Murphy, "Conservative Group Keeps Up Fight to End Same-Day Registration Used by Many Black Voters," *The Daily Beast*, December 8, 2016 (www.thedailybeast.com/conservative-group-keeps-up-fight-to-end-same-day-registration-used-by-many-black-voters).

47 Ibid.

48 Steven Levitsky and Daniel Ziblatt, *How Democracies Die* (New York: Crown Publishing Group, 2018), 212.

49 Yvonne Wenger, "Debate Rages Over South Carolina's Voter ID Law," *The Post and Courier*, May 18, 2011 (www.postandcourier.com/politics/state_politics/debate-rages-over-south-carolina-s-voter-id-law/article_dd22c213-bcac-54d2-9d87-3c9841ea84a4.html).

50 Kevin Dolak, "State Voter ID Laws Draw National Scrutiny," *ABCNEWS.com,* September 8, 2011.

51 *New York Times* Editorial Board, "The Big Lie Behind Voter ID Laws," *New York Times* website, October 13, 2014 (www.nytimes.com/2014/10/13/opinion/the-big-lie-behind-voter-id-laws.html).

52 Native American Rights Fund website, "North Dakota Again Passes Discriminatory Voter ID Law," May 9, 2017 (www.narf.org/north-dakota-voter-id-law/).

53 Ibid.

54 Ibid.

55 Michael Wines, "Voting Rights Use to Have an Ally in Government. That's Changing," *New York Times*, August 12, 2018.

56 Vann R. Newkirk II, "North Carolina's Voter ID Law Is Defeated, For Now," *The Atlantic* website, May 15, 2017 (www.theatlantic.com/politics/archive/2017/05/north-carolinas-voter-id-law-supreme-court-cert/526713/).

57 Gustavo López and Antonio Flores, "Dislike of Candidates or Campaign Issues Was Most Common Reason for Not Voting in 2016," Pew Research Center, June 1, 2017 (www.pewresearch.org/fact-tank/2017/06/01/dislike-of-candidates-or-campaign-issues-was-most-common-reason-for-not-voting-in-2016/).

58 Scott Sikich, "Young Voter Turnout Declines During Midterm Elections," *TommieMedia,* October 29, 2014 (www.tommiemedia.com/news/young-voter-turnout-declines-during-midterm-elections/).

59 Christopher Famighetti, "Long Voting Lines: Explained," *Brennan Center for Justice* website, November 4, 2016 (www.brennancenter.org/analysis/long-voting-lines-explained).

60 Juliet Lapidos, "Doing Democracy Right," *Slate*, October 17, 2008 (www.slate.com/articles/news_and_politics/how_they_do_it/2008/10/doing_democracy_right.html).

61 Barry C. Burden, David T. Canon, Kenneth R. Mayer and Donald P. Moynihan, "The Effects and Costs of Early Voting, Election Day Registration, and Same Day Registration in the 2008 Elections," Paper presented to the Pew Charitable Trusts, December 21, 2009 (www.pewcenteronthestates.org/uploadedFiles/wwwpewcenteronthestatesorg/Initiatives/MVW/UWisconsin.pdf).

62 Alicia M. Ollstein, "North Carolina Counties Slashed their Early Voting Hours and Now This is What the Lines Look Like," *ThinkProgress,* October 21, 2016 (https://thinkprogress.org/north-carolina-counties-that-slashed-early-voting-sites-see-hours-long-lines-fcffa0151748/).

63 Mark Joseph Stern, "Those Insane Early Voting Lines Were a Direct Result of Republican Voter Suppression," *Slate*, November 7, 2016.

64 Matthew Green, "MAP: States Where Convicted Felons Can't Vote," *KQED Public Media,* November 8, 2016 (www.kqed.org/lowdown/11897/map-felon-voter-disenfranchisement-by-the-numbers).

65 Ibid.

66 Ibid.

67 Ibid.

68 Steve Chapman, "Too Many Ex-Convicts Aren't Able to Vote," *StarTribune of Minneapolis-St. Paul,* August 15, 2006 (https://felonvoting.procon.org/view.resource.php?resourceID=000283#1).

69 Hannah Kozlowska, "What Would Happen if Felons Could Vote in the US?," *Quartz* website, October 6, 2016 (https://qz.com/784503/what-would-happen-if-felons-could-vote/).

70 Ibid.

71 Laura Vozzella, "Va. Gov. McAuliffe Says he has Broken US record for Restoring Voting Rights," *Washington Post* website, April 27, 2017 (www.washingtonpost.com/local/virginia-politics/va-gov-mcauliffe-says-he-has-broken-us-record-for-restoring-voting-rights/2017/04/27/55b5591a-2b8b-11e7-be51-b3fc6ff7faee_story.html?utm_term=.d534f0578098).

72 Ibid.

73 Steven Levitsky and Daniel Ziblatt, *How Democracies Die* (New York: Crown Publishing Group, 2018), 88.

74 Ibid.

75 Ibid., 90–93.

76 Frances Piven and Richard Cloward, *Why Americans Still Don't Vote: And Why Politicians Want It That Way* (Boston: Beacon Press, 2000), 16.

77 Steven Levitsky and Daniel Ziblatt, *How Democracies Die* (New York: Crown Publishing Group, 2018), 92.

78 Brennan Center for Justice, "Debunking the Voter Fraud Myth," January 31, 2017 (www.brennancenter.org/analysis/debunking-voter-fraud-myth).

79 Ibid.

80 Ibid.

81 Spencer Woodman, "Register Minority Voters in Georgia, Go to Jail," *New Republic*, May 5, 2015.

82 Ibid.

83 Carol Anderson, "Brian Kemp, Enemy of Democracy," *New York Times*, August 11, 2018.

84 Dana Milbank, "The GOP Turns to Toilets to Suppress More Votes," *Washington Post*, August 21, 2018.
85 As noted in Jack Healy, "Arrested, Charged and Jailed With a Felony. For Voting," *New York Times*, August 2, 2018.
86 Ibid.
87 Ibid.

4 Turning Out to Vote … Or Not
Is the Youth Apathy Rap Justified?

The popular narrative about Donald Trump's victory in 2016 centers on a surge of white working-class voters, motivated by economic fears. Good jobs had been slipping away, and along with them, the American dream of a bright future and a better life for their kids. Voters in Rust Belt states stuck with the business entrepreneur and reality television star because he promised revitalization – or at least a future that looked more like the past. Conversely, Hillary Clinton lost her bid because she paid scant attention to the woes of white working-class voters. Enough traditionally Democratic voters switched sides in a few key states to give Trump an Electoral College victory, even though Clinton won the national popular. The story hinges on shifting voter allegiance in a few swing states.

The only problem with this narrative is that it is mostly fiction. As noted by University of Chicago law professor, Omri Ben-Shahar, "The story of Hillary Clinton's defeat is not the Trump Movement erupting in the ballots, nor the fable that some 'Reagan Democrats' flipped again from Obama to Trump. Democrats stayed home."[1] A few simple statistics are illustrative: Wisconsin is a state that most analysts believed would be easy-pickings for Clinton; she did not even visit the state during the general election campaign, assuming it was already in her column. But on Election Day, Trump netted 1,405,284 votes to Clinton's 1,382,536 – a difference of just under 23,000 votes, or about 1 percent. Four years earlier, however, Republican Mitt Romney actually got *more* votes than Trump, but he lost the state because Barack Obama netted 1.6 million votes. In other words, it appears that Clinton lost the Badger State because a lot of Democratic voters stayed home.

The same process played out in Michigan. Trump and Romney netted about the same vote total, but in 2012 Obama beat Romney by 350,000 votes. Clinton lost it by 10,000. Ohio was also tight. Trump got about the same number of votes as Romney, but Clinton received about half a million *fewer* votes than Obama. This dynamic extended to a few southern states as well, such as in North Carolina, where Clinton probably lost to Trump because fewer voters came to the polls in 2016 than in 2012.

The same dynamic could be seen with important demographic groups. Across the nation, turnout for African Americans, a key voting bloc for Democratic candidates, dropped by 11 percent between 2012 and 2016. Turnout for those under 30, also a critical group for Democratic candidates, was lackluster in 2016. Young citizens supported Clinton by a huge margin, but their turnout was 12 percent lower than for older Americans.[2]

So while the nationwide turnout for the 2016 election was similar to 2012 (about 56 percent), variations in key states like Wisconsin, Ohio, Iowa and Michigan helped tilt the election to Donald Trump. His leap from long-shot candidate to the most powerful position in the world happened in large measure because of lackluster turnout among the Democratic base.[3] David Becker of the Center for Election Innovation and Research put it this way: "Several million voters didn't come out to vote ... [T]his idea of the Trump wave, a huge number of voters shifting over to Trump, is certainly not the story."[4] Bernard Fraga, author of a telling post-2016 election volume called *The Turnout Gap*, wrote, "If everybody voted, Clinton wins. If minority turnout was equal to white turnout, Clinton wins."[5]

It should also be noted that the assumption Trump supporters were primarily concerned with economic issues has been debunked, too. A number of studies since the election have shown that the foremost worry of Trump voters, particularly his white working-class supporters, was immigration politics.[6] A team of authors penned an important book in the wake of the election dubbed *Identity Crisis*. These scholars argue that Trump was successful because he activated long-standing sentiments surrounding race, immigration and religion – and that these attitudes shaped perceptions of other issues.[7]

This story is really nothing new. Fluctuations in turnout have propelled candidates of both parties to office, and have kept others in private life. The so-called "enthusiasm gap" is a critically important force in elections. In Clinton's case it is only fair to say that she failed to inspire important elements of her base – and it probably cost her the election. But it is entirely likely that the Democratic candidates for Congress and state and local offices who stormed into office during Trump's first two years in office benefited from an especially motivated base. Democrats had a historic win in the 2017 Virginia gubernatorial and state legislative elections, for example, because of a surge in enthusiasm in their ranks. Democratic candidates that year outperformed Clinton's 2016 margin by 11 points and Barack Obama's 2012 margin by nine points.[8] The 2018 midterm also yielded big Democratic gains due to a riled base – a so-called blue wave. As they say, what goes around, comes around.

Which brings up a broader issue of why so many Americans of all ideologies and persuasions, and in any given race, stay home on Election Day? Even though we are anxious to link the democratic character of our system to elections, and we see voting as a basic civic duty, voter turnout is sporadic and usually weak – especially compared to other nations. As noted by the editorial board at the *New York Times* in the spring of 2018, "It's a perennial conundrum for the world's oldest democracy: Why do so many Americans fail to go to the polls?"[9]

Much of the electoral engagement problem in the United States can be placed at the door of policy makers, as noted in the previous chapter. Federal and especially state laws have created barriers to voting for large swaths of Americans – and today registration and residency requirements are among a host of other issues that stunt turnout. There is growing evidence to suggest that the latest round of restrictive voting laws may have pushed turnout down in states like Ohio and Wisconsin in 2016. One estimate is that voter identification laws in Milwaukee led to 41,000 fewer voters in high-poverty areas.[10] (Recall that Trump won the state by just 23,000.)

But formal barriers are not the end of the story. In his widely read book, *Is Voting for Young People?*, scholar Martin Wattenberg put it this way: "Registration has been made significantly easier in the United States – most notably by the passage of the 1993 Motor Voter Act. [And yet,] just 54 percent of 18 to 24-year old citizens were registered to vote in 2012 as compared to 61 percent in 1972."[11] The 2016 presidential campaign was everywhere, extremely hard to tune out, but more than 100 million eligible citizens failed to vote. Setting aside 2018, where turnout rose to the 49 percent mark, congressional midterms generally bring out only about 40 percent of eligible Americans. The figure is even lower in state and local elections. We know it is important to vote and we struggle for the right to participate, but often blow it off on the day that matters. This chapter will explore a host of complex issues related to electoral engagement in the United States.

"Good Citizens" Vote, Right?

What do we mean by "electoral engagement?" Is it synonymous with voting? Some pundits argue that voting is the foundational means for involvement in the electoral process; very few become involved in other activities, such as attending political events or sending a check to a candidate, without first voting. Non-voters do not engage in other electoral activities, we are told. This is probably not true, however. Many citizens are politically active but do not vote. For some, not voting is either a statement of contentment or a form of political protest, and even if there may be some sort of pyramid of electoral participation, voting should probably not be considered the base. Talking about different candidates with friends and family, for example, or reading news stories or watching programs about an election are important forms of electoral participation. Any action broadly linked to the conduct or outcome of an election can be considered electoral behavior. Helping with a campaign, donating money, joining an election-centered group, attending rallies, commenting about campaign issues on social media, placing a yard sign in front of our house or a bumper sticker on our car, or even wearing a button are all forms of political engagement. This is only a partial list. The point is that citizens can become involved in the election process in many ways – voting being just one of them.

Another way to think about forms of electoral engagement is to consider the difference between individualistic and collective participation. Individualistic participation is where the citizen engages in activity aimed at changing the outcome of government action (i.e., public policy) without interacting with other citizens. Examples here include voting, giving money to a candidate or party, watching political news on television or writing a letter to an elected official. Collective participation is where the citizen's action is in partnership with other like-minded citizens, such as attending a rally, discussing politics with friends and family, working at a party or candidate headquarters, joining others in a protest, or engaging in political-oriented social media. While each can be seen in the American setting, clearly individualistic participation occurs more frequently. Many hold that our default toward individualistic acts is unfortunate given most significant changes in public policy come from collective action.

Why would anyone engage in electoral participation in any form? Are there not more interesting and entertaining things to do with your time? Americans are drawn to elections for many reasons, including the belief that the outcome of elections matter, that they are an important tradition, and that they are, yes, entertaining. At the heart of things, Americans believe involvement in elections is part of our civic duty. Polling data suggest that about 90 percent of Americans believe it is the duty of good citizens to become involved in the election process.[12]

Which begs the question of how individuals come to learn what is expected of them in civic life. Socialization is the process by which new members of a society come to learn the norms, values, and customs of their country. In most instances the "new members" are children – that is, socialization implies the passing on of customs, beliefs, and values from one generation to the next – but it can also take place for newly arrived adults. Socialization agents refer to the avenues through which this information is transmitted. The principal socialization agent in the American setting has been the family, followed by schools, the media, peer groups, and religious institutions.

Some time ago, scholars Gabriel Almond and Sidney Verba set out to chart the socialization process in numerous countries. Their book,

The Civic Culture, set the bar for scores of subsequent studies.[13] They found that the socialization process in the United States does a better job promoting the importance of voting and political participation than any other Western democracy.[14] There was some variation due to social class, levels of education, and race (poor African Americans were less sure about voting than affluent white citizens were), but for the most part Americans were socialized to be involved in civic life and to vote.

The Civic Culture was published in 1963, with most of its data coming from the 1950s. Much has changed. Americans have become cynical about the election process, public officials and government. According to the American National Election Study, in the 1960s, about 70 percent of Americans trusted the federal government to do the right thing most of the time, but in recent years this figure has dropped to about 20 percent. In the 1960s about two-thirds of Americans believed elections made government pay attention. In 2016, that figure stood at about one-third. Has mounting cynicism and distrust tempered our willingness to vote? Has the premise of *The Civic Culture* been turned on its head?

Levels of Participation throughout American History

Turnout is a ratio, where those who come to the polls are divided by those who are legally entitled to participate. As discussed in the introductory chapter, there was not a great deal of interest in federal elections in the early days of the republic. Turnout for presidential elections reached only into the teens until the contentious election of 1800, when it jumped to 31 percent. It slipped again during the Era of Good Feelings to roughly 25 percent, but after the Corrupt Deal of 1824 turnout rose dramatically. By the 1840s it leveled off at around 80 percent, where it remained for generations. It is worth noting that turnout for state and local offices was often higher than for presidential and congressional contests – in contrast to modern times.

By the turn of the 20th century, election turnout had begun to slip. There are a number of likely causes, including a flood of immigration. While these new arrivals would soon be assimilated into the political process, many did not or could not immediately vote. As part of the Progressive Movement, most states passed strict voter registration laws, residency requirements, and other regulations – as noted in the previous chapter. On their face, these new laws were designed to reduce voter fraud, which was rampant during the party machine heyday, but below the surface they made it harder for a certain group of citizens to participate. The 19th Amendment to the Constitution granted women the right to vote in 1920, but some women were slow to exercise their new rights, pushing turnout numbers down. The percentage of women voters gradually improved, but even as late as 1960 turnout among women was nearly 10 percentage points below that of men.[15] In fact, the 2008 election was the first time in American history when the percentage of women coming to the polls outpaced men. The turnout gender gap in 2016 was about 4 percentage points[16] and in 2018 it was a bit higher.

In the 1960 presidential contest between Richard Nixon and John Kennedy, some 63 percent of the electorate turned out to vote. This was lower than the heyday of political participation in the late 19th century, but nearly two-thirds of the electorate at the polls was encouraging. Between that election and 2004, however, there was a consistent decline to about 50 percent. In the dramatic race between Barack Obama and John McCain in 2008 that figure bumped up to 59 percent, but since then has slipped back to roughly 55 percent. In each of the last three presidential elections more than 100 million citizens sat on the sidelines. The picture of participation in midterm congressional elections is even worse. In the 1960s, about 50 percent of Americans made it to the polls for these elections, but by the 1970s it had dropped to just over 40 percent. In the 2014 midterms, less than 37 percent of eligible voters went to the polls – the lowest turnout in more than 70 years. Moreover, the decline in participation in state and local elections has been worse. Many cities have seen their voter turnouts for municipal posts, such as mayor and city councilors, drop to their lowest level ever.

Given these data, one might be surprised to hear that some scholars and pundits believe the turnout decline might be a myth or, at the very least, less significant than what it might appear on its face.[17] They argue that turnout figures are based on US Census Bureau estimates of the adult population, a figure that includes individuals who cannot legally vote – such as prison inmates and convicted felons. It is difficult to know precisely how many people this adds up to, but a reasonable estimate is roughly six million citizens, as noted in the last chapter. On top of this, there has been a liberalization of immigration laws since the 1960s, which has led to one of the largest influxes of immigrants since World War I. "Non-citizens were 2 percent of the population in 1960 and today they account for 7 percent."[18] Simply put, these scholars argue that when adjusted for *ineligible* adults, the picture of turnout in America is less stark – and in fact it has probably been stable since the 1960s.

Other scholars are ready with a response, including Patterson in *The Vanishing Voter*. Even when we adjust for ineligible voters, the picture is still one of decline – perhaps not as steep, but a decline nonetheless. This is puzzling, he argues, given that higher levels of education, a factor highly correlated with voting, have not produced the 15–20 percent rise in turnout that voting theories would have predicted.[19] Most significantly, prior to the 1960s, southern blacks and many poor whites were disenfranchised. Patterson writes: "The clearest picture of what's been happening with turnout in recent decades emerges from a look at non-southern states only ... The non-South voting rate is now near the levels of the 1820s, a time when many eligible voters could not read or write and had to travel by foot or on horseback for hours to get to the nearest polling place … [T]he flight from electoral politics is not illusory."[20]

How Do We Stack up Across the Globe?

The authors of *The Civic Culture* wrote that the socialization process in the United States was more effectual at promoting the importance of voting and elections than in most other countries, but in 2016 nearly half of eligible citizens – some 132 million – stayed home on Election Day. But how does this compare to turnout in other nations? Sure, levels of involvement in the United States are less than perfect, but what about citizens in democracies across the globe? Perhaps the decline that we see in the United States has been occurring in other nations as well.

Voting rates in the United States are low not only in historic terms, but in comparison to the rest of the world. Data collected by the Pew Research Center in 2018 charted the turnout of the 35 nations in the Organization for Economic Co-operation and Development. The United States ranks 28th.[21] This is not a new development. Turnout has declined in most of these nations during the second half of the 20th century, but the decline in the United States has been more pronounced and, when combined with traditionally lower levels of voting, places our country near the bottom.[22]

What might explain this relative disparity? One of the most common explanations for high voting rates in other nations is compulsory voting, meaning that in many nations there is some form of requirement for voting or fee for failing to come to the polls. Twenty-four nations across the globe have compulsory voting. Turnout in Australia is often above 80 percent, where the fine is about $15 for anyone who fails to come to the polls.[23] However, only six of the nations included in the Pew data use compulsory voting. In other words, 22 of the nations in the Organisation for Economic Co-operation and Development that rank higher than the United States do *not* have compulsory voting.[24]

One cause might be that in the United States citizens have to register to vote; they have to take concerted steps to sign up. In many other democracies it is automatic. In other words, in many countries it is incumbent upon the government to register each citizen to vote, while in the United States it is up to the individual to take the necessary steps. Some states appreciate the impact of "automatic registration." In 2015, Oregon took the bold move of registering every citizen of voting age. Since then nine other states and the District of Columbia have done the same, and several others are considering it.

Another structural difference is the day voting takes place. General elections in the United States take place on the first Tuesday after the first Monday in November, yet in many other nations Election Day is a

Saturday or Sunday, allowing citizens more flexibility in getting to the polls. In some nations elections take place over two days. Italians, for example, can vote on both Saturday and Sunday. The goal is to lower the cost of voting – the effort a citizen must expend to cast his or her vote.

A growing chorus of election reformers in the United States argue low voter turnout is a result of the two-party system – more precisely, how we define winners. In most democracies across the globe a proportional system is used, where parties vying for seats in governing (usually a parliament) are awarded seats based on the proportion of votes their candidates receive on Election Day. If a party nets one-fifth of the vote, for instance, they are awarded about 20 percent of the seats. This gives minor-party backers a reason to turn out; their party might not win the election outright, but will get something for their efforts. There is a consolation prize, so to speak. In the United States a plurality "first-past-the-post" system is used, where the candidate with the most votes wins. There is no consolation prize. Minor parties can fight it out in a series of elections without ever taking a seat in Congress or in a state legislature. This dynamic propels a two-party model, where minor parties eventually merge with other parties, and this discourages citizens who back minor parties from voting. By one estimate, a proportional scheme (leading to a multi-party model) in the United States would boost turnout by about 10 percent.[25] Although a change along these lines might be far off, as will be discussed in a subsequent chapter, this may help us better appreciate why turnout in the United States might be lower than in other nations.

It should also be noted that while Americans vote at lower rates than citizens of other democracies, this does not mean they are less politically engaged. Paradoxically, the opposite seems to be true. Surveys over the past 20 years have consistently found that Americans lead the world in most forms of non-electoral political participation, such as being a member of a political group or reading about politics in newspapers. Voting, it turns out, may be a weak predictor of other forms of participation.[26] Some countries with the highest election turnout rates rank far behind the United States in other categories of political participation.

These other forms of participation may be more common and important in the United States than in other countries because of the structural barriers, detailed in the previous chapter, and it might also be due to our unique form of government. The United States features more elective offices, a clear separation of powers between branches and levels of government, and loose party discipline in legislatures. One might conclude that individual elections matter less in America than they do in other countries. For instance, a British Member of Parliament deals not only with national matters – concerns we generally associate with Congress – but also with many things we would consider within the scope of a state or local government, such as school issues and highway maintenance.

From this perspective, a British voter's choice for Parliament might be more important than an American's vote for a member of Congress. Seeing that they cannot dramatically change public policy with a single vote, perhaps Americans try to influence the government in other ways.

Sitting Out Elections

A robust debate has centered on the cause(s) of lackluster electoral participation in the United States. As noted earlier in the chapter, turnout has been sliding even though more Americans than ever attend college, some registration barriers have been lowered, and the civil rights movement has opened the door to greater African American involvement. Only one group of citizens is legally barred from the ballot box – those with felony records in certain states. There has been a list of hot-button issues that motivated Americans in recent years, including a plethora of highly charged cultural disputes. With so many positive changes and so many points of contention, why would levels of electoral participation remain lackluster? There is no clear answer, but theories abound.

Some speculate that the root of the change is that members of the generation first turned off to politics – the "counterculture" protest generation of the 1960s – have passed on their ambivalence for traditional modes of activism to their children. In the 1960s, many thought elections and political parties were part of the problem, a means to maintain the status quo. Other modes of activism, like protests and demonstrations, seemed more effective, especially for traditionally disenfranchised groups (such as women and African Americans). As the protest generation aged, they passed on their lukewarm interest in voting to their children. These children, now adults, continue to doubt the utility of elections.

Another theory is that the media has become the primary socialization agent, leading to huge changes in our outlook about politics. We know that the amount of time Americans spend on screens has skyrocketed in recent years. By one estimate, we spend nearly 11 hours per day looking at our tablets, smartphones, personal computers, multimedia devices, video games, radios, and televisions.[27] Some eight in ten Americans have a smartphone, spending about 1.5 hours each day glued to it. Roughly half of the overall screen time is spent with the television. Another study found that teens are spending more than one-third of their days watching videos or listening to music online – nearly nine hours on average.[28] Ninety percent of people ages 18 to 29 use social media today – with a vast majority on Facebook – and access the web and social media several times a day.[29]

What difference might screen and social media use have on the political socialization process? On the one hand, some studies have found citizens have a deeper understanding of issues and trends, and perhaps a greater sympathy for other groups because of their time online. That is to say, Americans are increasingly aware of current events and are more tolerant.[30] As noted by a team of scholars, "Our research clearly concluded that social media positively influences political interest due to the constant exposure to concise, accurate, global information; and use of social media has the potential to increase political interest."[31] On the other hand, the evidence to suggest social media-based involvement actually increases real-world engagement is thin. Data from the 2016 election finds that much of the hostile, negative material found on social media may have created higher levels of cynicism about the process and distrust toward other Americans, thereby lowing voter turnout. A study conducted by the Pew Research Center in the fall of 2016, for instance, found that 59 percent of social media users saw exchanges about politics "stressful and frustrating." Six in ten said their online encounters with people on the opposite side of the political spectrum left them feeling as if they have even less in common than they thought.[32] Other studies point to a growing link between social media use and cynicism about government – and society more generally.[33]

We also know that scandal-based news reporting, what one scholar has dubbed the rise of "feeding frenzies,"[34] bombards Americans. According to this author, "The new media's greatest impact on voters is not in the winnowing of candidates but in the encouragement of cynicism."[35] It is no wonder that levels of pessimism and alienation have skyrocketed, precisely at the same time that a burgeoning number of news outlets vie for higher ratings. If all politicians are crooked and the system is broken, why take time out of your busy day to vote? As noted in a *New York Times* editorial, "Some people wouldn't vote if you put a ballot box in their living room. Whether they believe there is no meaningful difference between the major parties or that the government doesn't care what they think regardless of who is in power, they have detached themselves from the political process."[36]

Another perspective is what we might call the "lifestyle change supposition." Simply put, life today is busier and offers more distractions than in previous periods. According to Robert Putnam, author of *Bowling Alone: The Collapse and Revival of American Community*, "I don't have enough time" and "I'm too busy" are the most often heard excuses for social disengagement.[37] Let us take, for instance, the number of dual-income families. Today, a majority of families have two wage earners, a massive shift from the 1950s when few women worked outside the home. "[A]nd since there are only 24 hours in the day," writes Putnam, "something had to give … [and] it seems plausible that the cutbacks also affected community involvement."[38] The same sort of argument is often made with regard to the shrinking number of non-working hours for all Americans. We are too distracted by new technologies, namely television and the internet, to be heavily involved in politics. Studies suggest that "TV watching comes at the expense of nearly every social activity outside the home."[39] These changes likely play some role in the decline of voting, but many, including Putnam, are quick to caution against overstating the case. With regard to women in the workplace, for example, while it may be true that they have less time to vote, they also have more opportunities to vote given they are often outside the home on Election Day. More importantly, employed women are actually more involved in civic life than are stay-at-home women.[40] As for television, Putnam's best guess is that around 15 percent of the decline in civic participation, more generally, can be attributed to our love affair with television screens.[41]

Another perspective centers on the costs versus benefits of participation. Voting only happens, this approach holds, when the benefits equal or exceed the costs. Believe it or not, there are some costs associated with voting: one has to register, find time to cast a ballot, and know enough about the candidates to make informed decisions. Although many would suggest the costs are minor, social scientists believe they are enough to keep many voters from participating, particularly if they see few benefits. As fewer and fewer races are competitive, due, for instance, to partisan-gerrymandering, the rationale for voting declines. An important characteristic here seems to be levels of education; the costs of voting decline as one's level of formal education increases. Not only does awareness of the mechanics of elections increase with formal education, so too do the benefits of voting. One's sense of civic duty seems to increase through education. As noted in one study, "Length of education is one of the best predictors of an individual's likelihood of voting."[42] But there is a snag to this argument: the percentage of Americans who have attended at least some college has grown steadily since the end of World War II.[43] Perhaps better educated citizens realize their efforts are less important when the outcome of the election seems a foregone conclusion. An analysis conducted by the *Wall Street Journal* found that in presidential elections, states that are the least contested also had the lowest turnout; competitive states had the highest turnout.[44]

Local political parties historically have been the institutions that pulled citizens to the polls on Election Day. Legions of party workers, nearly always volunteers, would keep track of which party members had voted and which had not. Empirical data confirms that turnout is much higher in communities that still have strong local parties.[45] The problem, however, is that fewer and fewer communities have these organizations.

Campaigns, especially for the presidency, have become much longer, conceivably leading to voter burnout. "The long campaign of today runs in spurts, taxes people's attention, and dulls their sensibilities."[46] It used to be common for presidential candidates to kick off their campaigns in the fall, a year before the general election, but in 2016 nearly all of the major candidates had done so by spring of 2015. Along with the length of campaigns, they have become impersonal, relying on television and internet advertisements. In the not-too-distant past, much campaign work was done face to face, likely leading to greater interest among citizens and higher levels of turnout.

There is also the issue of negative campaigning. There is little question that the tone of campaigns has become more negative in recent decades. Hard-hitting, shrill campaigns have always been part of the political landscape in the United States, but the frequency these days, due in large measure to the rise of hyper-partisanship and expenditures by groups not connected to candidates, is unprecedented. Do attack ads turn off voters? The first scholarly take on the issue seemed to confirm this theory, but upon closer inspection we find it is more complicated. Many studies suggest that negative campaigning seems to turn voters off, but many others find that turnout actually increases in negative races.[47] One impressive study suggests that while some voters (namely, the less partisan ones) are turned off, others (the most partisan) are likely activated by negative campaigning.[48] Another promising line of research on this topic suggests that the effects of negative campaigning on voter turnout might be dependent upon the citizen's local political culture.[49] A citizen in Provo, Utah, might respond differently to attack ads than, say, a voter in Newark, New Jersey. At present, there seems to be no scholarly consensus on the effects of attack ads on levels of turnout; we cannot simply tag negative campaigns as the culprit.

A new line of research underscores the role of declining faith in the integrity of elections. Shortly before the 2016 election, Gallup issued a report showing that only 30 percent of Americans had confidence in the honesty of elections. That was a sharp decline from the three previous elections, and it put the United States at 90th out of 112 nations across the globe.[50] Harvard scholar Pippa Norris and a group of her graduate students zeroed in on the turnout piece. "When people believe that electoral malpractice is common, they are significantly less likely to vote," she writes.[51] By surveying over 700 political scientists who evaluated the integrity of their own state's election process during the 2016 election, and by overlaying the actual turnout, a telling portrait emerges: the states thought to have the most problems with elections tended to have the lowest levels of turnout. Conversely, states ranked high in election integrity generally had higher levels of turnout. For instance, many New England states were ranked high – and they had above average levels of turnout. Many southern states were ranked low, and turnout was below average.[52]

There was a dramatic increase in the number of non-partisan voters, particularly from the 1950s to the end of the 1990s – as will be discussed in detail in subsequent chapters. Is it just a coincidence that the number of independents increased at precisely the same time that fewer citizens came to the polls? Scholars have long noted a strong relationship between one's partisan intensity and willingness to vote: those individuals most committed to a party are also the ones most likely to turn out on Election Day. So, it is quite likely that changing attitudes toward party identification may have had a bearing on overall voting rates. Along similar lines, in his study of thousands of citizens during the 2000 election, Thomas Patterson found that those who believed that the parties are alike were much *less* likely to vote.[53]

And yet, there has been a stark increase in partisan polarization – as will be discussed in the next chapter. Partisan polarization is one of the defining characteristics of American politics in the early part of the 21st century. Stanford political scientist Morris Fiorina has argued that the root of the change stems from activists at the ends of the ideological spectrum; hard-core liberals and hard-core conservatives have become especially informed, vocal and engaged. Most citizens remain moderate, but the wings of the party have become loud and active. And because hard-core activists are more likely to vote, particularly in primary elections, the winners tend to be more ideological than their constituent base. Ironically, as middle-of-the-road citizens see their member of Congress and state legislature as firmly committed to either far-left or far-right policies, they veer away from the process. These citizens also notice that the tone of politics, given this polarization, has become shrill. It is possible, then, that this type of polarization contributes to lower levels of voting. True ideologues turn out to vote, certainly, but moderates, who tend to be much less engaged in the process, may be staying home. In his book *Disconnect: The Breakdown in Representation in American Politics*, Fiorina writes:

> [C]ross-sectional evidence does not rule out the possibility that the long-term decline in voting by independents and ideological moderates is relative to the growing negativity of contemporary politics ... [O]rdinary Americans are turned off by the uncivil manner of many members of the political class, their emphasis on issues of limited importance to most people ...[54]

Other scholars have suggested the polarization is much more widespread than merely among those at the ideological extremes – and there is a growing pool of data to back this view. But has this shift brought more to the polls or kept higher numbers of moderates at home? It is difficult to pin down the timing of the steep rise of polarization, but many believe the seeds of dysfunction were planted in the early 1990s, with the rise of a more strident wing of the Republican Party (and their leader, Newt Gingrich) and the emergence of hard-core conservative talk radio.[55] The widening gap between Democratic and Republican partisans did not show up until about 2004.[56] That might explain the modest jump in turnout in 2008, and an upswing in several measures of electoral engagement in recent years. But turnout – the percentage of Americans heading to the polls – has not increased appreciably since the hardening of partisanship. In other words, while Americans have become more polarized and ever-more concerned about the policies of the other party, there has not been a groundswell of voting. At best we might say that the growing number of hard-core partisans has stabilized an otherwise downward turnout trend.

It would be a mistake to assume that all forms of political participation have declined. A rather novel perspective suggests the emergence of a new type of politics, dubbed "lifestyle politics." This view holds that while Americans may be less engaged in traditional forms of political action, like voting, they are increasingly involved in matters that concern their own well-being. At the forefront of this list of concerns is one's economic condition. As noted by a prominent scholar, "The psychological energy (cathexis) people once devoted to the grand political projects of economic integration and nation-building in industrial democracies is now increasingly directed toward personal projects of managing and expressing complex identities in a fragmented society."[57] While some might suggest this perspective is little more than a cop-out, at the very least it underscores transformations brought upon by the Information Revolution and the new economy.

Then there is online activism. We know that online activism can lead to offline engagement, such as the wearing of particular clothing or buttons, boycotting products, or attending rallies or protests. While the exact origins of the phenomena are unclear, we all learned of the ALS Ice Bucket Challenge in the summer of 2014 after several videos went viral. The #MeToo movement spread in October 2017 as a hashtag used on social media to draw attention to the prevalence of sexual assault and harassment, especially in the workplace. There is growing literature on the link between social media and real-world politics.[58] One of the earliest and most cited works on the potential of social-media activism is Shirky's *Here Comes Everybody*, published in 2009.

But does social media-based involvement spur a broader array of political activities or act like a placebo? Social media engagement has mockingly been dubbed slacktivism and armchair activism by some. Malcolm Gladwell scoffed at any relationship between social networking sites and broad democratic engagement.[59] Contrary to the hopes of the "evangelists of social media," he argues new modes of communication have not drawn young citizens into the political fray. "Social networks are effective at increasing participation – by lessening the level of motivation that participation requires." Social media is designed to allow access to information, he argues, but it does not forge connections to other political actors or to the larger political system. "It makes it easier for activists to express themselves, and harder for that expression to have an impact." Moreover, by definition networks provide little structure and certainly no hierarchy. Given low levels of trust of traditional hierarchical structures, the attraction of networks would make sense. A "network" is fine, Gladwell writes, "if it just wants to frighten or humiliate or make a splash – or if it doesn't need to think strategically." If you're taking on a powerful and organized establishment, you have a hierarchy. Even Barack Obama, who seemed to benefit from a huge "net-root" campaign in 2008, took a stab at online engagement in the fall of 2018: "If you don't like what's going on right now, and you shouldn't, do not complain, don't hashtag, don't get anxious, don't retreat, don't binge on whatever it is you're bingeing on, don't lose yourself in ironic detachment, don't put your head in the sand, don't boo. Vote!"[60]

Empirical work connecting acts of support online and subsequent cost-intensive behaviors has yielded mixed findings. Sociologist Shelley Boulianne conducted a meta-analysis (a study of the studies) of 38 recent works on the relationship between social network engagement and broader political involvement.[61] Her findings suggest a small positive relationship. She writes, "popular discourse has focused on the use of social media by the Obama campaigns ... [and] while these campaigns may have revolutionized aspects of election campaigning online, such as gathering donations, the metadata provide little evidence that the social media aspects of the campaigns were successful in changing people's levels of participation."[62] In other words, there is little hard evidence to say social media affects people's likelihood of voting or participating in a campaign.

Conclusion: Is the Young Voter Apathy Rap Justified?

As the 20th century was drawing to a close, young Americans were tagged as apathetic, self-absorbed, lazy and indifferent. It had become a near truism that young Americans were unmoved by public affairs. Scholar James Q. Wilson wrote that America's youth represent nothing more than "30,000 more muggers, killers, and thieves than we have now," all of whom come from "dysfunctional families" and "disorderly neighborhoods."[63] Just one in three adults thought youth, once grown, would make the world a better place.[64] It was, after all, a generation reared under the omnipotent buzz of video games, instant messaging, cell phones, high-definition television, and iPhones. They were thought violent, promiscuous, lazy, angry, whiny, insolent and self-indulgent.[65] And the sense of entitlement – the certainty that everyone owed them something – seemed overwhelming.

The "apathy rap" was launched, in part, by *The Book of Virtues*, a hefty volume written in 1993 by William Bennett, Secretary of Education in the Reagan Administration. Things were different with this generation and America would turn its back on the sweeping changes at its peril. Yale law professor Robert Bork followed with *Slouching Towards Gomorrah* in 1996, where he charted the roots of American decline – and perhaps even Western decline. "Every generation," wrote Bork, "constitutes a wave of savages who must be civilized by their families, schools, and churches."[66] The problem was that an exceptionally large generation was coming of age during an exceptionally transformative period.

And yet, the preponderance of empirical studies on youth engagement shed a much different light. A series of reports by a number of organizations, particularly the Center for Information and Research on Civic Learning and Engagement (CIRCLE), suggested young citizens are deeply involved in their communities and truly concerned about public matters. Their data told, for example, that 18- to 25-year-olds volunteered in their communities at higher rates than any other age group.[67] Russell Dalton, in *The Good Citizen* (2008), offered evidence that young citizens are more engaged and more tolerant than previous generations, and Martin Wattenberg noted, "there are a variety of surveys that provide evidence regarding the increase of youth volunteerism in recent years."[68]

The rap was not completely baseless, however. Until 2008, low levels of *political* engagement among younger citizens were startling. Election turnout had dropped precipitously for three decades: in 1972, when 18-year-olds were first given the right to vote, 50 percent of those under 30 years old came to the polls. By 2004, it had dropped to just 34 percent. As for midterm congressional elections, one in four of those under 30 were making it to the polls by the end of the century. A CIRCLE study in 2002 found only about two-thirds of 18- to 25-year-olds had even registered to vote, and 49 percent of those under 25 said that voting is "a little important" or "not at all important" to them. Only 20 percent said that voting was a responsibility of citizenship.[69] Robert Putnam summed up the young voter problem this way: "Very little of the net decline in voting is attributable to individual change, and virtually all of it is generational."[70]

The response to the youth voting crisis was swift and comprehensive. A number of youth-centered political mobilization efforts took root, including Rock-the-Vote, Redeem the Vote, Choose or Lose, Head Count, Hip Hop Summit Action Network, Citizen Change, Punk Voter, Your Country, Your Vote, Declare Yourself and Smackdown Your Vote. Hefty philanthropic initiatives were launched, most notably Pew Charitable Trust's "New Voters Project"; the Youth Vote Coalition (an umbrella organization for a number of youth engagement initiatives); and several programs by the Carnegie Corporation. A number of college and university programs were created. Both the major parties, but especially the Democrats, allocated unprecedented resources to youth engagement efforts – likely due to the shrinking number of persuadable older voters.

Although a direct causal connection to these initiatives is difficult to verify, we know that youth interest in politics grew in the 2008 elections; turnout for those under 30 rose to 51 percent. Many other indicators of political behavior, such as participating in campaign events, talking about politics with friends and family, and paying attention to the news also increased. While many have speculated that the surge in 2008 may have been somewhat artificial, driven mostly by an extensive Obama net-roots campaign, few questioned the significance. Given the role that young voters played in several of the early presidential nomination contests, it seemed to make sense that *Time* would dub 2008 the "Year of the Youth Vote."[71] Those fretting about the long-term stability of our system breathed a sigh of relief. An article in *Wiretap* magazine proclaimed, "This year the epithet of youth apathy was finally laid to rest."[72] Young citizens had rediscovered the potential of politics and they were once again making their voices heard. Never shy about proclaiming the impact of their efforts, the folks at Rock the Vote noted, "2008 is the year of the young voter. We're not going to take politics as usual anymore, and we won't be ignored. We're taking the country into our hands ... Today's youth are a political powerhouse."[73]

Perhaps not. Was the reemergence of young voters a sea change or data blip? Consider that just one year after RTV's proclamation, voters under age 30 accounted for just 9 percent of the voters in the New Jersey gubernatorial election and only 10 percent in the Virginia gubernatorial race. By the 2010 midterm election it seemed quite clear that the youth engagement bubble had burst, given their meager involvement in that race. Young voter turnout in the 2012 presidential election was down to 44 percent, and by the summer of 2015 the scholars at CIRCLE issued an uncharacteristically gloomy press release. Census data had confirmed that turnout for voters under 30 in the 2014 midterm election was the lowest on record – just 20 percent. The proportion of young people who said that they were registered to vote in 2014 was also down to 47 percent – the lowest in 40 years. Turnout for this group in 2016 was on par with 2012 – a mediocre 45 percent. To add insult to injury, in a comparative sense youth turnout in the United States is bleak. According to scholar Paul Beck, co-director of the Comparative National Elections Project, "The US has the largest gap between ages out of the whole democratic world."[74]

It should be noted that youth turnout climbed considerably in the 2018 midterm election, with 31 percent of those under 30 coming to the polls.[75] That just one in three young voters took the time to cast a ballot in such a historic election might seem a rather modest accomplishment (turnout for those *over* 30 was roughly 50 percent), but it was a big improvement over the previous midterm.

What is going on? Are young citizens disengaged, indifferent to the big issue of our day? Is the apathy rap justified? Prior to the bump in 2008, a group of students representing 27 colleges and universities gathered for a conference in Racine, Wisconsin to discuss these contradictory trends. These students did not see their community work as an alternative to politics, but rather a way to create positive change through community-building efforts. Out of this, a new concept emerged: service politics. Younger citizens have become cynical and distrustful about the political process and they believe the best way for them to stay involved is to volunteer. Columnist Jane Eisner put it this way:

> [T]he attraction of service for young people is undeniable, and growing. It is propelled by the characteristics of this generation – their tendency toward compassion and their nonjudgmental concern for others, and away from what they see as a political system driven by conflict and ego.[76]

In other words, maybe young people remain deeply concerned and connected, but many choose to channel their engagement in different ways – namely through community work and online efforts. Conceivably, the withdrawal from the electoral process may reflect a conscious choice to reject ineffectual, flawed modes of participation in favor of concrete, tangible activities. Can we blame them?

It seems we are entering uncharted territory. It would be easy, perhaps even rote, to detail the dangers of a generation of citizens coming of age divorced from politics. How could a limited government, a government by the people, function when an entire cohort turns its back on voting and elections? But that is not the story of today's generation of young citizens. They are coming of age in a very cynical time, with historic low levels of trust in governing institutions. They doubt the capacity of politics to spur meaningful change, and certainly question their capacity to influence public policy. Instead of withdrawing from public life all together, they have chosen to stay connected through social media and other online tools, and to do community work. With the exception of the pre-Civil War era, it is likely that no other generation of Americans has come of political age during a period of such deep partisan divisions. Yet, the young seem reluctant to vilify those on the other side.

The withdrawal of so many Americans from traditional modes of political action will have an impact on the nation's policy agenda. "Casting a ballot is the best opportunity most of us will ever get to have a say in who will represent us, what issues they will address and how they will spend our money."[77] One might wonder if Barack Obama's aggressive college tuition/student loan proposals, introduced in the spring of 2015, might not have languished if legislators feared a surge of young voters in 2016? As noted at the start of this chapter, even a slightly higher turnout of young voters in a few key states might have flipped the outcome of the 2016 presidential election. We also know that a full 67 percent of this age group supported Democratic candidates in the 2018 midterms, adding to the wave that flipped 40 House seats, 333 state legislative seats, and seven governors' mansions.[78] Young voters had a big role in the wave.

The irony, of course, is that the slow-moving, often ugly process that young citizens reject could also reshape the conditions they struggle to change through volunteer work. Volunteer work, while essential, can sometimes mask the broader systemic forces that define relationships and cause the conditions that are disguised in the ordinary. In the fall of 2018, shortly before the midterm election, Barack Obama made a special appeal to young citizens:

> The biggest threat to our democracy is indifference. The biggest threat to our democracy is cynicism. To all the young people who are here today, there are now more eligible voters in your generation than in any other, which means your generation now has more power than anybody to change things. If you want it, you can make sure America gets out of its current funk.[79]

Greater youth engagement in politics might transform the process itself. From the weight of big money, to the prevalence of negative, shrill campaign rhetoric, to the vitriol spewed by media pundits, a groundswell of reform-minded activists could alter the way we do politics in America. In the spring of 2018, a *Washington Post* essay declared: "Millennials disrupted the system. Gen Z is here to fix the mess."[80] Perhaps so, but we have to wonder if a generation that only sporadically engages in traditional modes of political activism will have the verve to make real changes. We need only recount the frustration that progressives must have felt after retaking the reigns of the federal government in 2008, only to see their agenda crippled two years later due to young citizens standing on the sidelines.

Volunteer work is critically important in our system, and online organizing and information sharing has the potential to invigorate our democracy. Young Americans are caring, compassionate, tolerant, and in many respects the exemplars of democratic citizenship. But our governing institutions will not be changing any time soon, and while it might be a tough business, retreating to the sidelines to watch others battle it out is not an option. Voting matters. Writing a few days before the 2018 midterms, columnist Roxane Gay offered a rather stern message for young Americans: "I have no patience for disillusionment. I have no patience for the audacious luxury of choosing not to vote because of that disillusionment, as if not voting is the best choice a person could make. Not voting is, in fact, the worst choice a person could make."[81]

Perhaps, also, young Americans should take to heart the comments of Andrea Anthony, a Wisconsin woman who was barred from voting in the 2016 presidential election due to a new ID law – after voting for her entire adult life: "Voting is important to me because I know I have a little, teeny, tiny voice, but that is a way for it to be heard. Even though it's one vote, I feel it needs to count."[82]

Notes

1 Omri Ben-Shahar, "The Non-Voters Who Decided the Election: Trump Won Because Of Lower Democratic Turnout," *Forbes* website, November 17, 2016 (www.forbes.com/sites/omribenshahar/2016/11/17/the-non-voters-who-decided-the-election-trump-won-because-of-lower-democratic-turnout/#76a292df53ab).

2 Charles Prysby, "The Republican Appeal to Working-Class Whites in 2016," Department of Political Science University of North Carolina at Greensboro, Conference on the State of the Parties: 2016 and Beyond, November 9–10, 2017.

3 Michael D. Regan, "What Does Voter Turnout Tell us About the 2016 Election?," *PBS NewsHour* website, November 20, 2016 (www.pbs.org/newshour/politics/voter-turnout-2016-elections).

4 Ibid.

5 As cited in Emily Badger, "What if Everyone Voted?," *New York Times*, October 29, 2018.

6 Charles Prysby, "The Republican Appeal to Working-Class Whites in 2016," Department of Political Science University of North Carolina at Greensboro, Conference on the State of the Parties: 2016 and Beyond, November 9–10, 2017.

7 John Sides, Michael Tesler, and Lynn Vavreck, *Identity Crisis: The 2016 Presidential Campaign and the Battle for the Meaning of America* (Princeton, NJ: Princeton University Press, 2018).

8 Ezra Klein, "Ed Gillespie's Loss Shows Donald Trump has Made Trumpism Toxic," *Vox Media*, November 17, 2017 (www.vox.com/policy-and-politics/2017/11/7/16621994/ed-gillespie-ralph-northam-va-gov-trump).

9 *New York Times* Editorial Board, "Vote. That's Just What They Don't Want You to Do," *New York Times* website, March 10, 2018 (www.nytimes.com/2018/03/10/opinion/sunday/go-vote.html?action=click&pgtype=Homepage&clickSource=story-heading&module=opinion-c-col-left-region&region=opinion-c-col-left-region&WT.nav=opinion-c-col-left-region).

10 Michael D. Regan, "What Does Voter Turnout Tell us About the 2016 Election?," *PBS NewsHour*, November 20, 2016 (www.pbs.org/newshour/politics/voter-turnout-2016-elections).

11 Martin P. Wattenberg, *Is Voting for Young People?* (New York: Pearson Longman, 2012), 201.

12 William H. Flanigan and Nancy H. Zingal, *Political Behavior and the American Electorate*, 9th Edition (Washington, DC: Congressional Quarterly Press, 1998), 12.

13 Gabriel Almond and Sidney Verba, *The Civic Culture* (Princeton, NJ: Princeton University Press, 1963).

14 As cited in William H. Flanigan and Nancy H. Zingal, *Political Behavior and the American Electorate*, 9th Edition (Washington, DC: Congressional Quarterly Press, 1998), 20.

15 Thomas E. Patterson, *The Vanishing Voter: Public Involvement in an Age of Uncertainty* (New York: Knopf, 2002), 6.

16 Center for American Women and Politics, "Gender Differences in Voter Turnout," *Eagleton Institute of Politics, Rutgers University*, July 20, 2017.

17 See, for example, Michael McDonald and Samuel Popkin, "The Myth of the Vanishing Voter," a paper presented at the annual meeting of the American Political Science Association (Washington, DC, August 30–September 3, 2000), as cited in Patterson, *The Vanishing Voter* (2002), 198.

18 Thomas E. Patterson, *The Vanishing Voter: Public Involvement in an Age of Uncertainty* (New York: Knopf, 2002), 8.

19 Ibid., 9.

20 Ibid.

21 Drew Desilver, "U.S. Trails Most Developed Countries in Voter Turnout," Pew Research Center, May 15, 2017 (www.pewresearch.org/fact-tank/2017/05/15/u-s-voter-turnout-trails-most-developed-countries/).

22 Rafael López Pintor et al., *Voter Turnout Since 1945: A Global Report* (Stockholm: International Institute for Democracy and Electoral Assistance, 2002), 78–85.

23 Aamna Mohdin, "There Is a Way Democracies Can Create Better-informed Voters – But You're Probably Not Going to Like It," *Quartz*, August 1, 2016 (https://qz.com/746737/there-is-a-way-democracies-can-create-better-informed-voters-but-youre-not-going-to-like-it/).

24 Drew Desilver, "U.S. Trails Most Developed Countries in Voter Turnout," Pew Research Center, May 15, 2017 (www.pewresearch.org/fact-tank/2017/05/15/u-s-voter-turnout-trails-most-developed-countries/).

25 George Cheung, "Strengthening Democracy by Embracing a Multi-Party System," *Stanford Social Innovation Review*, February 4, 2016 (https://ssir.org/articles/entry/strengthening_democracy_by_embracing_a_multi_party_system).

26 Samuel H. Barnes et al., *Political Action: Mass Participation in Five Western Democracies* (Beverly Hills: Sage Publications, 1979), 85.

27 Jacqueline Howard, "Americans Devote More than 10 Hours a Day to Screen Time, and Growing," *Cable News Network*, July 29, 2016 (www.cnn.com/2016/06/30/health/americans-screen-time-nielsen/index.html).

28 Hayley Tsukayama, "Teens Spend Nearly Nine Hours Every Day Consuming Media," *Washington Post* website, November 3, 2015 (www.washingtonpost.com/news/the-switch/wp/2015/11/03/teens-spend-nearly-nine-hours-every-day-consuming-media/?utm_term=.be780ab9d6fd).

29 Veranike Collazo, "Peers, Social Media Play Increasingly Large Role in Youth Political Socialization," *The Columbia Missourian* website, October 30, 2015 (www.columbiamissourian.com/news/local/peers-social-media-play-increasingly-large-role-in-youth-political/article_ff969934-7ea9-11e5-8bf4-fb73f63c5057.html).

30 Kate Dunsmore and Taso G. Lagos, "Politics, Media and Youth: Understanding Political Socialization Via Video Production in Secondary Schools," *Learning, Media and Technology* 33 (March 2008), 1–10.

31 Florentina-Alina Vasile, "Social Media Can Increase Youth's Political Interest," *School of Politics and International Relations, University of Nottingham*, September 9, 2014.

32 Maeve Duggan and Aaron Smith, "The Political Environment on Social Media," Pew Research Center, October 25, 2016 (www.pewinternet.org/2016/10/25/the-political-environment-on-social-media/).

33 Kristen Bialik and Katerina Eva Matsa, "Key Trends in Social and Digital Media Usage," Pew Research Center, October 4, 2017 (www.pewresearch.org/fact-tank/2017/10/04/key-trends-in-social-and-digital-news-media/).

34 Larry Sabato, *Feeding Frenzies: How Attack Journalism and Transformed American Politics* (New York: Free Press, 1993).

35 Ibid., 207.

36 *New York Times* Editorial Board, "Vote. That's Just What They Don't Want You to Do," *New York Times* website, March 10, 2018 (www.nytimes.com/2018/03/10/opinion/sunday/go-vote.html?action=click&pgtype=Homepage&clickSource=story-heading&module=opinion-c-col-left-region&region=opinion-c-col-left-region&WT.nav=opinion-c-col-left-region).

37 Robert D. Putnam, *Bowling Alone: The Collapse and Revival of American Community* (New York: Simon and Schuster, 2000), 189.

38 Ibid., 194.

39 Ibid., 237.

40 Ibid., 196.

41 Ibid., 284.

42 William H. Flanigan and Nancy H. Zingal, *Political Behavior and the American Electorate* (Washington, DC: Congressional Quarterly Press, 1998), 40.

43 Camille L. Ryan and Kurt Bauman, "Educational Attainment in the United States: 2015," *US Census Bureau*, March 2016.

44 Evan Comen et al., "States with the Highest (and Lowest) Voter Turnout," *24/7 Wall Street*, February 4, 2016 (https://247wallst.com/special-report/2016/02/04/voter-turnout-in-each-state/11/).

45 John P. Frendreis, James L. Gibson and Laura L. Vertz, "Electoral Relevance of Local Party Organization," *American Political Science Review* 84 (1990), 225–235.

46 Patterson, *The Vanishing Voter*, 127.

47 For a meta-analysis on the topic – that is, a study of the studies – see Richard Lau, Lee Sigelman, Caroline Heldman and Paul Babbit, "The Effects of Negative Political Advertising: A Meta-analytic Assessment," *American Political Science Review* 93 (December 1999), 851–875.

48 Stephen Ansolabehere and Shanto Iyenger, *Going Negative: How Political Advertisements Shrink and Polarize the Electorate* (New York: Free Press, 1997), Chapter 5.

49 Kelly Patterson and Daniel M. Shea, "Local Political Context and Negative Campaigns: A Test of Negative Effect Across State Party Systems," *The Journal of Political Marketing* 3 (December 2003), 1–20.

50 Justin McCarthy and Jon Clifton, "Update: Americans' Confidence in Voting, Election," *Gallup*, November 1, 2016 (http://news.gallup.com/poll/196976/update-americans-confidence-voting-election.aspx).

51 Pippa Norris, Holly Ann Garnett, and Max Gromping, "Why Don't More Americans Vote? Maybe Because they Don't Trust US Elections," *Washington Post* website, December 26, 2016 (www.washingtonpost.com/news/monkey-cage/wp/2016/12/26/why-dont-more-americans-vote-maybe-because-they-dont-trust-u-s-elections/?utm_term=.75384de5870c).

52 Ibid.

53 Thomas E. Patterson, *The Vanishing Voter: Public Involvement in an Age of Uncertainty* (New York: Knopf, 2002), 59.

54 Morris P. Fiorina with Samuel J. Abrams, *Disconnect: The Breakdown of Representation in American Politics* (Norman, OK: University of Oklahoma Press, 2009), 41.

55 Thomas E. Mann and Norman J. Ornstein, *It's Even Worse Than it Looks* (New York: Basic Books, 2012), Chapter 2.

56 Pew Research Center, "Partisan Divides Over Political Values Widen," October 5, 2017 (www.people-press.org/2017/10/05/1-partisan-divides-over-political-values-widen/).

57 W. Lance Bennett, "The Uncivic Culture: Communication, Identity, and the Rise of Lifestyle Politics," *PS – Political Science and Politics* 31 (December 1998), 755, 758.

58 Daniel Trottier and Christian Fuchs, *Social Media, Politics and the State* (New York: Routledge Press, 2015), Chapter 1.

59 Malcolm Gladwell, "Small Change: Why the Revolution Will Not Be Tweeted." *New Yorker* website, October 4, 2010 (www.newyorker.com/magazine/2010/10/04/small-change-malcolm-gladwell).

60 Isaac Saul, "Obama Says the Next Election is More Important than the One that Elected Him," APlus, September 7, 2018 (https://aplus.com/a/barack-obama-young-people-vote-november-elections?no_monetization=true).

61 Shelley Boulianne, "Does Internet Use Affect Engagement? A Meta-Analysis of Research," *Political Communication* 26 (May 2009).

62 Ibid.

63 James Q. Wilson, *On Character* (Washington, DC: American Enterprise Institute for Public Policy Research, 1995), 507.

64 Neil Howe, William Strauss, and R.J. Matson, *Millennials Rising: The Next Great Generation* (New York: Vintage Books, 2000), 3.

65 Daniel M. Shea and John C. Green, *Fountain of Youth: Strategies and Tactics for Mobilizing America's Young Voters* (Lanham, MD: Rowman and Littlefield, 2007), 3.

66 Robert Bork, *Slouching Toward Gomorrah: Modern Liberalism and American Decline* (New York: Harper Perennial, 1996), 21.

67 The Center for Information and Research on Civic Learning and Engagement, "The Civic and Political Health of the Nation: National Civic Engagement Survey II," December 2002.

68 Martin P. Wattenberg, *Is Voting for Young People?* (New York: Pearson Longman, 2012), 151.

69 The Center for Information and Research on Civic Learning and Engagement, "The Civic and Political Health of the Nation: National Civic Engagement Survey II," December 2002.

70 Putnam, *Bowling Alone*, 35.

71 David Von Drehle, "The Year of the Youth Vote," *Time* website, January 31, 2008 (http://content.time.com/time/magazine/article/0,9171,1708836,00.html).

72 Martin P. Wattenberg, *Is Voting for Young People?* (New York: Pearson Longman, 2012), 172.

73 Rock the Vote, 2008.

74 Richard Gunther, "About the Comparative National Elections Project," *Mershon Center for International Security Studies, The Ohio State University,* November 20, 2017 (http://u.osu.edu/cnep/).

75 Center for Information and Research on Civic Learning and Engagement, "Young People Dramatically Increased Their Turnout to 31%," November 9, 2018 (https://civicyouth.org/young-people-dramatically-increase-their-turnout-31-percent-shape-2018-midterm-elections/).

76 Jane Eisner, *Taking Back the Vote: Getting Youth Involved in Our Democracy* (Boston: Beacon Press, 2004), 80.

77 *New York Times* Editorial Board, "Vote. That's Just What They Don't Want You to Do," *New York Times* website, March 10, 2018 (www.nytimes.com/2018/03/10/opinion/sunday/go-vote.html?action=click&pgtype=Homepage&clickSource=story-heading&module=opinion-c-col-left-region&region=opinion-c-col-left-region&WT.nav=opinion-c-col-left-region).

78 Center for Information and Research on Civic Learning and Engagement, "Young People Dramatically Increased Their Turnout to 31%," November 9, 2018 (https://civicyouth.org/young-people-dramatically-increase-their-turnout-31-percent-shape-2018-midterm-elections/).

79 *The Guardian,* "Barack Obama's Rebuke of Donald Trump's America," September 7, 2018 (www.theguardian.com/us-news/2018/sep/07/barack-obama-speech-rebukes-donald-trump).

80 Rhonda Colvin, "Millennials Disrupted the System. Gen Z is Here to Fix the Mess," *Washington Post* website, February 24, 2018 (www.washingtonpost.com/news/post-nation/wp/2018/02/24/millennials-disrupted-the-system-gen-z-is-here-to-fix-the-mess/?utm_term=.68c1f01cd1a7).

81 Roxane Gay, "You're Disillusioned. That's Fine. Vote Anyway" *New York Times,* October 30, 2018.

82 *New York Times* Editorial Board, "Vote. That's Just What They Don't Want You to Do," *New York Times* website, March 10, 2018 (www.nytimes.com/2018/03/10/opinion/sunday/go-vote.html?action=click&pgtype=Homepage&clickSource=story-heading&module=opinion-c-col-left-region&region=opinion-c-col-left-region&WT.nav=opinion-c-col-left-region).

5   Partisanship, 21st-Century Style

Can We Break from the Shelter of Our Tribe?

From their extensive reading of history, the framers of our system understood the dangers of unchecked ambition and the necessities of free speech and minority protections that are so vital in a representative democracy. The government they created, with checks, balances, and shared powers, has endured with only modest revisions for over 230 years. It was in creating a *political system* that the framers were less than successful.

One of the first problems they confronted was how to organize elections. Popular, democratic elections were a novel experiment at the time that many believed could only happen with widespread turmoil and violence. Who would run for office and how would they conduct their campaigns? How would unscrupulous, corrupt citizens be kept off the ballot and would voters really sort through candidate qualifications, policy planks and competing claims? How would disparate elements of the government come together after turbulent elections? Would the entire works collapse into a chaotic mess? To their astonishment, political parties proved to be the glue that held the system together. Today, there is not a modern democracy across the globe that does not boast a viable party system. Decades ago, a prominent political scientist put the matter bluntly: "It should be flatly stated that political parties created democracy and that modern democracy is unthinkable save in terms of political parties."[1]

Even so, the American party system has changed and contorted over the centuries. Parties emerged in the late 1790s over a set of controversial issues, only to fade throughout the following decades. As part of a broader effort to wrest control from elites, astute political operatives formed vibrant local party organizations in the 1840s, fueled by a vicious, omnipotent partisan press. Electoral politics were thrust into the very fabric of American life, and it lasted for generations. Local party organizations took a hit during the Progressive Era, as noted in previous chapters, but state and national party committees grew after the Great Depression. With the rise of television advertisements and campaign professionals in the 1960s, "candidate-centered" politics threatened the very rationale for parties, and some scholars warned of their pending demise. But political parties are adaptive creatures and by the 1990s they had morphed into "service organizations," fueled by massive soft money contributions. The phoenix had risen from the ashes.

All along the journey, individuals have been attached to party labels; what we call party identification or individual-level partisanship. In many ways, it is *this* component of party politics that set the foundation for elections and governance in the United States. It allowed party committees to organize and recruit volunteers, and candidates to secure a base of support (rather than starting from scratch each election). Party identification channeled the behavior of elected officials and offered average citizens a rational, cost-saving cue on Election Day. It added a deliberative, policy-centered component to an otherwise tumultuous process. Party identification has sometimes been scorned – usually when voters are being charged with blindly following a party allegiance instead of considering more pressing concerns, or when legislators are compelled to abandon the general good to appease their base – but one would be hard pressed to point to a force that has had a greater impact on American politics. American governance has changed as voter partisanship shifted.

In a relatively short period of time, roughly two decades, and to the astonishment of scholars, pundits and politicians, an exceptionally large swath of Americans have become deeply partisan. It is a unique brand of party identification, too, centered on the fear and loathing of the other party, and an affinity to groups of like-minded citizens. The fervor of today's party identification has turned the entire system on its head, leading to gridlock in Congress, declining trust in the media and other institutions, an ugliness in our political discourse, and more. Much of the crisis in American politics outlined at the start of this book springs from this unique brand of party identification. It certainly helped bring Donald Trump to power. It is the manifestation of several other changes, and it has become one of the great challenges to the American system. As noted by columnist David Brooks, we are in an "era where the very preservation of our democratic structures is under threat from [partisan] tribalism."[2]

Certainly, the results of the 2018 midterm elections added fuel to the tribalism fire. As noted by one commentator, "red states got redder, blue states got bluer."[3] An exit poll found eight in ten Americans said the nation is more divided than ever. Even criminal charges against candidates did not break tribal bonds. Republican Chris Collins of Buffalo was one of the first officials to endorse Donald Trump. He won reelection in 2018 in his heavily Republican district, even though he was under indictment for insider trading. Republican Duncan Hunter of California was reelected by a whopping 11 percentage points while facing criminal charges for misusing campaign funds. And on the other side, New Jersey voters returned

Democratic Senator Bob Menendez to office even though he had been "severely admonished" by the Senate for a host of ethical violations.[4]

The question guiding this chapter is whether average Americans can break free from hyper-partisanship and the belief that members of the opposing party are evil and a threat to the country. Can we come together and find common ground on big issues? The reader will note an important irony in this chapter: while the constitutional framers were uncertain about the particulars of the political process, to their surprise it was political parties that made things work. James Madison railed against factions and Washington warned about the "spirit of party," but these institutions nurtured a democracy for over 200 years. In the last two decades, however, hyper-partisanship has created a distinct threat to our system. Much of the dysfunction we now see in Washington, state capitals and city halls across the country can be laid at the door of the party system. Are we overdosing on partisanship?

Political Parties: Institutions Americans Love to Hate

The men who pulled the American system together fretted about a lot of things, but they were especially fearful of political parties. Instead of parties, they hoped other mediating institutions would "refine and enlarge the public views by passing them through the medium of a chosen body of citizens, whose wisdom may best discern the true interest of their country and whose patriotism and love of justice will be least likely to sacrifice it to temporary or partial conditions."[5] But the view that mediating institutions would consider public sentiments and translate them into public policies whenever it was judged to be timely and appropriate did not include political parties. George Washington was especially critical of partisan demagogues whose objective, he claimed, was not to give the people the facts from which they could make up their own minds but to make them followers instead of thinkers. Washington maintained that "we are *all* children of the same country... [and] that our interest, however diversified in local and smaller matters, is the same in all the great and essential concerns of the nation."[6] Determined to make good on his intention to leave office in 1796, Washington issued his now-famous Farewell Address, where he admonished his fellow citizens to avoid partisanship at any cost: "Let me ... warn you in the most solemn manner against the baneful effects of the spirit of party... It exists under different shapes in all governments, more or less stifled, controlled, or repressed; but, in those of the popular form, it is seen in its greatest rankness and is truly their worst enemy."[7]

Observing the effects of partisan attacks on her husband, John, during his presidency, Abigail Adams wrote: "Party spirit is blind, malevolent, un-candid, ungenerous, unjust, and unforgiving."[8] James Monroe, who would become the nation's fifth chief executive, urged his backers to obliterate all party divisions in our country. Other presidents have voiced similar sentiments. When Abraham Lincoln sought reelection in 1864 under the newly created National Union banner, 500,000 pamphlets were published bearing titles such as "No Party Now but All for Our Country."[9] Campaigning for president in 1992, then-Governor Bill Clinton denounced the "brain-dead politics" of both political parties.

The idea that political parties are the proverbial scarlet letter of American politics has not been shared by the vast majority of political scientists.[10] In his book *The American Commonwealth,* published in 1888, James Bryce began a tradition of scholarly investigation of political parties devoting more than 200 pages to the subject. His treatment was laudatory: "Parties are inevitable. No free large country has been without them. No-one has shown how representative government could be worked without them. They bring order out of chaos to a multitude of voters."[11] More than a century later, scores of other academics agree with Bryce. In an amicus curiae (friend-of-the-court) brief filed at the US Supreme Court, a bipartisan team of scholars calling themselves the Committee for Party Renewal suggested political parties play a unique and crucial role in our democratic system of government. They enable citizens to participate coherently in a system of government allowing for a substantial number of popularly elected offices; bring fractured and diverse groups together as a unified force; provide a necessary link between the distinct branches and levels of government; and provide continuity that lasts beyond terms of office. Parties also play an important role in encouraging active participation in politics, holding politicians accountable for their actions, and encouraging debate and discussion of important issues.[12]

Generally, scholars have argued that without parties, civic life would be reduced to "a politics of celebrities, of excessive media influence, of political fad-of-the-month clubs, of massive private financing by various 'fat cats' of state and congressional campaigns, of gun-for-hire campaign managers, of heightened interest in 'personalities' and lowered concern for policy, of manipulation and maneuver and management by self-chosen political elites."[13] Such statements buttressed the consensus that strong, vital parties are a prerequisite for a healthy democracy.

The Elements of Parties

One of the most confusing aspects of political parties is precisely what the term implies. By the 1950s, political scientists developed what is called the tripartite view of parties. Political parties boast three inter-related elements: party-in-government (PIG), party-as-organization (PO) and party-in-the-electorate (PIE). This is often referred to as the "tripod" model of political parties.

Party-in-government refers to the officials elected under a particular party banner. All the Republicans in the House of Representatives, for example, make up one piece of party-in-government. They call themselves the House Republican Conference. If they have a majority in the chamber their leader is the Speaker of the House; if not, he or she is the Minority Leader. Other segments of the Republican party-in-government include the Republicans in the Senate, and the president when he or she is a member of the GOP. There are also sub-branches of the national party-in-government, such as governors, state-level elected officials, municipal officials, and so on. The Democrats, of course, have a parallel structure.

The American system is unusual in that party-in-government structures are weak. In many other democracies there is an expectation that elected officials will vote with their party on most matters. Dissenters, or those who vote with the opposition party on key issues, are rare. At times, there is a great deal of pressure designed to force officials to stay in line, but in the American system, elected officials can stray without serious repercussions. For example, Maine Republican Senator Susan Collins essentially killed GOP efforts to rescind the Affordable Care Act in 2017, but there was never any suggestion that she should leave the party.

There are several ways to measure how often legislators stick with their party, the most common being party unity scores. This is the percentage of votes on legislation when a majority of one party oppose a majority of the other. It is a measure that can be used to describe the partisan nature of any legislative body, including Congress, state legislatures, county legislatures, and city councils. Regarding Congress, party unity scores have shifted over time, with the average being about 70 percent of votes. A low point was the middle decades of the 20th century when the Democrats controlled Congress, given that their caucus was made up of an awkward mix of northeastern liberals and southern conservatives – the latter being dubbed "Boll Weevils." The two wings of the Democratic Party disagreed passionately on many issues, especially civil rights legislation, leading unity scores to drop into the 30 percent range. By the 1990s, the Republican Party in the South grew, making it a more comfortable home for conservative politicians. Today, most federal legislators from the South are Republican and party unity scores are at record highs. In fact, the exceptional level of party unity in Congress and most legislative bodies across the country is a manifestation of individual-level polarization, as will be discussed below.

Party-as-organizations (PO) refers to the formal apparatus of the party, including party headquarters, offices, and leaders. Party organizations exist at each of the layers of our political system. At the national level, there is the Democratic National Committee (DNC) and the Republican National Committee (RNC). Each state has both a Republican and Democratic party. There is an Indiana Democratic Party, a New York State Democratic Committee, an Arizona Democratic Party, a Republican Party of Texas, and a California Republican Party, for instance. Much the same can be found at the county and municipal levels; there is a

Crawford County Republican Committee in western Pennsylvania, and a Farmington Democratic Town Committee in Massachusetts. At the very bottom of the structure one occasionally finds ward or precinct organizations. The Chicago Democratic Committee is comprised of numerous precinct organizations.

Throughout much of our history, local party organizations took on a rather distinctive, aggressive form. These units, sometimes called party machines, were especially strong in larger cities around the turn of the 20th century, such as in New York City, Boston, Chicago, Philadelphia, and Kansas City. The leader of a machine was referred to as "the boss." Party machines carried a double-edged sword: on the one hand, their strong desire to win elections in order to control patronage jobs, city contracts, and regulations, coupled with an efficient, military-like organization, had the effect of bringing otherwise disenfranchised citizens into the process. This was particularly important for newly arrived immigrants, of which there was a flood in the second half of the 19th century. In exchange for their help on Election Day, party bosses and their machines provided a social safety net. If someone needed a job, if they were evicted from their apartment and needed another place to live, if they sought a loan to pay for a funeral, or if some cash was needed to post bond for a "confused" son, the machine would often lend a hand. In exchange for this help, voters would support the party's slate of candidates on Election Day. To many – including many of the residents of these cities – machines created a perfect democratic accountability mechanism: if the machine failed to take care of the citizens in the community they were simply voted out of office and the other party was given a chance.

On the other hand, a great deal of corruption was thrown into the mix of machine politics. Election fraud was rampant. One of the last of the big city bosses, Richard J. Daley of Chicago, would proclaim to his workers on Election Day, with only a veneer of levity, that they should "vote early and vote often."[14] As the machines controlled the reins of government, they also rigged the workings of the government to suit their political needs and to line their own pockets. For example, in many cities public employees were required to kick back a portion of their pay to the machine – generally about 3 percent. Their humanitarian efforts only extended to supporters and to those who were able to vote. Many minority groups, namely African Americans, did not benefit from machine assistance because they were of no use, given that most could not vote.

For these reasons and others, a series of reforms were ushered in at the end of the 19th century, collectively called the Progressive Movement, as discussed in previous chapters. For instance, the Civil Service robbed machines of patronage (jobs to hand out to loyal supporters), the secret ballot removed the machine's control of votes on Election Day, and the direct primary stripped them of their ability to control nominations.

Local party organizations survived these changes, but machines, for the most part, faced overwhelming challenges and slowly faded from the American scene.

It should also be noted that several scholars have sought to broaden the definition of party organization to a "network of aligned actors." These networks would include an array of candidates, activists, donors, media personalities (and outlets), political action committees, and elected officials. Much of the work in this area has been on campaign funding networks, coupled with campaign service vendors. According to one such analysis, "The way we think of parties is vitally important to how we treat them. If we want to regulate parties or restrict their activities or even ban them, that's far easier to do if they're rigid hierarchies than if they're flexible networks. The latter can adapt to a great many impediments."[15]

Party-in-the-electorate (PIE) refers to those who attach themselves to a particular party. This is a somewhat ambiguous concept and thus the source of much scholarly debate. Some scholars hold that one's *attitude*, or self-proclaimed party identification, provides enough evidence to consider them partisan. Party identification (ID), they argue, is a feeling that a particular party best represents their interests and outlook toward government and society. For example, if a citizen tells a pollster that he thinks of himself as a "strong Republican," this person would be considered part of the party-in-electorate. He would have a party ID. Most assessments of PIE in America rely upon attitudinal measures – the most common being a seven-point scale where "strong Democrat" and "strong Republican" are at the ends, and true "independents" are at the midpoint.

Other social scientists suggest that a person's *behavior* is more important than their attitude when it comes to defining partisanship. If a person votes for Democrats most of the time, they should be tagged a Democrat regardless of what she says to a pollster or a friend. Straight-ticket voters are those who support candidates of the same party in each race, one election after another. Voters that switch back and forth from one election to the next are called split-ticket voters. These voters might support the Republican gubernatorial candidate, the Democratic candidate for the House of Representatives, and the Green Party candidate for mayor. Voting behavior of this sort would suggest that citizen is a non-partisan, or what we often call an independent. (Contrary to what many believe, as of yet there is no official "Independent Party.")

Another way to define one's party ID would be to rely on official voter registration lists. In most states, voters are asked to enroll in a party as they register to vote. This approach to measuring PIE might make sense, except that many citizens register with a party when they reach voting age, only to change their attitudes and voting habits over time. Some of them might head off to their local board of elections to change their enrollment, but most would probably not. A core group of Donald Trump supporters in the 2016 election were blue-collar workers, many of whom were likely enrolled with the Democratic Party. This was the same type of voter that helped put Republican Ronald Reagan in the White House in the 1980s – a group dubbed "Reagan Democrats."

Still another possibility is that true membership in PIE comes from an active involvement with a party. There are two options here: voting in primary elections and helping parties undertake activities. Primaries are elections that allow citizens to select party nominees for the general election ballot. Candidates on a primary election ballot are vying for the party's nomination, the privilege of representing the party in the general election in November. In 2016, for example, about one-third of the electorate came to the polls to pick party nominees for the presidency.[16] The second way citizens can actively support a party is by helping undertake activities. This would be the most rigorous way of deciding which citizens are in PIE. Only about 5 percent of Americans either give money or help parties undertake activities.

The Roots of Party Identification

Early studies of partisanship and voter behavior centered on demographic factors, such as religious affiliations, workplace organizations, and social acquaintances. That is to say, one's partisanship seemed to be a function of social and economic factors. In *The People's Choice*, written in 1944, authors Paul Lazarsfeld, Bernard Berelson and Hazel Gaudet surveyed a massive pool of voters, finding a close fit between a set of long-standing factors, partisanship and vote choice. This point was reiterated a few years later in *Voting*, by Berelson, Lazarsfeld and William McPhee: "Like music, literature, recreational activities, dress, ethics, speech, [and] social behavior," the scholars wrote, political decisions "have their origin in ethnic, sectional, class, and family traditions" and "exhibit stability and resistance to change … While both are responsive to changed conditions and unusual stimuli, they are relatively invulnerable to direct argumentation and vulnerable to indirect social influences."[17] Briefly veering from one's partisanship usually only happened when there was a significant cross-pressure. Voters had to decide among pressures, and they did so by talking to people within their social circles. If social alliances were aligned, no real decision was required and a voter knew early in the season who he or she would vote for. The book also suggested cross-pressured voters tended to decide late in the election or opt not to vote at all.

By the late 1950s, scholars began exploring the role of historical context and early childhood socialization in the development of party identification. We learned that party attachments develop early in life, usually by about ten years of age, and typically go unchanged. A religious analogy was used: a youngster raised a Baptist would likely remain a Baptist throughout his life, just as a son of a Republican would become a Republican, and remain so throughout his life. And again, a person's party ID was the single best predictor of vote choice; the vast majority of partisans stuck with their party's candidates each election.

The snag with both the socioeconomic and socialization perspectives was that they offered a bleak view of voter deliberation because issues, candidates, and even the voter's personal circumstances took a back seat to pre-existing partisanship. There was little room for persuasion by candidates, the impact of campaign events, or deliberation. These models seem to imply that voters acted like lemmings, following their party off the cliff each election. In fact, some scholars began to argue that all of what happens during elections does not matter – a school of thought called the "minimal effects perspective."[18]

The American Voter, published in 1960, came to the rescue. Authors Angus Campbell, Phillip Converse, Warren Miller and Donald Stokes argued that voting behavior worked its way through a "funnel of causality" that began with a voter's demographic position, but proceeded through the development of party identification (largely inherited from parents) and later to short-term factors like perceptions of candidates, campaign developments and issues. They agreed that party identification is powerful and generally gained early in life, but voters also considered short-term factors. They were deliberative. However, and this was the key point, each person's partisanship filters the interpretation of new information. In other words, the way most voters see candidates and issues is a function of their own partisan lens. It was a way to reconcile both perspectives: the correlation between party ID and vote choice was exceedingly high, but voters *did* consider short-term factors. The authors of *The American Voter, Revisited* (a different set of scholars in 2008), argued much the same: "Once an individual has formed a party attachment, however embryonic, and whatever stage in life it happened, a self-reinforcing process of momentum takes over."[19]

Fear and Loathing of the Other Side

In recent decades, there has been a stunning change in individual-level partisanship. Emory University scholar Alan Abramowitz has written extensively about this issue. He argues that polarization has become a defining characteristic of modern electoral politics. In *The Disappearing Center* (2010), Abramowitz shows a steady, powerful realignment in the American electorate. The ideological center of the parties has moved further and further apart – meaning there is little policy overlap among partisans. Most Republicans have become very conservative and most Democrats are now quite liberal. Furthermore, as the electorate has become more polarized, with a smaller and smaller buffer zone, the stakes of winning and losing have increased. As a consequence, the voting public has become more engaged.

The Pew Research Center has carried out a series of studies over the last several years, finding much the same. Their data show that while the gulf between the average policy positions of Democrats and Republicans has widened to historic levels, so too has political antipathy. Partisans on each side dislike and fear those on the other side – and the most active partisans are the most fearful of the other side. For example, in 1994, 21 percent of self-identified Republicans had a very unfavorable view of Democrats. By 2017, that figure had nearly tripled to 58 percent. Some 17 percent of self-identified Democrats had a very unfavorable view of Republicans in 1994, but by 2017 that figure had climbed to 55 percent.[20] In an eye-opening 2018 report, a full 71 percent of Republicans and 63 percent of Democrats said the harm that the opposing party's policies might cause the nation was a major reason for their own party affiliation. In other words, partisans on both sides believe not only that their party's policies are right, but that the other party's ideas are dangerous. Nearly two-thirds of both Democratic and Republican identifiers said the other side's policies are harmful for the country.[21] A similar finding was that 62 percent of highly engaged Republicans say Democrats made them feel afraid, and a stunning 70 percent of Democrats said the same about Republicans.[22] Fifty-two percent of Republicans said Democrats are "closed minded," and 70 percent of Democrats believed the same thing about Republicans.

Worries about the other party have spilled into social relationships. Many now check the partisan leanings of parents before sanctioning a child's play-date. Political intermarriage has become a problem, too. Roughly equal percentages of Democrats (15%) and Republicans (17%) say they would be unhappy welcoming someone from the other party into their family.

Furthermore, a recent study conducted by a team of scholars demonstrates the new and extreme boundaries of partisan behavior. A surprising number of strong partisans are willing to explicitly state that members of the opposing party are like animals, that they lack essential human traits, and that they are less evolved than members of their own party.[23]

In a 2018 paper, Abramowitz and his colleague Steven Webster labeled this change the rise of "negative partisanship." They note that both Hillary Clinton and Donald Trump were the most unpopular presidential candidates since polling data was compiled (the late 1940s). What was particularly startling is the incredibly low ratings given to the opposing party's candidate – that is, what Democrats thought of Trump and what Republicans thought of Clinton. Using a 100-point scale, where 0 is very negative and 100 is very positive, the average score given to both candidates from members of the other side was 11. More than half of Democrats and Republicans gave the other party's candidate a zero.[24] "Even though both major party nominees in 2016 were quite unpopular, partisan loyalty remained very high because both Democratic and Republican identifiers overwhelmingly viewed the opposing party's candidate with deep hostility."[25] Voters did not dislike the other party's candidate – they hated him/her.

Another 2018 study by a team of scholars from the University of Missouri–St. Louis label this change "affective polarization." They write, "supporters of both parties express increasing levels of contempt toward the opposite party and its presidential candidates, with the 2016 election cycle producing record levels of out-party demonization."[26]

Two years earlier, a Pew Research Center poll found that 40 percent of Republicans gave Michelle Obama, the former First Lady, a "0" on a scale of 0 to 100.[27] Certainly most Republicans disagreed with her husband's policies, and may have even disliked Mrs. Obama. But that nearly half of Republicans could give her a zero seems exceptional and clearly illustrative of the breadth of partisan animosities we see in contemporary politics.

There is evidence to suggest anger-centered polarization has increased, by leaps and bounds, during the first two years of the Trump Administration. A piece in the *New York Times* in the summer of 2018 charted how discussions about politics and Trump are tearing apart relationships.[28] Siblings are finding it hard to come together for barbeques, budding courtships are being cut short, and even decades-old marriages are under stress because of divergent views about Trump and his policies. Babysitters are being fired, long-standing friendships are being dropped. One statistic jumps out: a poll of 1,000 Americans conduced a few weeks earlier had found nearly a third of respondents saying they stopped talking to a friend or a family member because of disagreements over politics. "This is very different," said GOP consultant Frank Luntz, who conducted the study. "With Obama, people hated him or people loved him. But you weren't evil for how you felt. You might be accused of being a racist or a socialist. It still wasn't the same."[29] Carolyn Lukensmeyer, Director of the National Center for Civil Discourse, added, "This is now deep in our homes, deep in our neighborhoods, deep in our places of worship and deep in our workplaces. It really is a virus."[30]

Hyper-polarization can also be seen in media consumption patterns. Research into viewing habits reveals that conservatives get their news from Fox News and liberals get theirs from MSNBC, CNN, NPR and the *New York Times*.[31] And, there is less and less trust of media. Another study done by the Pew Research Center found a majority of self-described conservatives distrusted a whopping 24 of 36 major news outlets. Liberals distrusted eight of 36 outlets. Conservatives were more likely to have online friends who share their own political views than are liberals, and liberals were more likely than those in other ideological groups to block or defriend someone on a social network – as well as to end a personal friendship – because of politics.[32]

If voters are becoming more trustful of their own sources and more distrustful of the other side's sources, as seems to be the case, it is easy to see why partisans talk past one another, and are unable to agree on simple facts. "Alternative facts" was first used by Trump advisor Kellyanne Conway during a television interview in which she defended a false statement about the size of the crowd at Donald Trump's inauguration. Conway seemed surprisingly confident during the interview, perhaps knowing that facts have become subjective in today's hyper-partisan media world. According to a piece of scholarship published by the American Psychological Association, "Research shows we also interpret facts differently if they challenge our personal beliefs, group identity or moral values." Also, for people who identify strongly with a party, it can feel like their opponents are willfully ignoring the facts. "But right or left, both sides believe their positions are grounded in evidence."[33]

What Caused the Change?

Although we do not have polling data before the 1940s to help fine-tune our understanding of this change, we know that Americans have attached themselves to a partisan badge since the 1830s. Electoral politics were very passionate during much of the 19th century, so it is likely polarization was just as intense then as it is now – and perhaps more so. We do know with certainty, however, that since the advent of sophisticated polling, the level of issue coherence among partisans and disdain of the other side is at record levels. Even during the contentious, turbulent 1960s, the divide was not as great. Many voters had what we might today call rigid policy views, and although many thought the other side's positions were wrongheaded, few believed the their agenda would destroy the nation. Split-ticket voting was much more common than it is today. In fact, some have suggested that split-ticket voting is essentially dead in America.[34] The 2016 election was the first time in American history – going back to 1913 when Senators were first elected by citizens (and not the state legislatures) – that every state won by a Republican Senate candidate also supported the Republican candidate for president, and every state that sent a Democrat to the Senate also supported the Democrat for the White House.[35] As noted by Geoffrey Skelley of the University of Virginia, "It's a dramatic reversal from much of the middle of the 20th century, when voters frequently backed senators of one party while *also* supporting the opposing party's presidential nominee.[36] "Partisan polarization" write the authors of an oft-cited book on the dysfunction of American politics, "is undeniably the central and most problematic feature of contemporary American politics."[37]

So what has changed? What are the forces that have propelled this hyper-partisanship? The list of potential culprits is long and contentious.

The next chapter will explore cross-cutting issues, especially the growing importance of social policy and issues related to race and immigration. For this chapter, a starting point might be the new breed of Republicans that stormed into government, particularly the House of Representatives, in the late 1980s and early 1990s. At the helm of this crew was a fire-brand conservative from Georgia named Newt Gingrich. When Gingrich took his seat in the House in 1978, the Republicans had been in the minority for nearly 50 years – with the brief exception of four years after World War II. From his perspective, the only way to break the domination of the Democrats was to create gridlock in the system by destroying many of the historic routes of moderation and compromise, and obliterate many of the norms and customs of the chamber. Gingrich ushered in a new brand of bare-knuckle, take-no-prisoners politics in which the opposing side was demonized. As noted by two prominent authors, "His attacks on partisan adversaries in the White House and Congress created a norm in which colleagues with different views became mortal enemies."[38]

Closely linked, conservative talk radio gained traction at roughly the same time. Rush Limbaugh led the way, but there were many others. In 1987, the Federal Communications Commission repealed the Fairness Doctrine, allowing broadcast media stations to air con-troversial material without having to offer those on the other side time for rebuttal. A host of political shock-jocks and conservative/religious commentators were soon preaching on the airways. Limbaugh set the mold through a keen understanding of the issues, an entertaining style and a willingness to break conventions of traditional political rhet-oric. He became the champion of the conservative right. His audience swelled – and so too did his power and prestige in Republican circles. Many believe Limbaugh was a key factor behind the high turnout of Republicans in the 1994 election which led to the capture of both chambers of Congress.

There was an added element to Limbaugh's appeal, used by liberals a generation earlier. He was skillful at turning policy disputes into battles over rights, patriotism, and the future of the nation. As politics moves from disputes over policy questions to notions of values and rights, compromise becomes difficult and rhetoric more heated. Mary Ann Glendon charted the rise of "rights" politics in the 1970s – a ten-dency to frame nearly every social controversy in terms of a clash of rights (a woman's right to her own body versus a fetus' right to life, for example). When this happens, compromise, mutual understanding and the discovery of common ground become almost impossible.[39] There is no middle ground on issues of rights, as anyone opposed to your rights is an oppressor.

This approach was used by the Tea Party after the election of Barack Obama in 2008. It became common to challenge Democratic policies by calling into question their constitutional validity. When policy questions such as health care reform, gun control, federal mandates to states, or even the entire Social Security system are deemed unconstitutional, compromise is out of the question, and efforts to find any middle ground are deemed unpatriotic. This helps explain why most GOP House and Senate candidates during those years frequently proclaimed their intention to "uphold the Constitution," a rather strange, ambiguous assertion uncommon in previous elections. The implication was that those on the other side of the policy dispute are not simply wrong-headed, but willing to throw the nation's sacred document out the window. The other side's positions are illegitimate because they are unconstitutional. Scholars Theda Skocpol and Vanessa Williamson penned an important book on the formation of the Tea Party movement in the Obama years.[40] At the center of the movement, the authors say, is a direct link between Christian doctrine and constitutional principles, as well as a tribal notion of us versus them.

Cable news is part of the story, too. As the number of options grew, a novel model of profitability took hold. Smaller audiences could prove lucrative, but only if they continue to tune in night after night. The way to keep an audience loyal was to merge sensationalism with ideology. Fox News was launched as an alternative to the increasingly profitable CNN, and it was initially considered centrist. But within a few years, due in no small measure to the ideological leaning of its owner, Fox News shifted its approach to appeal to conservative voters. Issues were presented as a battle between right and wrong, between good Americans and traitors. Coupled with the news programs were several charismatic commentators, including Laura Ingraham, Glenn Beck and Sean Hannity. It is hard to overstate the importance of Fox News in the story of hyper-polarization in America – a topic that will be discussed in a later chapter. Similar programs emerged for liberal voters, most notably MSNBC, but their audience has never approached the size of Fox's.

Another reason for polarization may lie in geographic sorting. This idea was first introduced by journalist Bill Bishop in *The Big Sort: Why the Clustering of Like-Minded America Is Tearing Us Apart*. Bishop argued that partisanship extends beyond labels and issues into fundamental differences of lifestyle and outlook. People with similar hobbies, incomes, religious beliefs, sources of news, and work tend to sort themselves into the same neighborhoods, and these neighborhoods tend to have explicit partisan characteristics. Many communities have become politically homogeneous. Bishop observed the increasing number of "landslide counties," defined as counties in which the margin of victory in presidential elections exceeded 20 percent. In the 1970s, roughly 20 percent fell into this category. Three decades later it approach 50 percent.[41]

By 2004, Bishop writes, "nearly half of all voters lived in landslide counties."[42] In Bishop's view, "Pockets of like-minded citizens that have become so ideologically inbred that we don't know, can't understand, and can barely conceive of 'those people' who live just a few miles away."[43] Bishop found that women in Democratic landslide counties were strongly against the war in Iraq while Democratic women in Republican blowout counties were strongly supportive of the war. Democrats in Republican landslide districts were much more likely to attend church than were Democrats in Democratic landslide districts.

In the 2016 presidential election, a stunning 71 percent of counties had a landslide outcome. Even though the overall outcome was close, there was a blowout in nearly three-quarters of the roughly 3,200 counties (or county equivalents). Hillary Clinton won 199 counties by 60 percent or more, and Donald Trump won a staggering 2,035 by that margin. A whopping 40 percent of counties yielded a winner who received over 70 percent of the vote! Flipping it the other way and keeping in mind the additional drag of minor-party candidates, the losing presidential candidate received less than one-third of the vote in an astonishing 62 percent of counties.

Another way to look at this is with standard deviation – that is, the average spread around the mean. The standard deviation for the presidential vote outcome in counties has grown steadily in the last three decades and nearly doubled from 2000 to 2016. And it is more than just vote totals: a 2014 Pew Research Center survey found that roughly 50 percent of true conservatives and hard-core liberals thought it was important to live in a place where most people share their politics.

And of course there is sorting of a different kind – on the internet, where we are flooded with concordant information and our circle of "friends" (through social networks) is vastly narrower than in the pre-digital age. Early thinking about the internet was that nearly unlimited information and the ability to connect with diverse citizens would broaden knowledge and shrink tribal instincts. Several years ago, Roger Cohen of the *New York Times* wrote that this is probably not happening: "The internet opens worlds and minds, but also offers opinions to reinforce every prejudice. You're never alone out there; some idiot will always back you. The online world doesn't dissolve tribes. It gives them global reach."[44] As citizens of all ideological stripes escape to an enclave of consistent news information, they become reluctant to hear opposing points of view. While noting the possibility of some positive developments with the rise of partisan media, *Echo Chamber* scholars Kathleen Hall Jamison and Joseph Cappella suggest audiences are held to a station or commentator by value-centered politics, with consequences: "A steady diet of moral outrage feeds the assumption that the opponent is the enemy." Partisan news pundits encourage their audiences to see the world as "unburdened by either ambiguity or common ground across the ideological divide."[45]

Law and political science scholar Cass Sunstein has also written on this subject. He argued that the ability to self-sort through the media is nothing new. We have always picked different newspapers and magazines, and to some extent television and radio programs, to reduce the likelihood of cognitive dissonance (hearing discordant points of view). The great difference with modern technologies is the power to "fence in and to fence out." We live increasingly in an era of enclaves and niches, once again leading to more extreme positions. He calls this "enclave extremism," with the outcome being "serious problems of mutual suspicion, unjustified rage, and social fragmentation."[46]

In the summer of 2018, Americans were introduced to a growing right-wing underground movement dubbed QAnon. By one account, it is a "deranged conspiracy cult," dedicated to the theory that Donald Trump is at the forefront of a counter-coup – where the first coup is being waged against "core American values" and being led by the Clintons, Barack Obama and Robert Mueller. This account writes,

> "Q" feeds disciples, or "bakers," scraps of intelligence, or "bread crumbs," that they scramble to bake into an understanding of the "storm" – the community's term, drawn from Trump's cryptic reference last year to "the calm before the storm" – for the president's final conquest over elites, globalists and deep-state saboteurs.[47]

It seemed that movement's followers had been growing since Trump's candidacy, driven by their own verification of information on the internet. They are, it seems, frustrated by how authority over information and verification is allocated. That is to say, QAnon followers resent the self-righteous assumption of expertise made by members of the media and academia. QAnon "marks the emergence of long-hidden communities of people who want to decide for themselves what the truth is."[48]

As a final note in this section, it is worth brief mention that many scholars suggest contemporary partisan polarization is asymmetric.[49] That is, Democrats have become more liberal, to be sure, and they certainly view the other side with suspicion. But an array of data suggests a larger dose of the strident, hard-line partisan politics we see in America comes from the sharp right turn made by Republicans. A series of polls conducted by the author of this volume, for example, found that those who identified as Republicans were vastly less interested in finding compromise solutions than were those who identified as Democrats.[50] In a 2016 report, respondents were asked, "Which is more important in a politician: the ability to compromise to get things done or a determination to stand firm in support of principles?" Three-quarters of Democrats chose the compromise position, but only 49 percent of Republicans did the same. That figure drops to 40 percent for "strong conservatives."[51] A Gallup study found that upwards of 70 percent of Republicans call themselves conservative or very conservative, whereas 40 percent of

Democrats say they are liberal or very liberal.[52] The Pew Research Center polls cited throughout this chapter show Republicans are more disdainful of Democrats than the other way around, and the heated rhetoric common on conservative radio and television programs is probably a bit sharper than what is heard on left-leaning programs. The degree of GOP party unity in Congress and in state legislatures is much higher than it is for Democrats. In other words, while there has been an ideological purification on both sides, and each side worries about the other, Republicans seem particularly strident. A likely cause for this will be discussed in the next chapter.

It should also be noted, however, that Democratic anger in the Trump era seems out-of-the-ordinary. A study conducted in 2017 found that liberals are much more likely to drop a friend because they voted for Donald Trump than the other way around. Thirty-five percent of Democrats said learning that a friend had voted for Trump would put a strain on their relationship, but only 13 percent of Republicans said that of a friend's vote for Hillary Clinton. The most educated and most liberal Democrats were most likely to say a Trump vote would "complicate" their friendships.[53] "There is a sense, especially among Democrats who recoil at Mr. Trump's style of politics, that partisan affiliation reflects more than just a voting preference. Rather, it says something about your character."[54] But, as noted in a separate account of growing partisan strains since the 2016 election, conservative intolerance is hardly uncommon. "In the Texas Panhandle this summer, motorists passed a billboard along the interstate that read: 'Liberals, please continue on I-40 until you have left our GREAT STATE OF TEXAS.' "[55]

Conclusion: Can We Break from the Shelter of Our Tribe?

Elections should serve as an expression of popular will. "The people are a sovereign whose vocabulary is limited to two words, 'yes' and 'no,' " wrote a famous political scientist more than 70 years ago.[56] We select leaders based on their experience, character and intelligence, and also their policy positions. This process, where elections are thought to direct the course of public policy, can work in different ways, but it centers on rationality – both that of voters and that of elected officials. We vote in particular ways because we want certain changes.

But do voters pay enough attention to public policy questions to redirect the course of government? Maybe it is not policy issues that drive vote choice, but rather vague, nebulous views of candidate traits and other idiosyncratic factors. Throughout this discussion of partisanship and party identification, there has been the nagging question of voter rationality. How much time do voters spend thinking about issues or candidates? It has never been clear that voters absorbed a broad range of information or sifted through competing evidence. It is likely elites have always been able to manipulate mass opinion to some degree. Heuristics, especially party identification, are used to sort and filter – as noted earlier in this chapter.

Some scholars have been a bit more optimistic about voter capacities than others. "Voters are not fools," declared Harvard political scientist V.O. Key Jr. in 1966.[57] He reasoned that people look at recent history and decide whether incumbents are worth keeping or if they should be thrown out. A voter can make a rational decision to stand pat or to switch. From Key's perspective, voters make policy choices even if they lack comprehensive knowledge of public policy.

Along similar lines, other political scientists write of prospective versus retrospective evaluations. Prospective evaluations are anticipatory. A voter looks at a candidate – his or her qualifications, party label, personality, and campaign promises – and then guesses what kind of job he or she will do. When Donald Trump vowed to "make America great again," he was asking voters to view his candidacy prospectively. Retrospective evaluations look in the opposite direction. Past actions are weighed in order to judge a candidate's future behavior. When Obama charged that John McCain consistently voted in line with George W. Bush, he was inviting citizens to think about the problems of the outgoing administration, a call to retrospective assessments. The most celebrated example of a campaign appeal to a retrospective evaluation was Ronald Reagan's question to the American people in 1980 when the economy under President Jimmy Carter seemed in deep trouble: "Are you better off than you were four years ago?" It was an attempt to convey the perils of supporting Carter by pointing to the president's past performance. Voters are confronted with a choice – either look at each candidate's plans for the future (a speculative, time-consuming chore), or examine what has happened in the recent past (a quick, "factual" process). If backwardlooking clues are unflattering, the evaluation of the candidate will be negative. The power of retrospection carries an obvious appeal, and as more and more candidates use negative advertising, voters might become accustomed to the attacks and depend on them for information even as they decry mean-spirited politics.

And yet, both prospective and retrospective models hinge on voter rationality; that idea that issues, trends, candidate characteristics and more become part of a calculation. But is that really what happens? In the 1960s, scholars began a deep-dive into how voters assessed candidates and parties. The historian Richard Hofstadter offered a rather controversial perspective, in his lecture dubbed "The Paranoid Style in American Politics":

> Political life is not simply an arena in which the conflicting interests of various social groups in concrete material gains are fought out; it is also an arena into which status aspirations and frustrations are, as the psychologist would say, projected. It is at this point that the issues

of politics, or the pretended issues of politics, become interwoven with and dependent upon the personal problems of individuals. We have, at all times, two kinds of processes going on inextricably connected with each other: *interest politics*, the clash of material aims and needs among various groups and blocs; and *status politics*, the clash of various projective rationalizations arising from status aspirations and other personal motives.[58]

Echoing this theme, *Democracy for Realists: Why Elections Do Not Produce Responsive Government,* was penned by Christopher Achen and Larry Bartels shortly after the 2016 election. They find that "issue congruence [between voters and parties], in so far as it exists, is mostly a byproduct of other connections, most of them lacking policy content."[59] That is, voters align themselves with racial, ethnic, occupational, religious, recreational and other groups. It is their group identity that determines vote choice, not a particular policy concern or array of policy preferences. People do not seem to like or even understand the policy choices they make, they argue.

What difference does it make if voters link themselves to particular groups and spend little time evaluating candidate positions? How would the transformation of policy disputes into symbolic, value-centered differences – combined with the tendency to merge with like-minded citizens – shape the conduct of our politics? What is wrong with group-based voting decisions?

For one, there is also evidence to support the notion that like-minded groups foster extremism. Social psychological research has identified what is called the "risky shift phenomenon."[60] Whereas we might expect group decisions to reflect the average opinions of those in the group, researchers have found that group positions become more extreme than the average position of members. In other words, our positions become more radical as we merge with others. In politics, the implication is that a group's policy position will become more extreme over time, particularly if these positions are symbolic, continually reinforced by a partisan media, and rarely challenged. It is no wonder that gridlock seems fixed in Congress and in state legislatures across the country. Columnist David Brooks put it this way: "Once politics became a contest pitting one identity group against another, it was no longer possible to compromise. Everything became a status war between my kind of people and your kind of people."[61]

We might ponder if antipathy toward the other side could propel the majority to enact changes that undermine core democratic institutions, such as freedom of the press and access to the polling booth? One might recall a quote in a previous chapter from the chair of a redistricting committee in North Carolina: "I think electing Republicans is better than electing Democrats, so I drew this map to help foster what I think is better for the country."[62] If they are not part of our tribe, exclusion from the process becomes a snap. Does abridging our opponent's democratic freedoms become justified because they are not one of us? Can freedom of the press be curtailed if the criticism of your side becomes too intense?

Might some Americans even accept an assault on our election process by foreign actors – so long as it helps their side win? By the summer of 2018, after two years of media accounts and unambiguous proclamations from US intelligence agencies (overseen by Republicans) that it happened, just 32 percent of self-identified Republicans agreed that Russia interfered in the 2016 election. Did the others really doubt that it took place – or refuse to say so, given that their candidate won? Americans have always used their partisanship to filter information, to weed out discordant messages, but this seems exceptional.

Finally, and potentially most important, will there be an erosion of our willingness to accept election outcomes? One of the guardrails of our system is to graciously accept defeat, even after hotly contested races. This extends back to the election of 1800, when John Adams was thrown from the presidency by his former friend, Thomas Jefferson. Adams was humiliated and disgruntled, and he departed the White House in the dead of night. But he accepted the outcome – as did his followers. Jefferson, understanding the importance of post-election acts, set forth one of the most sacred principles of electoral politics in his inaugural address:

> [All must] bear in mind this sacred principle, that though the will of the majority is in all cases to prevail, that will to be rightful must be reasonable; that the minority possess their equal rights, which equal law must protect, and to violate would be oppression. Let us, then, fellow-citizens, unite with one heart and one mind. Let us restore to social intercourse that harmony and affection without which liberty and even life itself are but dreary things ... [E]very difference of opinion is not a difference of principle. We have called by different names brethren of the same principle. We are all Republicans, we are all Federalists.[63]

Can Americans come together after a heated, intense election? Will they cast aside tribal impulses in the name of compromise and pragmatic policy solutions, as was routine throughout our history? If the losing side sees the outcome as fraudulent, what would be the incentive to negotiate, to find common ground? The election of Donald Trump has done little to calm the partisan waters, and in 2018 there was uproar over the legitimacy of election results in Georgia and Florida. Can voters once again have faith in the election process if they see the other side as the enemy? The question of whether we can overcome our increasingly deep-seated partisanship and visceral fear of the other side is one of the great questions facing America.

Notes

1　E.E. Schattschneider, *Party Government* (New York: Rinehart, 1942), 1.
2　David Brooks, "Worthy Is the Lamb," *New York Times* website, March 15, 2018 (www.nytimes.com/2018/03/15/opinion/conor-lamb-democrats-pennsylvania.html).
3　James Hohmann, "Daily 202: 10 Take Midterm Takeaway," *Washington Post*, November 7, 2018.
4　Ibid.
5　Ibid.
6　Quoted in James Thomas Flexner, *Washington: The Indispensable Man* (New York: New American Library, 1974), 263.
7　Washington, "Farewell Address."
8　Quoted in A. James Reichley, *The Life of the Parties: A History of American Political Parties* (New York: Free Press, 1992), 29.
9　David Herbert Donald, *Lincoln* (New York: Touchstone Books, 1995), 537.
10　John White and Daniel Shea, *New Party Politics* (Belmont, CA: Thompson, 2004), 21.
11　Quoted in Leon D. Epstein, *Political Parties in the American Mold* (Madison: University of Wisconsin Press, 1986), 18.
12　Amicus Curiae Brief filed by the Committee for Party Renewal in *Colorado Republican Federal Campaign Committee v. Federal Election Commission*, February 1996, 3.
13　Committee for Party Renewal, *Statement of Principles*, September 1977.
14　Ibid., 50.
15　Seth Masket, "Political Parties are Networks, and You Want Them on Your Side," *Pacific Standard Magazine* website, June 9, 2014 (https://psmag.com/news/parties-networks-want-side-82888).
16　Pew Research Center, "Turnout was High in the 2016 Primary Season, but Just Short of 2008 Record," June 10, 2016 (www.pewresearch.org/fact-tank/2016/06/10/turnout-was-high-in-the-2016-primary-season-but-just-short-of-2008-record/).
17　Bernard R. Berelson, Paul F. Lazarsfeld, and William N. McPhee, *Voting: A Study of Opinion Formation in a Presidential Campaign* (Chicago, IL: University of Chicago Press, 1954), 310–311.
18　Thomas M. Holbrook, *Do Campaigns Matter?* (Thousand Oaks, CA: SAGE Publications, 1996).
19　Michael S. Lewis-Beck, Helmut Norpoth, William G. Jacoby and Herbert F. Weisberg, *The American Voter Revisited* (Ann Arbor, MI: University of Michigan Press, 2008), 149–150.
20　Pew Research Center, "Partisanship and Political Animosity in 2016," June 22, 2016 (www.people-press.org/2016/06/22/partisanship-and-political-animosity-in-2016/).
21　Hannah Fingerhut, "Why do People Belong to a Party? Negative Views of the Opposing Party are a Major Factor," Pew Research Center, March 29, 2018 (www.pewresearch.org/fact-tank/2018/03/29/why-do-people-belong-to-a-party-negative-views-of-the-opposing-party-are-a-major-factor/).
22　Pew Research Center, "Partisanship and Political Animosity in 2016," June 22, 2016 (www.people-press.org/2016/06/22/partisanship-and-political-animosity-in-2016/).

23 Alexander G. Theodoridis and James L. Martherus, "Trump is Not the Only One Who Calls Opponents 'Animals.' Democrats and Republicans do it to Each Other." *Washington Post* website, May 21, 2018 (www.washingtonpost.com/news/monkey-cage/wp/2018/05/21/trump-isnt-the-only-one-who-calls-opponents-animals-democrats-and-republicans-do-it-to-each-other/?utm_term=.d5c37899820b).

24 Alan I. Abramowitz and Steven W. Webster, *Taking it to a New Level: Negative Partisanship, Voter Anger and the 2016 Presidential Election.* Paper presented at the State of the Parties Conference, Akron Ohio, November 4, 2017.

25 Ibid., 7.

26 David C. Kimball, Joseph Anthony and Tyler Chance "Political Identity and Party Polarization in the American Electorate," prepared for presentation at the State of the Parties 2016 Conference, University of Akron, November 9, 2017.

27 Pew Research Center, "Partisanship and Political Animosity in 2016," June 22, 2016. Accessed at: www.people-press.org/2016/06/22/partisanship-and-political-animosity-in-2016/.

28 Jeremy Peters, "In a Divided Era, One Thing Seems to Unite: Political Anger," *New York Times*, August 16, 2018.

29 Ibid.

30 Ibid.

31 Amy Mitchell, Jeffrey Gottfried, Jocelyn Kiley and Katerina Eva Matsa, "Political Polarization & Media Habits," Pew Research Center, October 21, 2014 (www.journalism.org/2014/10/21/political-polarization-media-habits/).

32 Ibid.

33 Kirsten Weir, "Why We Believe Alternative Facts," *American Psychological Association Journal* 48 (May 2017).

34 Jeff Stein, "Ticket Splitting is Dead. National Parties are Now Everything." *Vox*, November 17, 2016 (www.vox.com/policy-and-politics/2016/11/17/13666192/voting-congress-presidency).

35 Ibid.

36 Ibid.

37 Thomas E. Mann and Norman J. Ornstein, *It's Even Worse Than It Looks: How the American Constitutional System Collided with the New Politics of Extremism* (New York: Basic Books, 2016), 44.

38 Ibid., 43.

39 Mary Ann Glendon, *Rights Talk: The Impoverishment of Political Discourse* (New York: Free Press, 1991), xi.

40 Theda Skocpol and Vanessa Williamson, *The Tea Party and the Remaking of Republican Conservatism* (New York: Oxford University Press, 2012).

41 Bill Bishop, *The Big Sort: Why the Clustering of Like-Minded America is Tearing Us Apart* (Boston: Mariner Books, 2008), 6.

42 Ibid., 1.

43 Ibid., 40.

44 Roger Cohen, "Tribalism Here, and There," *New York Times* website, March 10, 2008 (www.nytimes.com/2008/03/09/opinion/09iht-edcohen.1.10836343.html).

45 Kathleen Hall Jamison and Joseph N. Cappella, *Echo Chamber: Rush Limbaugh and the Conservative Media Establishment* (New York: Oxford University Press, 2008), 245.

46 Ibid.

47 Isaac Stanley-Becker, "We are 'Q': A Deranged Conspiracy Cult Leaps From the Internet to the Crowd at Trump's MAGA Tour," *Washington Post,* August 1, 2018.

48 Isaac Stanley-Becker, "QAnon: Meet a Real-life Believer in the Online, Pro-Trump Conspiracy Theory that's Bursting into View," *Washington Post*, August 3, 2018.

49 One of the most frequently cited works on the effects of hyper-partisanship is Thomas E. Mann and Norman J. Ornstein, *It's Even Worse Than It Looks: How the American Constitutional System Collided with the New Politics of Extremism* (New York: Basic Books, 2016). They also argue that the change is asymmetric, essentially the function of Republican extremism.

50 Daniel M. Shea, "Colby College-*Boston Globe* 2016 Civility Poll," *Colby College,* 2016 (www.colby.edu/goldfarb/civilitypoll/).

51 Ibid.

52 Lydia Saad, "Conservatives Finish 2009 as No. 1 Ideological Group," *Gallup,* January 7, 2010 (http://news.gallup.com/poll/124958/conservatives-finish-2009-no-1-ideological-group.aspx).

53 Pew Research Center, "Since Trump's Election, Increased Attention to Politics – Especially Among Women," July 20, 2017 (www.people-press.org/2017/07/20/since-trumps-election-increased-attention-to-politics-especially-among-women/).

54 Jeremy Peters, "In a Divided Era, One Thing Seems to Unite: Political Anger," *New York Times*, August 16, 2018.

55 Ibid.

56 E.E. Schattschneider, *Party Government* (New York: Rinehart, 1942), 52.

57 V.O. Key, Jr. and Milton C. Cummings, Jr., *The Responsible Electorate: Rationality in Presidential Voting, 1936–1960* (Cambridge, MA: Harvard University Press, 1966), 7.

58 Richard Hofstadter, "Paranoid Style in American Politics," *Harpers Magazine*, 1964, 52–53.

59 Christopher H. Achen and Larry M. Bartels, *Democracy for Realists: Why Elections Do Not Produce Responsive Government* (Princeton, NJ: Princeton University Press, 2017), 301.

60 Bill Bishop, *The Big Sort: Why the Clustering of Like-Minded America is Tearing Us Apart* (Boston: Mariner Books, 2008), 66.

61 David Brooks, *The Social Animal* (New York: Random House, 2011), 319.

62 Richard Fausset, "North Carolina Exemplifies National Battle Over Voting Laws," *New York Times* website, March 10, 2016 (www.nytimes.com/2016/03/11/us/north-carolina-voting-rights-redistictricting-battles.html?_r=0).

63 Thomas Jefferson's Inaugural Address, March 4, 1801 (http://avalon.law.yale.edu/19th_century/jefinau1.asp).

6 Realignment Redux

Is There a "Unifying Theory" for Today's Electoral Alignment?

It was a given that Republicans would lose seats in the 2018 congressional elections. Their supporters tend to turn out in higher numbers than Democratic voters in midterm contests, but the president's party usually takes a hit in these elections. It might be a tidal wave of change, as was the case in 1994 when Republicans picked up 54 seats in the House, or maybe a modest boost, like in 2002 when the Democrats picked up eight spots. There would be some losses, sure, but whether the GOP would lose control of either branch of Congress was far from certain. (In the end, the Democrats netted some 40 seats in the House, but the Republicans picked up two seats in the Senate.)

That is why it seemed strange that so many Republicans, in both the House and Senate, decided not to run for reelection. By May of 2018, some 40 House Republicans had called it quits, and in the Senate, several high-profile members were ending their careers. Even the Speaker of the House, Paul Ryan, a rising star in the party, decided it was time to head home to Wisconsin. Donald Trump's rocky first year in office probably had something to do with it, and the Democrats were gunning for a fight – as evidenced by a record number of candidates entering in primary elections and their robust fundraising. But were things all that grim for the GOP?

At the heart of the mass exodus from Congress was the growing belief that the Republican Party had changed, dramatically, and that it no longer fit the ideological outlook of many GOP officials. They no longer felt at home in the party, and there was a real chance that they might lose their primary election – historically a rare occurrence for incumbents of either party. In a widely covered speech in March of that year at the National Press Club, Arizona Senator Jeff Flake, who himself had chosen to step down, seemed to hit the nail on the head: "Never has a party abandoned, fled its principles and deeply held beliefs so quickly as my party did in the face of the nativist juggernaut. We have become strangers to ourselves."[1]

What was particularly odd about the departure of so many Republicans was that the party seemed, by some measures, on the ascent. Just two years earlier they had captured the rare prize in contemporary American politics: unified control of the federal government (the White House, Senate, and House). They held an unprecedented number of state legislative seats and a whopping 33 governorships. The head of their ticket in 2016, Donald Trump, had pulled together a unique coalition of supporters in a diverse set of states, perhaps creating a route for future wins.

But there was a rub. Rarely have we seen in American history a greater shift in the governing philosophy of a party in such a short period of time. Many issues tell the story, but Trump's position on trade tariffs tops the list. He ran for the presidency promising to scrap many of the trade deals that previous administrations, both Democratic and Republican, had pulled together. Many of those accords, like NAFTA, had broad Republican backing. But they were "disastrous," according to Trump, and he planned to start from scratch. After his inauguration, he moved in that direction – with modest grumbling from his party's ranks – but in March of 2018 he stunned the nation by tweeting that he would impose a 20 percent tariff on imported steel and a 10 percent tax on imported aluminum. This was a huge development, sending ripples across the economy and leading other nations to levy tariffs on important American products. China responded with a laundry list of duties on products and commodities. Among the items on the list was a 25 percent tax on soybeans, America's second largest export to China. According to one account, "By proposing the tariffs, Mr. Trump has moved to fulfill a central promise of his campaign: confronting those countries he believes are undermining American industry. Yet ... he has effectively prioritized one element of the Trump political coalition over another."[2] A farmer who had supported Trump in 2016 put the matter this way: "If he doesn't understand what he's doing to the nation by doing what he's doing, he's going to be a one-term president, plain and simple."[3] It was a far cry from Reagan's declaration in 1986 that, "Our trade policy rests firmly on the foundation of free and open markets. ... The freer the flow of world trade, the stronger the tides of human progress and peace among nations."[4]

Trump was striking at the heart of the Republican free trade ideology, and that was just the tip of the iceberg. For decades, Republicans had extolled the virtues of family values, integrity and honesty, but Trump lied incessantly (the *Washington Post* claimed to document well over 4,228 falsehoods in less than two years).[5] His use of crude, ugly language, often in the form of tweets, was ubiquitous. More significantly, by about the time many Republicans decided to step down from Congress, it was alleged that Trump had paid hush money to both a porn star and a Playboy model to hide his sexual liaisons with them – all while he was married to Melania. He spoke of the "very fine people" on both sides of confrontations between white supremacist neo-Nazis and counter-protesters in Charlottesville, Virginia, and he took the unprecedented move, particularly for a Republican, of repeatedly attacking the FBI and other law enforcement agencies. Through all of this, the vast majority of self-identified Republicans, the people who brought him to office, stood by him. A full 85 percent still backed the president in the summer of 2018.[6]

Why were there not greater defections, particularly over key issues for the Republican Party like free trade and family values? Republican Senator Bob Corker of Tennessee, who had also decided to step down, said what many were coming to learn. Republican voters "don't care about issues. They just want to know if you're with Trump."[7] The Republican Party had transformed; it had become the party of Trump. A journalist put it this way: "What he offers politics is not a conservative agenda. It is not an agenda, or an ideology, at all. It is a set of feelings about patriotism, about who is a proper American and who is not, about foreigners, about elites, about sovereignty and about power."[8]

By the spring of 2018, there was broad recognition that the Republican Party had changed; that it was no longer the party of Ronald Reagan or even George W. Bush. As suggested in the previous chapter, the history of parties in the United States is one of adaptation, and we explored partisan polarization and how a growing disdain for the "other" side is reshaping elections and the very nature of American politics. We also said that one's perceived group membership might be more important than policy positions. This chapter will set our gaze on the broader party system – the electorate *as a whole.*

Aggregate party affiliations and voting behaviors form electoral coalitions, and these coalitions matter a great deal. When Franklin D. Roosevelt won a landslide victory in 1936, one analyst declared that he could "see no interpretation of the returns which does not suggest that the people of America want the president to proceed along progressive or liberal lines."[9] The so-called New Deal Coalition structured American politics and public policy for generations. Similarly, after Ronald Reagan's stunningly large victory in 1980, many agreed with pollster Richard Wirthlin that the result implied "a mandate for change" that included "a rejection of the New Deal agenda."[10] In each case, the *structure* of the American party system had undergone a transformation. The question guiding this chapter is what the rise of Donald Trump tells us about new electoral coalitions and the nature of electoral politics in the years to come. What are the contours of the transformation and what will they mean for big policy questions and future elections? Finally, might there be a "unifying theory" for today's electoral alignment?

Critical Realignment ... Redux?[11]

One of the first political scientists to explore coalitions and the weight of particular elections was, once again, V.O. Key, Jr. Who remembers, for example, whether Franklin Pierce won the presidency in 1852, or James Buchanan in 1856, or James Garfield in 1880? But from Key's perspective, "realigning elections" are those in which upheaval plays a significant role. The impending Civil War consumed everything in its wake in 1860, for example. Lincoln's successful prosecution of that war along with his proclamation of a "new birth of freedom" in the Gettysburg Address convinced most voters that the Republican Party could be trusted to steer the ship of state. Several decades later, fellow Republican William McKinley shifted the foundation of the party from a more agrarian, working-class model to a pro-business, small government approach. Likewise, Franklin D. Roosevelt's hodgepodge of government programs to combat the Great Depression convinced most voters that the Democratic Party could best handle the nation's economy and look after the interests of the "common man." When voters were asked in 1951 who they would tell young people the parties stood for, most said that the Democrats represented the "working man" while Republicans promoted the "privileged few."[12]

Building on this idea, in 1955 Key developed a category of elections he described as critical elections – contests characterized by sharp reorganizations of party loyalties over short periods of time. In these contests, voter turnout is high and new party coalitions are formed. Studying the election outcomes of several New England towns from 1916 to 1952, Key found that when the Democrats nominated Catholic New York governor Alfred E. Smith in 1928, party support in urban areas increased significantly and remained high, while Democratic backing in rural, Protestant-dominated enclaves fell to record lows and remained there for decades.[13]

Shortly after Key came up with the concept of critical elections, he published a major modification of his original idea. He wrote that changes in partisanship are sometimes not as dramatic as what occurred in 1928. Instead, party loyalties can erode among some groups and regions over many years. Key termed these changes "secular realignments," defining them as "a movement of the members of a population category from party to party that extends over several presidential elections and appears to be independent of the peculiar factors influencing the vote at individual elections."[14] Key placed no time limit on the pace of change, noting that it could take as long as 50 years. But the premise was clear: secular realignments were characterized by gradual alterations in voting behavior, not a sharp reorganization of party loyalties.

Ideas about critical elections and secular realignment gained popularity in the political science community. Walter Dean Burnham, a major proponent of the realignment concept and a student of Key's, published an important book in 1970 titled *Critical Elections and the Mainsprings of American Politics*. Burnham transformed the simple idea of critical elections into a generalized theory of coalitional change. He outlined the conditions that characterized the partisan realignments. There are sharp reorganizations of the major party voter coalitions that occur at periodic intervals, quite often when there is abnormal stress in the socioeconomic system. During these periods, the ideological polarizations between the major parties become exceptionally large, leading to durable, long-term consequences on important public policies.[15]

Using this classification scheme, Burnham cited the elections of Andrew Jackson in 1828, Abraham Lincoln in 1860, William McKinley in 1896, and Franklin D. Roosevelt in 1932 as having met the conditions of party realignment. In each case, voter interest and turnout was high, there were significant third-party revolts either in the election or in the contests leading up to it, and the differences between the parties were exceptionally large by American standards. Burnham also discovered a rhythm to American politics – namely, that realigning elections occur once every 28 to 36 years. Thus, if a realigning election happened in 1932 (as Burnham suggests) or in 1928 (as Key found in New England), one could expect another realignment to occur circa 1968.

Indeed, many believe that Richard Nixon's close victory over Hubert Humphrey in 1968 met the conditions of a classic party realignment. The issue differences between Democratic and Republican on civil rights, the Vietnam War, and what became known as the social issues (crime, abortion, pornography) were significant. Moreover, there was a major third-party revolt in the person of Alabama Governor George Wallace, whose presidential candidacy garnered 14 percent of the popular vote – a feat not exceeded until Ross Perot captured 19 percent in 1992. Kevin Phillips, an astute Republican political analyst, wrote in his 1969 book *The Emerging Republican Majority*, "Far from being the tenuous and unmeaningful victory suggested by critical observers, the election of Richard M. Nixon as president of the United States in November, 1968, bespoke the end of the New Deal Democratic hegemony and the beginning of a new era in American politics."[16] The elections that followed Nixon's 1968 win gave credence to Phillip's vision of a Republican realignment. From 1968 to 1988, Republicans won five of the six presidential contests (Nixon in 1968 and 1972, Reagan in 1980 and 1984, and Bush in 1988). Only Nixon's Watergate scandal permitted a lone Democratic victory – Jimmy Carter in 1976 – and that was for just one term. The Republican hold on the presidency was so great that some analysts thought the GOP had an impenetrable lock on the Electoral College that would prevent future Democratic victories.

But the Republican realignment in 1968 had a very different feel from those that preceded it. Far from being vanquished, Democrats retained comfortable majorities in both houses of Congress for most of this period. Democrats controlled the Senate from 1968 to 1980 – narrowly losing control in the 1980 Reagan landslide – yet reclaiming majority status in 1986. The House showed an even greater Democratic advantage. When Ronald Reagan won reelection in 1984, Democrats had a 71-seat margin in the House – the largest edge given to a party that did not control the presidency since 1895. Thus, while the party system created by Franklin D. Roosevelt had died, the ideal-type party realignment forecast by Burnham had failed to take its place.[17]

What happened? Some attributed the Republican failure to produce a classic realignment to the aftereffects of Watergate. In 1974, Democrats added 49 seats in the House – enough to ensure control until Newt Gingrich and his partisans took over 20 years later. Others attributed the failure of either party to achieve a classic realignment to presidents who eschew their party affiliations in order to win more votes. This separation of president from party – coupled with television's capacity to allow candidates to highlight style and image – meant that voters could pick a presidential candidate without regard to how he might link to other candidates running on the same ballot.

Despite the attempts of Key, Burnham and many others to develop an iron-clad theory of party realignment, one problem persisted: voters refused to cooperate. During the 1970s and early 1980s, new terms to describe how the electorate was behaving came into *vogue*. The most common of these was dealignment, meaning that voters were moving away from *both* political parties. In 1980, political scientist Everett Carll Ladd wrote: "All the anchors are being raised at the same moment in American politics, and the electoral ship is drifting as never before."[18] A new way of talking about politics was suddenly in style. Phrases like "Tweedledum and Tweedledee" or "There's not a dime's worth of difference between the two parties" were commonly heard. Instead of rooting for their "home team," Democrats or Republicans, voters adopted neutral attitudes.

In a major critique of party realignment theory entitled "Like Waiting for Godot," Ladd maintained that the New Deal was a unique period when parties mattered and Franklin D. Roosevelt loomed over the political horizon. Key, Burnham, and others who believed in the party realignment idea grew up during the New Deal era and were shaped by it. Focusing on whether or not a party realignment happened in such interesting contests as 1968, 1980, 1992, or 1994, political scientists have been asking the wrong question. Rather than wondering whether each of these elections constituted a party realignment, Ladd suggested better questions, such as "What are the major issues and policy differences between the two major parties?" and "How do these differences separate political elites and the voting public?"

And yet, the 1994 midterm election gave party realignment theorists ammunition as a reorganization of voter loyalties seemed to have occurred – and nearly on schedule (26 years after Richard Nixon's 1968 victory). For the first time in 40 years, Republicans won majorities in both houses of Congress, gaining 53 seats in the House and eight seats in the Senate. Newt Gingrich and his fellow Republicans campaigned on a simple theme, the Contract with America, a document signed by all but four Republican House contenders in a flashy Capitol Hill ceremony. The contract promised that if Republicans won, party leaders would schedule votes during the first 100 days of the new Congress on such issues as term limits, a line-item veto for the president, and a balanced budget amendment. Republicans were winning the war of ideas, and the word "revolution," commonly associated with ideal-type party realignments, was in fashion. Burnham claimed that the 1994 results closely resembled an old-fashioned party realignment and challenged his critics to disagree: "Those who have stressed partisan dealignment will now have to consider how this abrupt emergence of something remarkably like an old-fashioned partisan election fits their models. And those who have placed their bets on the argument that critical-realignment analysis is irrelevant to this modern candidate-driven electoral universe will have to reconsider their position."[19]

The Break Up of the New Deal Coalition

As the New Deal–like party system became unanchored, a large number of Americans were willing to split their ballots among candidates of all parties. According to American National Election Study data, those who voted for House candidates of one party and a president of another totaled 10 percent in the early 1950s, 15 percent in the 1960s, and 30 percent in the early 1970s – where it remained stable for over three decades. Even self-identified Republicans and Democrats regularly split their tickets. During the 1998 midterm elections, for example, ticket-splitting was rampant. In New York and Connecticut, voters returned Republican governors George Pataki and John Rowland to office, while choosing Democrats Chuck Schumer and Christopher Dodd to represent them in the US Senate. Of the 22 gubernatorial races where the winning candidate won by 10 percentage points or more, the winning governor's party did not net a single additional congressional seat. In fact, in two of these states – California and Kansas – the party of the losing gubernatorial candidate actually won a House seat.

The rise of the ticket-splitters led to a bewildering array of extremely close presidential elections followed by landslides with the winning party often switching back and forth. Close elections, defined by the percentage of popular vote (as opposed to Electoral College votes), occurred in 1960, 1968, 1976, 1988, 1992, and 2000. Landslide elections appeared in 1952, 1956, 1964, 1972 and 1984. The alternation between squeakers and blowouts was yet another illustration of the decline in party loyalty. There was much speculation as to why a growing number of voters shifted away from political parties, including that the nature of issues changed during the 1960s and 1970s and the extent to which voters were guided by them increased; the rise of interest groups as important competitors vying with parties for the voters' attention; candidate-centered politics causing voters to think of politicians as individuals rather than party advocates; campaign consultants encouraging candidates to take popular positions and soften their images rather than be depicted as uncompromising partisans; and the news media which portrayed partisanship in a negative light. About the same time party identification began to wane, incumbent reelection rates soared. Incumbents, in effect, created their own "party" as they sought reelection. (A congressional term that limits movement was launched in response to these high re-election rates.)

The New Electoral Alignment

When Bill Clinton won the presidency in 1992 and again in 1996, the coalition he and his fellow Democrats assembled differed dramatically from Franklin D. Roosevelt's 60 years before. Democrats, including Clinton, won backing from women, unmarried voters, divorcees, Hispanics, West Coast and Northeast residents, Jews, those who infrequently attend church, and those with post-graduate degrees. Republicans won the support of white men, members of the Christian Right, married voters, white southerners, libertarians, and regular church-goers. White Catholics, employees in the new Information Age technologies, middle-income voters, moderates, those who live in the Midwest, those with some college exposure, and true independents were the new swing voters. The portraits of the two parties were starting to look fundamentally different than they were a mere three decades earlier. Like mosaics, the tiles shifted – some taken away from the Democratic portrait and added to the Republican one (and vice versa) – and new tiles (e.g., the LGBTQ community, unmarried women, churched versus un-churched) have been added.[20]

Many observers came to believe the American political system was undergoing a slow but steady recalibration – precisely what Key conjectured. Unlike previous realignments, where intense cross-cutting issues divided the electorate and reconfigured voting patterns in a single election or two, the recent process has happened slowly but steadily. The tectonic plates of politics had shifted, but the roots of the change were a bit unclear. Below is a list of what might be the top five elements of this secular realignment.

Element #1: A Widening Gender Gap. A central piece of the new electoral order is the gender gap – the variance between the voting preferences of men and women. After women were permitted to go to the polls thanks to the passage of the 19th Amendment, politics changed but only marginally. Women often followed their husbands' leads, and partisan differences between the two sexes were negligible. Things began to shift in 1964, however, when, for the first time women voted in slightly greater numbers than men for Democrat Lyndon Johnson. Johnson offered himself as the "peace candidate" and exploited the public fears of his opponent, Arizona Senator Barry Goldwater, by running a series of hard-hitting television commercials. Many women were frightened of losing their sons in another war and cast 62 percent of their votes for Johnson (men were not far behind, with 60 percent siding with Johnson).

In the elections that followed, there were only small differences in male–female voting behavior. This changed in 1980. Divorced women with children were not charmed by Ronald Reagan and the revolution he promised in downsizing the federal government. Many depended on government help to make ends meet. In addition, many women, regardless of their marital status, were frightened by Reagan's pledge to drastically increase military spending. Because the economy was in poor shape with high inflation and unemployment, Reagan was able to beat Carter among women by the narrow margin of 47 percent to 45 percent. Among men, the race was no contest; men liked Reagan's rugged individualism and his projection of US military might, giving him 55 percent of their votes to just 36 percent for Carter. The gender gap was born.

Instead of being a flash in a pan, the gender gap persisted long after Reagan left the White House. In 1992 the gap slightly narrowed, but it widened once more four years later as men chose Bob Dole (44 percent to 43 percent) while women picked Bill Clinton (54 percent to 38 percent). Clinton won a second term propelled by the exceptionally strong support from women, and this pattern continued with Barack Obama. Some 56 percent of women voted for Obama, compared to 49 percent of men. In the 2012 contest, the spread was a bit more pronounced.

The contest between Hillary Clinton and Donald Trump in 2016 yielded one of the widest gender gaps in history, with the Democrat winning women by 12 percentage points and losing men by 12 points as well – a 24-point spread.[21] A hefty chunk of the disparity can probably be explained by what many saw as insensitive, even vulgar acts and behavior by Trump during the campaign, including the infamous *Access Hollywood* video where he boasted about groping women without their consent. The opportunity to finally break the toughest glass ceiling in electoral politics probably increased Clinton's support among women, too, and once again women differed from men on several big issues. It should be noted that the gender gap in 2016 was also rooted in the changing behavior of men, particularly white men. Democratic presidential candidates have not fared well with this group for decades, but in 2016 the figure was stark: Clinton netted just 36 percent of the vote from white men.[22]

As predicted, the gender gap persisted in the 2018 midterms, with women voters supporting Democratic candidates by a stunning 21-point margin (60 percent to 39 percent). This time, however, male voters favored Republican candidates by a small margin (50 percent to 48 percent).[23] Perhaps more significantly, a vast number of the women entered the fray in 2018, and a record number were elected to the US House. For the first time in history, more than 100 women will fill seats in the Lower Chamber. There will also be 22 women in the Senate and nine will serve as governor. The great majority of these officials are Democrats.

Element #2: Geographic Shifts. From the earliest days of the republic, geographic blocs of voters were tightly linked to party coalitions. Each party could count on particular states or regions in national elections, and these patterns generally lasted for decades. In the election of 1800, for example, nearly all Federalist support came from New England states, and Jefferson's Republican backers were located in the mid-Atlantic and southern states. At times, these geographic coalitions were linked to economic issues, such as agricultural interests or manufacturing, but at other times social or cultural issues formed the basis of the division.

The most important of these blocs was the "Solid South." Given the election of Republican Abraham Lincoln in 1860, and the difficulties the former Confederate states confronted in the post-Civil War Reconstruction period levied by the so-called Radical Republicans in Congress, few voters throughout the entire southeastern region wanted to ally themselves with the Republican Party. There were roughly 16 states that boasted a one-party system with the only electoral competition happening in primary elections. It was a foregone conclusion that nearly all elected posts, from county sheriff to governor and US Senate, would be held by Democrats. Many in the region were conservative, especially when it came to issues related to racial segregation, but they were die-hard Democrats nevertheless. In a number of distinct, important ways, the Solid South shaped politics and governance in the United States for generations. Of course, the systematic disenfranchisement of blacks in the region, discussed in Chapter 3, was due to the hegemony of the Democratic Party.

While Woodrow Wilson, a Democrat, was brought to office in 1912 and reelected in 1916 in large measure by nearly unanimous support of southern states, isolationist sentiment in the two subsequent elections allowed the Republican presidential candidate to win two states (Tennessee and Missouri in 1920, and Kentucky and Missouri in 1924). Likely because the Democrats nominated the first Catholic candidate for president in 1928, and because the South was overwhelmingly Protestant, the Republican candidate that year, Herbert Hoover, got the backing of seven southern states.

It was not until 1948 that large fissures emerged. That year, President Harry Truman, a Democrat, issued an executive order desegregating the military, a move strongly opposed by most voters in the South. He pushed forward with a number of other changes designed to bolster civil rights for African Americans. At the Democratic National Convention, a young firebrand liberal from Minnesota, Hubert Humphrey, proceeded to scold the party in a primetime speech for turning a blind-eye to the treatment of blacks in the South. "To those who say that we are rushing this issue of civil rights, I say to them we are 172 years [too] late! To those who say this civil rights program is an infringement on states' rights, I say this: the time has arrived in America for the Democratic Party to get out of the shadow of states' rights and walk forthrightly into the bright sunshine of human rights."[24] He was cheered on by many of the delegates, but booed by those from the South. Humphrey also spearheaded a move to include a plank in the Democratic platform calling for federal legislation against lynching, to end race-based job discrimination and to desegregate schools. By a narrow margin, the plank was accepted, leading delegates from several southern states to leave the convention. The States Rights Democratic Party, or Dixiecrats, was formed and their nominee for the president would be the staunch conservative and pro-segregationist Senator from South Carolina, Strom Thurmond (a lifelong Democrat). He won four southern states in 1948, but most of the bloc narrowly stuck with Truman.

In subsequent years, a different dynamic began to take hold, called the "southern strategy." Republican candidates appeared to discover that a winning route to the White House was to rally support in their traditional regions of the country, but also appeal to white voters in the South. In 1968, for example, Republican Richard Nixon ran as the "law and order" candidate, which implied he would get tough on civil rights and anti-Vietnam War protesters. It is a controversial topic, but some suggest both Ronald Reagan and George H.W. Bush also used this approach. In 1980, for instance, Reagan kicked off his campaign in Mississippi claiming, "I believe in states' rights," and in the 1988 campaign Bush aired the controversial and racially charged Willy Horton ad, which featured a black inmate who raped and murdered a family. In 2005, the chair of the Republican National Committee, Ken Mehlman, formally apologized to the National Association for the Advancement of Colored People (NAACP) for his party's history of exploiting racial polarization to win presidential election.[25]

It was not until 1994 that the Solid South would fully collapse. It was Bill Clinton's first midterm election and voters vented their displeasure with his administration's missteps by bringing a majority of Republicans to the House and Senate. The GOP picked up a whopping 54 seats in the House, sending the outspoken conservative Newt Gingrich to power as Speaker. The vast majority of their gains occurred in the South. Conservative voters had abandoned their historic connection to the Democratic Party. Exit polling confirmed there was a massive swing to the Republican Party in the South – almost all of it coming from whites, especially men.[26]

Since the 1994 election, a majority of elected officials from the South – at the federal, state and local level – have been Republican. Democratic officials have been limited, for the most part, to areas with high numbers of minority voters, mostly in urban areas. In 2014, *New York Times* analyst Nate Cohen went so far as to write, "Southern politics are deeply polarized along racial lines. It is no exaggeration to suggest that in these states the Democrats have become the party of African Americans and that the Republicans are the party of whites."[27]

To no one's surprise, Donald Trump ran the table in the South, with the exception of Virginia, where Clinton won by a whisker. In several states, like Arkansas, Kentucky, Tennessee, Mississippi and Louisiana, Trump's margin of victory was massive – more than 20 percentage points. Here again, exit polling underscored huge differences along racial lines: upwards of 90 percent of African American voters in the South voted for Clinton, but roughly 70 percent of white voters backed Trump.[28]

As a final note on geographic shifts, over the last few elections a massive partisan gap has emerged between urban and suburban voters, and those living in rural communities. A noteworthy city versus country divide appeared in several previous elections, but it was generally overshadowed by the region of the country and other factors. For example, during much of the 20th century, Democrats did well in the agricultural Midwest, but were swamped by Republicans in New England. As odd as it might seem, Vermont, still one of the most rural states in the union, was a consistent Republican stronghold throughout much of the 20th century. The only two states that Roosevelt lost in his 1936 reelection were Maine and Vermont. In the last few elections, a growing number of rural areas across the nation have become heavily Republican and Democrats have become increasingly concentrated in cities. There are shrinking numbers of Americans living in rural areas, certainly, but even so, the percentage of overall Democratic presidential vote coming from rural areas has gone from about 10 percent in 2000 to just 3 percent in 2016.[29] In scores of counties across the nation Barack Obama and Hillary Clinton netted well below one-third of the vote, and in many communities, they netted less than one-fifth. There are 3,141 counties in the United States, the vast majority of them rural. Hillary Clinton won just 487 of them.

In the wake of the 2018 midterm elections, where once again Democrats were trounced in non-urban areas, one commentator made an important observation: "The consistent pattern you're seeing is that Republicans are consolidating control of rural white America faster than Democrats are making inroads into educated suburbia."[30]

As to the root of the urban versus rural divide, many scholars point to cultural changes. For example, there is evidence to suggest support for gay marriage is lower in rural areas than in urban and suburban communities.[31] It is also difficult to downplay the likelihood that race is once again the dividing force. Especially since World War II, rural areas have been much less diverse; conversely urban areas have held a larger proportion of minority residents. Writing of the mounting problem Democratic candidates face in rural areas across the nation, one analyst noted, "Inextricably intertwined in the party's loss of political power – even as it made demographic strides – are uncomfortable questions about the deep racial divide that lingers in its broader traditional coalition."[32]

Element #3: Class Divisions. Economic issues have always been a key ingredient in American electoral coalitions. At the dawn of the party system, the late 1790s, sharp differences emerged over economic issues. The two leading characters in George Washington's cabinet were Alexander Hamilton, Secretary of the Treasury, and Thomas Jefferson, Secretary of State. They passionately disagreed about the future of the nation. Jefferson believed that America's hope lay in small, agricultural-based communities. He had faith in ordinary citizens, particularly the farmer: "Those who labor in the earth are the chosen people of God, if ever He had a chosen people."[33] Hamilton, on the other hand, believed that the future of the nation lay in the development of vibrant urban centers, based on a strong manufacturing sector. He was a capitalist through and through, and he believed that the strong central government was the best mechanism to ensure long-term economic growth.

The two men got along in Washington's cabinet for a while, but it was just a matter of time until their divergent philosophies would spill over into heated debate. The spark was a plan that Hamilton put forward to kick-start the nation's economy. Among other things, Hamilton called for the full payment of wartime debt, termed "full assumption," and heavy national investment in roads, bridges, ports, and canals. Doing so would increase the flow of goods and services, Hamilton argued, thus leading to a general increase in living standards.[34] To pay for these two projects Hamilton proposed a tax on distilled spirits, which became known as the Whiskey Tax. Whiskey producers in those days were farmers in the South and West, so to many, the plan reeked of northeastern industrial elites placing the burden of economic development on the backs of the working poor. Opposition to Hamilton's plans grew, with the leading critic being none other than Jefferson. In a surprise move, Jefferson actually endorsed the plan in exchange for Hamilton's support in moving the nation's capital from New York to a small piece of land on the Potomac River in Virginia. But the controversy surrounding the plan continued to simmer in the hinterlands. In 1794, shortly after the plan's approval, a group of farmers in Western Pennsylvania refused to pay the tax. Federal troops were sent to collect but they were met with armed resistance. This event, called the Whiskey Rebellion, was one of the first tests of the rule of national law in the states.

The episode underscored the importance that economic issues would play in American politics from that time forward. As Jeffrey Stonecash notes in *Class and Party in American Politics,* "It is through the [political process] that ideas filter about what constitutes [economic] fairness and justice … The mechanism to carry that debate on a mass scale is a political party."[35] One might go so far as to suggest that class dynamics have done more to structure party politics than any other dividing force.

Economic issues certainly jumped to the fore in the late 1800s. Farmers in the upper Midwest were especially hard hit by the flood of foreign commodities. This was occurring at nearly the same time as the Industrial Revolution. Business owners, dubbed robber barons, were making fortunes in the bourgeoning cities, often at the expense of the working class. Hardships and growing concerns about staggering inequities in wealth distribution led to the formation of several economic-based political parties, most notably the Populists in 1891. By 1896, the Populists had become a force to be reckoned with, merging with the Democrats in endorsing William Jennings Bryan. William McKinley, the Republican candidate, turned the Republican Party in a more business-friendly direction. McKinley won that contest and the Populist Party faded from the political scene, but many of their proposals were picked up by the Democrats and were eventually adopted into law. This election also solidified the Republican support for a laissez-faire national economy.

The perception that Democrats stand with the working class and Republicans side with big business was further locked in during the Great Depression. As the stock market crashed in 1929 and economic hardship took hold across the nation, Herbert Hoover and his Republicans in Congress offered little in the form of relief. The Democrats, beginning in Congress in 1930 and with the election of Franklin D. Roosevelt as president two years later, swept into power with a platform thought to be centered on the working class. From that point onward, the connection between class and party identification became a fixture in our politics. Writing in 1964, the esteemed political scientist and historian Clinton Rossiter noted, "The fact is that class has now become the most important single force in shaping the political behavior of Americans."[36] There were a few dents in the working class–New Deal Coalition, such as the robust support that Richard Nixon received from this group in 1968 and 1972, and Ronald Reagan's appeal among blue-collar workers in 1980 (dubbed "Reagan Democrats"), but working-class voters seemed to be loyal Democrats for the most part – that is, until 2016. Working-class voters supported Trump over Clinton by a two to one advantage.[37] As noted by analyst Nat Cohen, "Overall for Democrats, white voters without a degree have fallen from 43 percent of John Kerry's voters to 26 percent of Hillary Clinton's."[38]

But the story of class and partisanship may not be that simple. For one, over the last few decades a pattern emerged where Democratic presidential candidates were more likely to win affluent states. States with the highest average income, like Maryland, New Jersey, Connecticut, California and Washington, consistently supported Democratic candidates, while many of the poorest states, like Mississippi, Arkansas, West Virginia and Kentucky, regularly backed GOP candidates. In a series of articles and an important book, a team of political scientists led by Andrew Gelman of Columbia University unravel this apparent paradox by showing that income is a particularly powerful predictor of voter choice in affluent states, but less so in poor states. They write, "Within each state, richer people are more likely to vote Republican, but the states with higher income give more support to the Democrats."[39]

Once again, race is an important piece of the puzzle. When the voter's race is controlled, the income–party preference relationship changes – dramatically. Overall, lower income voters support Democrats, but that relationship holds because there are a disproportionate number of minority votes in this group. Put a bit differently, the percentage of white working-class voters casting their lot with Democrats has declined sharply in recent elections. Exit polling from the 2016 election shows Trump won a staggering 71 percent of white men without a college education.[40] Ron Brownstein of *The Atlantic* made a telling observation: After the 2016 election, two-thirds of Republican House members represented districts with a below-average level of education. After the 2018 midterms, that figure shot up to three-quarters.[41]

Many have speculated that the root of this shift is economic anxiety. A common narrative is that many voters, especially white men, feel that they have been left behind in the new, information-driven economy. "Hobbled by unemployment and locked out of the recovery, those voters turned out in force to send Mr. Trump, and a message, to Washington."[42] This view grew in popularity as Trump squeaked by Clinton in several swing states from the so-called Rust Belt region of the country (such as Pennsylvania, Wisconsin and Michigan). And yet, while there is no question that working-class white voters are shifting to the GOP, scholars are increasingly skeptical that the root of the change is economic insecurity. A comprehensive study conducted by Diana Mutz of the University of Pennsylvania suggests the core of the backlash is concern about cultural displacement – and not economic anxiety.[43] In other words, white working-class men feel their position in society has been threatened by a host of changes. As Mutz explains, "It's not a threat to their own economic well-being; it's a threat to their group's dominance in our country overall."[44] In this light, it is not surprising that white working-class voters who favored deporting immigrants living in the country illegally were 3.3 times more likely to express a preference for Trump than those who did not.[45]

Element #4: Cultural Issues. A long line of scholarship has explored the relationship between cross-cutting cultural issues and partisanship. Journalist Thomas Frank, for example, wrote a powerful, highly acclaimed book, titled *What's the Matter with Kansas?* Frank, a native of Kansas, charted the stunning transformation of the state's politics from progressive, sometimes radically liberal, to hard-core social conservatism and steadfast pro-business. At the heart of his inquiry is how low wage, blue-collar voters would jettison economic policies that might benefit them in favor of social concerns like abortion, gay marriage, evolution, school prayer and gun control. He writes,

> [In the past], when business screwed farmers and workers – when it implemented monopoly strategies invasive beyond the Populists' furthest imaginings – when it ripped off shareholders and casually tossed thousands out of work – you could be damned sure about what would follow. Not these days. Out here the gravity of discontent pulls in only one direction: to the right, to the right, further to the right. Strip today's Kansans of their job security, and they head out to become registered Republicans.[46]

Frank argued that conservative leaders in his state (and elsewhere) made a determined effort to shift voter concern away from economic policies by raising the specter of massive cultural decay, and by suggesting that we are in a quasi-civil war. Pitted against the "real Americans" are the liberal elite: the high-taxing, government-spending, latte-drinking, sushi-eating, Volvo-driving, *New York Times*–reading, Hollywood-loving, left-wing freak show.[47] The nation is divided between "red states" and "blue states," easily evident by looking at an Electoral College map from the past few elections. Red states are the heartland; blue states are at the coastal extremes. And there is so much red! This view, according to Frank, allowed conservatives to present their views as the philosophy of a region that Americans venerate – a repository of national virtue and down-home family values. It also brought majoritarian legitimacy to a president who had actually lost the popular vote (George W. Bush in 2000 and now Trump in 2016).[48]

"Us versus them" (or should we say, "red versus blue") rhetoric became commonplace by the early 1990s. In 1992, the chair of the Republican National Committee proclaimed to a national television audience that "we are America [and] those other people are not."[49] Former Speaker of the House Newt Gingrich described Democrats as "the enemy of normal Americans."[50] Vice-presidential candidate Sarah Palin proclaimed at a campaign stop in North Carolina, "We believe that the best of America is in these small towns that we get to visit and these wonderful little pockets of what I call the real America, being here with all of you hard-working, very patriotic, very pro-America areas of this great nation."[51] About the same time, John McCain stated, "Western Pennsylvania … is the most patriotic, most God-loving part of America," and Robin Hayes, a Republican congressman from North Carolina, extolled, "Liberals hate real Americans that work, and accomplish, and achieve, and believe in God."[52]

It seems possible that the nation is being divided into distinct cultural tribes. It is possible that grievances and moral concerns have replaced economic policy disputes as the dividing line between the parties, and by doing so the "us versus them" divide is made vivid. In turn, this perception shapes the tone and outcome of contemporary politics. As noted by scholar Morris Fiorina, "The symbolic nature of many contemporary political issues is another factor that makes compromise more difficult and contributes to the nasty quality of contemporary debate."[53]

While this might have been true a decade ago when McCain and Palin stumped for the presidency in 2008, some believed the Great Recession put economic concerns back to the forefront. The oft-told narrative regarding the rise of the Tea Party movement, for example, seemed to challenge Frank's supposition. Surely job loss, bank bailouts, huge deficits and wasteful government spending pulled activists to the streets and to the ballot box. Drawing on a pool of 3,000 citizens interviewed in 2006 and again in the summer of 2011, scholars Robert Putnam and David Campbell were able to uncover the motivations spurring those who would later back the Tea Party movement. "Next to being a Republican, the strongest predictor of being a Tea Party supporter today was a desire, back in 2006, to see religion play a prominent role in politics."

But other changes were also underway. By 2012, the US Census had reported that for the first time in American history most births in the United States would be of minority children. While some people welcome our growing diversity, others find these changes unsettling. We might also add that there have been dramatic changes in attitudes toward the LGBTQ movement.

It was within this context that the nation was introduced to Barack Obama. To say that Obama was different would be a vast understatement. For many, his difference was at the heart of Obama's appeal. He represented change, a new direction, a new America. As captured in an *Atlantic* article in 2007, "Obama's candidacy in this sense is a potentially transformational one. Unlike any of the other candidates, he could take America – finally – past the debilitating, self-perpetuating family quarrel of the Baby Boom generation that has long engulfed all of us."[54] His message of change and transformation was particularly potent for younger voters. But to others, Obama's message of change and biography represented a radical departure from the status quo. "As a new president of diverse heritage promised to 'transform America,' perceived threats to the very nature of 'our country' spurred many people, and particularly older people, to get involved with the Tea Party."[55] Whereas many on the left were giddy with the prospects of a transformational president, many on the right were springing to action to "take back their country." As noted by a team of scholars, "Rather than ushering in a new era of tolerance and cooperation, the Obama presidency was marked by rising extremism and partisan warfare."[56] By 2016, the theme had morphed into "make American great again."

Element #5: The Party of Trump. Finally, there is a growing view that "The Party of Trump" emerged from many of these long-simmering changes. During his campaign, Trump offered an unconventional mix of both liberal and conservative policy positions (such as trade tariffs *and* restrictions on immigration), and he had no prior experience in public office. And yet, he became the perfect vehicle for a backlash against political correctness, elitism, and the establishment. "[Trump] turned the anti-elitism the party has long fostered in its supporters against its own leadership. In breaking taboo after taboo he did what many in the base had long wanted to see."[57] This would help explain why several well-qualified "establishment" candidates, like Florida Senator Marco Rubio and former Florida Governor Jeb Bush, could not get any traction in the GOP presidential nomination race against Trump.

Trump was skilled at pushing tribal cues that resonated with white working-class voters, and those living in small cities and towns. At stake, supposedly, was unbridled gun control, abortion on demand, government sponsored health care, a complete disregard of religious tenets, and an end to the American way of life. This was not because he was a purist or had a long record working on these issues. Stretching back to 1999, Trump voiced support for gun restrictions, was supportive of a women's right to choose, and told an interviewer that he was very liberal on health care and even supported universal health care. Back then he thought highly of many GOP establishment types, including Jeb Bush.[58] He had a long record of giving money to liberal politicians, including Hillary Clinton. Somehow all of that did not matter in 2016. It is fair to say that few successful politicians in American history have undergone more of a wholesale conversion than Donald Trump.

More importantly, his past policy positions and current character flaws were set aside when Trump became the outspoken disrupter – the voice of angry Americans. Over and over, his supporters boasted that their champion, the former reality television star, would "tell it like it is," or "say things that everyone knows but are afraid to say." The fact that he was radically different from all politicians was precisely the point. How could the status quo be shattered with another Bush or Clinton? For decades, establishment Republicans drew support by railing against the elitism and arrogance of Democrats. It came back to bite them in the primaries and caucuses in 2016, as Trump, the true outsider, ran away with the contest. The list of Republican "Never Trump-ers" boasted former presidents, cabinet members, senators, governors, and scores of other prominent officials. But all that did not matter.

Today, the Party of Trump is more about attitude than any particular policy, save perhaps one exception – immigration. "Trump did not for the most part infect Republicans with new beliefs from beyond their ken. He connected, and continues to connect, with what a significant part of its base feels."[59] It is about patriotism, who is a proper American, foreigners, elites, and culture battles. Larry Bartels, a political scientist at Vanderbilt University, argues the Party of Trump is united by cultural issues, like respect for the flag and the English language, and negative feelings towards Muslims, immigrants, atheists, and gays and lesbians.[60]

This is why so many traditional Republicans, who would seem to be opposed to Trump's policies and might be shocked by his personal transgressions, seem to fall in line behind the president – or at the very least remain quiet. Many were puzzled, even shocked that House Speaker

Paul Ryan remained quiet when Trump spoke of "very fine people on both sides" of confrontations between white supremacists and protesters in Charlottesville, Virginia. Few want to face the wrath of angry Trump-supporting primary voters, though. And the more the mainstream media attacks Trump, the more his supporters dig in. Fox News has become an integral element of the Party of Trump.

By most measures, Trump seemed in a precarious place in spring of 2018. Robert Mueller, the special prosecutor investigating the president's possible ties to Russia during the 2016 campaign, was pushing forward on several fronts, the porn star Stormy Daniels was suing the president for defamation, several of his cabinet members had been caught in various scandals, his friend and former lawyer Michael Cohen's office had been raided by federal law enforcement officers, and one gaffe after another suggested the White House was in turmoil. Even so, Trump supporters remained resolute. Stanley Greenberg, one of the nation's premier pollsters, conducted a series of in-depth interviews in May of 2018 with voters in Macomb County, Michigan, a place Barack Obama won by 16 points in 2008, but Trump won by 12 points in 2018. He found no buyer's remorse among Trump supporters. They were pleased that the president continued his no nonsense approach, that he was a true patriot and was determined to make America great again. And what about the massive tax cut, his signature policy achievement of his first two years? "The Trump voters are constantly looking for evidence that they cast the right vote, yet the tax cut barely came up when talking about good things about Trump. There are much bigger, more defining issues for Trump voters, like immigration."[61]

Conclusion: Is There a Unifying Theory of Today's Electoral Alignment?

Not very long ago, scholars were poised to jettison the very idea of partisan realignments. Voters were less willing to link themselves to a partisan badge, and their voting behavior underscored their ambivalence. Split-ticket voting had shot up to record levels. Party control of the White House, Congress and state legislatures shifted back and forth, voters of a single state would select a member of one party to be their governor and of another party to be their senator. Dealignment seemed more apt than any sort of long-term party dominance. Demographic-based partisan coalitions seemed a thing of the past, too.

As noted throughout this book, however, the headline of contemporary American politics is about bourgeoning partisan polarization and the reemergence of powerful electoral coalitions – key elements of critical realignment theory. In fact, speculation regarding the new electoral order has been recurrent, and the 2016 presidential election added fuel to the fire. One analyst commented, "Political realignments are inevitable and natural transformations [that] clear away underbrush, and give way to new periods of growth [and] frenzied periods of activity."[62] Others caution against premature assertions. "Realignments are not made by proclamations by rabid partisans who desperately want to believe they occurred."[63] In any event, the fundamentals of partisanship and electoral coalitions have been redefined.

This chapter has explored the shifting coalitions, ranging from the widening gender gap to the movement of working-class white voters away from Democratic ranks. We know that while the 2016 election may have been the culminating event, big changes have been underway for some time – a process scholars call secular realignment. A nagging question remains: Is there some sort of coalescing force? For the New Deal alignment, class and economic issues were foundational. The Democratic Party became an umbrella for the working class and anyone who thought government should take steps to provide a basic standard of living for all Americans, and the Republican Party represented business interest and policies that promoted personal freedom, as opposed to big government.[64] In large measure, nevertheless, the two parties were moderate and heterogeneous, leading to a lower level of polarization than we see today. The two sides were often able to find common ground, as evidenced by lower party unity scores in Congress and the passage of many important pieces of legislation with bipartisan support. The first truly significant piece of legislation since World War II to pass on a party-line basis was Barack Obama's Affordable Care Act in 2010.

Are there forces or issues that form a foundational element of contemporary electoral politics? In particle physics, a unifying theory is an attempt to describe all the fundamental forces and relationships between elements in a single model. Is there a unifying theory to define today's electoral alignment?

A growing chorus of scholars and pundits believe attitudes toward race and immigration have redefined electoral coalitions. This argument – that partisanship and electoral dynamics are now largely defined by attitudes toward race – was detailed in a powerful book in the wake of Obama's election by Michael Tesler, dubbed *Post-Racial or Most Racial?*[65] This idea was echoed in Levitsky and Ziblatt's *How Democracies Die.* The provocative, disturbing hypothesis is that the key event shaping today's electoral politics happened more than 50 years ago when Congress passed the 1964 Civil Rights Act and the 1965 Voting Rights Act. The breakdown of the New Deal Coalition began a few decades earlier (recall our discussion of 1948), but these acts solidified the idea that Democrats were the civil rights party, and Republicans were the party of the status quo. The shift has been ongoing ever since.

The evidence supporting a race-centered realignment is robust, as noted throughout this chapter and at many points in the book. There is certainly a geographic component, with the resettlement of southern whites (especially men) to the Republican Party, a move that was hastened by the recurrent use of the southern strategy by many GOP presidential candidates. Bill Clinton, a "new Democrat," with a thick southern drawl, was able to slow the exodus and win several southern states in 1992, but the dam broke with the election of Barack Obama. The Great Recession coincided with Obama's move into the White House, and the popular narrative at the time was that the Tea Party movement, which sprang to life almost immediately after Obama's election, centered on dislocated blue-collar workers. The economy had shifted, and they were being left behind. But that may not have been the disturbance that propelled such anger and hostility. Any move that the Obama Administration made, including many that would aid working-class citizens, was vehemently opposed by Republicans. Republican Senate Leader Mitch McConnell's proclamation that his number one priority was to make Obama a one-term president accentuated the anger. Through a historical lens, many of Obama's policies were moderate, certainly not hyper-liberal. As most know, for example, the highly contentious individual mandate component of the Affordable Care Act was an idea hatched years earlier by a conservative think tank. But that did not matter. It seems unlikely that Obama's policies explain the asymmetric partisan polarization discussed in the previous chapter.

It was later revealed that the motivating force behind the Tea Party was not economic dislocation per se, but fears about changes in society and, in particular, concerns about race and immigration. In an extensive four-year study, a team of scholars found that attitudes about race were intimately linked to support for the Tea Party. In one rather simple experiment, pictures of Barack Obama with a different skin tone were shown to subjects. Those seeing the picture with Obama's face darkened were twice as likely to express support for the Tea Party than those who saw the picture of Obama with a lighter skin tone.[66] They write, "The Tea Party emerged during a period when white Americans' political power was threatened by the election of Barack Obama, their majority status was threatened by a rising minority population that received wide media coverage, and the Great Recession increased their economic insecurity, a factor previously shown to catalyze racial threats."[67]

It is within this context that the birther movement was formed. In spite of unequivocal evidence (including a copy of a Hawaiian birth certificate), huge numbers of Americans came to believe that Barack Obama was not a legitimate president, nor a "real" American, because he was not born in the United States. Donald Trump made the transition from a New York City Democrat, with questionable moral values and allegedly shady business practices, to the darling of the far right, which included Evangelical Christians, by being a steadfast champion of the birther movement even after many on the far right had abandoned the sham.

It bears repeating that the foremost issues for Trump voters – the issues that were mentioned more often than any other – were concerns about race and immigration. Most observers thought Trump's campaign would be over before it began when he called immigrants from Mexico "rapists and murderers" in his campaign announcement speech. Did he not understand electoral and demographic trends? One analysis found that while the perception of one's personal finances had little impact on vote choice, attitudes toward blacks and immigrants had a strong influence.[68] What is more, as the 2018 midterm elections neared, Mike Allen, co-founder of AXIOS, a political news and information website, noted new polling data found a near perfect relationship between voter attitudes toward race and immigration, and support for Trump.[69] In the final days of the campaign, Trump's speeches were laced with what many called race and immigration dog whistles. He repeatedly asserted that there was a caravan of dangerous immigrants poised at the southern border – and even went so far as to call up the military to thwart their "assault." The Democrats, he said, were for "open borders." He also falsely claimed that the Democrats were funding the caravan. One of his television ads was deemed so racist that it was pulled from most stations, including Fox.

We might note that Fox News is an essential piece of the Trump coalition, but only 1 percent of their viewership during primetime hours is black, compared to roughly 25 percent for most other cable news programs.[70] In the summer of 2018, their anti-immigration, anti-diversity message seemed overt. "What [Fox is] doing rather consistently is promoting ideas that derive from white nationalist places," noted Angelo Carusone of *Media Matters*. "It's moved beyond a wink and a nod."[71] A particular program on Fox drew wide attention. Laura Ingraham, one of the channel's most popular commentators, aired a segment on August 8, 2018, that laid the issue bare. "[I]n some parts of the country it does seem like the America we know and love doesn't exist anymore. Massive demographic changes have been foisted upon the American people, and they're changes that none of us ever voted for, and most of us don't like."[72] There was a backlash after the program, with one journalist noting, "Fox News is peddling white Christian fear of change – of losing power. It is one of the same veins that President Trump taps." Democratic Senator Tammy Duckworth of Illinois tweeted, "These comments from Laura Ingraham aren't just racist, they're wrong & shouldn't have been aired by Fox."

Moves to limit access to the polls in recent years, either by eliminating early voting or by mandating strict voter ID laws, disproportionally impact black Americans. Georgia Congressman John Lewis, an icon of the civil rights era, described these moves as a "modern day poll tax."[73] Republicans have been in charge in every state where these laws have been enacted.

One might also recall from the previous chapter that as the Obamas were leaving the White House, a full 40 percent of Republicans gave the First Lady a "0" on a scale from zero to 100. No First Lady has ever received lower approval scores from members of the opposing party. What did Michelle Obama do to raise such ire from Republicans?

Through a historical and comparative perspective, a team of scholars offer a stark assessment: Trump's election represents the intersection of polarized two-party politics, the erosion of democratic norms, and a polity divided over who should be members in the political community.[74] Through his "hostile comments about members of specific ethnic and religious groups during the presidential campaign, to the Muslim ban, his pardon of former Maricopa County, Arizona, Sheriff Joseph Arpaio, ... to his response to the 'Unite the Right' rally in Charlottesville, Virginia, [Trump] has given license to political forces that vociferously and publicly spurn these developments."[75] As noted by Thomas Edsel of the *New York Times*, "Trump's demonization of nonwhites was and remains essential to his takeover of the Republican Party."[76]

As Barack Obama was running for the presidency in the fall of 2008, an old sage of the House of Representatives, John Murtha, a Democrat, said out loud what many were thinking: "We cannot deny that race is a factor in this election."[77] He was not referring to the Deep South or even to border states but, rather, to his district in Western Pennsylvania. An outpouring of criticism pushed him to retract the comment, but Murtha had spent a career representing coal miners, farmers and steel workers. He knew white working-class Americans.

It is certainly not the case that all or even a majority of Trump supporters are driven by racial animus – just as the New Deal Coalition was not solely bound by working-class voters. As with the Tea Party followers, issues of race and immigration are mixed, often unconsciously, with a host of other concerns and motivations – many quite justified. In the spring of 2018, Pulitzer Prize–winning historian Jon Meacham published *The Soul of America* in an attempt to steady anxieties during the tumultuous first year of the Trump Administration. Don't worry, we've been through this before, Meacham argued. America will survive this heated, confrontational period. It is just that "extremism, racism, nativism and isolationism, driven by fear of the unknown tend to spike in periods of economic and social stress – periods like our own."[78]

Notes

1 Haley Britzky, "Flake: Never has a Party Fled Beliefs as Quickly as GOP under Trump," *Axios Media,* March 15, 2018 (www.axios.com/jeff-flake-trump-administration-2f1d8c16-3a0a-4df6-931d-5685fe0c5190.html).

2 Jonathan Martin, "Across Midwest, Farmers Warn of GOP Losses Over Trump's Trade Policy," *New York Times* website, April 18, 2018 (www.nytimes.com/2018/04/18/us/politics/trump-tariffs-china-soybeans-midterms.html).

3 Ibid.

4 April Kelly-Woessner, "Trump's Departures from GOP Policy May Signal Realignment," *Lancaster Online,* April 1, 2018 (https://lancasteronline. com/opinion/columnists/trump-s-departures-from-gop-policy-may-signal-realignment/article_276ef912-3391-11e8-b2d9-bba05957b138.html).

5 *Washington Post Fact Check,* "President Trump has Made 4,229 False or Misleading Claims in 558 Days," August 1, 2018.

6 Perry Bacon, Jr., and Dhrumil Mehta, "Republicans are Coming Home to Trump," *FiveThirtyEight,* February 16, 2018 (https://fivethirtyeight.com/ features/republicans-are-coming-home-to-trump/).

7 *The Economist,* "Donald Trump's Takeover of his Party is Near Complete," *The Economist* website, April 19, 2018 (www.economist.com/briefing/2018/ 04/19/donald-trumps-takeover-of-his-party-is-near-complete).

8 Ibid.

9 Quoted in Alan Brinkley, *The End of Reform: New Deal Liberalism and War* (New York: Alfred A. Knopf, 1995), 16.

10 "Moving Right Along? Campaign '84's Lessons for 1988: An Interview with Peter Hart and Richard Wirthlin," *Public Opinion,* December/January 1985–86, 8.

11 Large portions of this section first appeared in John K. White and Daniel M. Shea, *New Party Politics,* 2nd Edition (New York: Cengage Press, 2003).

12 Gallup poll, August 3–8, 1951. Text of question: "Suppose a young person just turned 21, asked you what the Republican party (Democratic party) stands for today – what would you tell them?" The number-one Republican response, 16 percent, was "for the privileged few, moneyed interests." The number-one Democratic response, 19 percent, was "for the working man, for the public benefit, for the common man."

13 V.O. Key, Jr., "A Theory of Critical Elections," *Journal of Politics* 17 (February 1955), 3–18.

14 V.O. Key, Jr., "Secular Realignment and the Party System," *Journal of Politics* 21 (May 1959), 199.

15 Walter Dean Burnham, *Critical Elections and the Mainsprings of American Politics* (New York: W. W. Norton, 1970), 10.

16 Kevin P. Phillips, *The Emerging Republican Majority* (New Rochelle, New York: Arlington House, 1969), 25.

17 John K. White and Daniel M. Shea, *New Party Politics: From Jefferson and Hamilton to the Information Age* (New York: Bedford/St. Martin's, 2000).

18 Everett C. Ladd, "Realignment? No. Dealignment? Yes," *Public Opinion,* October/November 1980, 55.

19 Walter Dean Burnham, "Realignment Lives: The 1994 Earthquake and Its Implications," in Colin Campbell and Bert A. Rockman, eds., *The Clinton Presidency: First Appraisals* (Chatham, New Jersey: Chatham House Publishers, 1996), 370.

20 White and Shea, *New Party Politics,* 2000.

21 Danielle Paquette, "The Unexpected Voters Behind the Widest Gender Gap in Recorded Election History," *Washington Post* website, November 9, 2016 (www.washingtonpost.com/news/wonk/wp/2016/11/09/men-handed-trump-the-election/?utm_term=.c3e198cd3200).

22 Alec Tyson and Shiva Maniam, "Behind Trump's Victory: Divisions by Race, Gender, Education," *Pew Research Center* website, November 9, 2016

(www.pewresearch.org/fact-tank/2016/11/09/behind-trumps-victory-divisions-by-race-gender-education/).

23 James Hohmann, "The Daily 202: 10 Midterm Takeaways," *Washington Post*, November 7, 2018.

24 Hubert H. Humphrey, "1948 Democratic National Convention Address," July 14, 1948 (www.americanrhetoric.com/speeches/huberthumphey1948dnc.html).

25 Bob Herbert, "An Empty Apology," *New York Times* website, July 18, 2005 (www.nytimes.com/2005/07/18/opinion/an-empty-apology.html?mtrrref=undefined&assetType=opinion).

26 Bill Marsh and Marjorie Connelly, "Dissecting the Midterm Exit Polls," *New York Times* website, November 6, 2010 (https://archive.nytimes.com/www.nytimes.com/interactive/2010/11/07/weekinreview/07marsh.html).

27 Nate Cohn, "Southern Whites' Loyalty to GOP Nearing That of Blacks to Democrats," *New York Times* website, April 23, 2014 (www.nytimes.com/2014/04/24/upshot/southern-whites-loyalty-to-gop-nearing-that-of-blacks-to-democrats.html).

28 K.K. Rebecca Lai, Alicia Parlapiano, Jeremy White, and Karen Yourish, "How Trump Won the Election According to Exit Polls," *New York Times* website, November 8, 2016 (www.nytimes.com/interactive/2016/11/08/us/elections/exit-poll-analysis.html?mtrrref=undefined).

29 Clare Malone and Harry Enten, "Barack Obama Won the White House, But Democrats Lost the Country," *FiveThirtyEight,* January 19, 2017 (https://fivethirtyeight.com/features/barack-obama-won-the-white-house-but-democrats-lost-the-country/).

30 David Klion, as noted in David Leonhardt, "A Smashing National Win," *New York Times*, November 7, 2018.

31 Tiffany Stanley, "The Last Frontier for Gay Rights," *Washington Post* website, April 2, 2018 (www.washingtonpost.com/news/style/wp/2018/04/02/feature/the-last-frontier-for-gay-rights/?noredirect=on&utm_term=.dd1d18a72a48).

32 Clare Malone and Harry Enten, "Barack Obama Won the White House, But Democrats Lost the Country," *FiveThirtyEight*, January 19, 2017 (https://fivethirtyeight.com/features/barack-obama-won-the-white-house-but-democrats-lost-the-country/).

33 As cited in John K. White and Daniel M. Shea, *New Party Politics: From Jefferson and Hamilton to the Information Age* (New York: Bedford/St. Martin's, 2000), 28.

34 White and Shea, *New Party Politics*, 2000, 37–38.

35 Jeffrey M. Stonecash, *Class and Party in American Politics* (Boulder, CO: Westview Press, 2000), 2.

36 Clinton Lawrence Rossiter, *Parties and Politics in America* (Ithaca, NY: Cornell University Press, 1964), 89.

37 Nate Cohen, "How Broad, and How Happy, is the Trump Coalition?" *New York Times*, August, 2018 (www.nytimes.com/interactive/2018/08/09/upshot/trump-voters-how-theyve-changed.html?hp&action=click&pgtype=Homepage&clickSource=story-heading&module=first-column-region&region=top-news&WT.nav=top-news).

38 Ibid.

39 Andrew Gelman, Boris Shor, Joseph Bafumi, and David Park, "Rich State, Poor State, Red State, Blue State: What's the Matter with Connecticut?" *Quarterly Journal of Political Science* 2 (2007), 355.

40 Matthew Yglesias, "What Really Happened in 2016, in 7 Charts," *Vox*, September 18, 2017 (www.vox.com/policy-and-politics/2017/9/18/16305486/what-really-happened-in-2016).

41 As cited in Dan Balz and Michael Scherer, "For Democrats, A Midterm Election that Keeps on Giving," *Washington Post*, November 9, 2018.

42 Niraj Chokshi, "Trump Voters Driven by Fear of Losing Status, Not Economic Anxiety, Study Finds," *New York Times* website, April 24, 2018 (www.nytimes.com/2018/04/24/us/politics/trump-economic-anxiety.html).

43 Daniel Cox, Rachel Lienesch, and Robert P. Jones, "Beyond Economics: Fears of Cultural Displacement Pushed the White Working Class to Trump," *Public Religion Research Institute* website, May 9, 2017 (www.prri.org/research/white-working-class-attitudes-economy-trade-immigration-election-donald-trump/).

44 Niraj Chokshi, "Trump Voters Driven by Fear of Losing Status, Not Economic Anxiety, Study Finds," *New York Times* website, April 24, 2018 (www.nytimes.com/2018/04/24/us/politics/trump-economic-anxiety.html).

45 Daniel Cox, Rachel Lienesch, and Robert P. Jones, "Beyond Economics: Fears of Cultural Displacement Pushed the White Working Class to Trump," *Public Religion Research Institute* website, May 9, 2017 (www.prri.org/research/white-working-class-attitudes-economy-trade-immigration-election-donald-trump/).

46 Thomas Frank, *What's the Matter with Kansas? How Conservatives Won the Heart of America* (New York: Metropolitan Books, 2004), 67–68.

47 Ibid., 17.

48 Ibid.

49 Ibid., 13.

50 Ibid.

51 Mark Leibovich, "Palin Visits a 'Pro-America' Kind of Town," *New York Times* website, October 17, 2008 (https://thecaucus.blogs.nytimes.com/2008/10/17/palin-visits-a-pro-america-kind-of-town/?mtrref=www.google.com).

52 Bernd Debusman, "Real vs Unreal Americans," *Reuters website*, October 29, 2008 (http://blogs.reuters.com/great-debate/2008/10/29/real-vs-unreal-americans/).

53 Morris Fiorina, *Disconnect; The Breakdown of Representation in American Politics* (Norman, OK: University of Oklahoma Press, 2009), 38.

54 Andrew Sullivan, "Goodbye to All That: Why Obama Matters," *The Atlantic* website, December 2007 (www.theatlantic.com/magazine/archive/2007/12/goodbye-to-all-that-why-obama-matters/6445/).

55 Theda Skocpol and Vanessa Williamson, *The Tea Party and the Remaking of Republican Conservatism* (New York: Oxford University Press, 2012), 7.

56 Steven Levitsky and Daniel Ziblatt, *How Democracies Die* (New York: Crown Publishing Group, 2018), 158.

57 *The Economist,* "Donald Trump's Takeover of His Party is Near Complete," *The Economist* website, April 19, 2018 (www.economist.com/briefing/2018/04/19/donald-trumps-takeover-of-his-party-is-near-complete).

58 Hunter Schwarz, "The Many Ways in Which Donald Trump Was Once a Liberal's Liberal," *Washington Post* website, July 9, 2015 (www. washingtonpost.com/news/the-fix/wp/2015/07/09/ths-many-ways-in-which-donald-trump-was-once-a-liberals-liberal/?utm_term=.436c280415b2).

59 *The Economist,* "Donald Trump's Takeover of His Party is Near Complete," *The Economist* website, April 19, 2018 (www.economist.com/briefing/2018/ 04/19/donald-trumps-takeover-of-his-party-is-near-complete).

60 Ibid.

61 Stanley Greenberg and Nancy Zdunkewicz, "Macomb and America's New Political Movement: Learning from Obama-Trump Working Class Voters in Macomb and Democratic Base Groups in Greater Detroit," *Democracy Corps*, May 7, 2018 (https://static1.squarespace.com/static/582e1a36e58c62cc 076cdc81/t/5af05743f950b7ef0550767f/1525700420093/Macomb%20 %26%20America%27s%20New%20Political%20Moment_Democracy%20 Corps_May%202018.pdf).

62 Ryan Bohl, "Donald Trump May Be Causing The Long-Awaited American Political Realignment," *Medium,* August 1, 2017 (https://medium.com/ u-s-politics-made-super/donald-trump-may-be-causing-the-long-awaited-american-political-realignment-74557d8ca25d).

63 Stan Collender, "Did Donald Trump Start a Political Realignment in the US?" *Forbes* website, November 6, 2016 (www.forbes.com/sites/stancollender/ 2016/11/06/did-donald-trump-start-a-political-realignment-in-the-us/ #5f3a5eb255ba).

64 April Kelly-Woessner, "Trump's Departures from GOP Policy May Signal Realignment," *Lancaster Online,* April 1, 2018 (https://lancasteronline. com/opinion/columnists/trump-s-departures-from-gop-policy-may-signal-realignment/article_276ef912-3391-11e8-b2d9-bba05957b138.html).

65 Michael Tesler, *Post-Racial or Most-Racial?: Race and Politics in the Obama Era* (Chicago, IL: University of Chicago Press, 2016).

66 Robb Willer, Matthew Feinberg, and Rachel Wetts, "Threats to Racial Status Promote Tea Party Support Among White Americans," *Social Science Research Network,* April 28, 2016 (https://papers.ssrn.com/sol3/papers. cfm?abstract_id=2770186).

67 Ibid.

68 Charles Prysby, "The Republican Appeal to Working-Class Whites in 2016," Department of Political Science University of North Carolina at Greensboro, Conference on the State of the Parties: 2016 and Beyond, November 9–10, 2017.

69 These comments were made on the MSNBC program, *Morning Joe*, on August 10, 2018.

70 Matt Wilstein, "Only 1% of Fox News Viewers Are Black," *Mediaite* website, December 15, 2014 (www.mediaite.com/tv/only-1-of-fox-news-viewers-are-black/).

71 These comments were made on a CNN program aired on August 9, 2018. They were echoed in a piece published on the Media Matters for America website, dubbed "White Supremacy on Fox News," August 10, 2018 (www. mediamatters.org/).

72 Greg Price, "Laura Ingraham Airs Racially Charged Segment," *Newsweek*, August 9, 2018 (www.newsweek.com/ingraham-race-charged-fox-warned-1066570).

73 As cited in Steven Levitsky and Daniel Ziblatt, *How Democracies Die* (New York: Crown Publishing Group, 2018), 184.

74 Robert Lieberman, Suzanne Mettler, Thomas B. Pepinsky, Kenneth M. Roberts, and Richard Valelly, "Trumpism and American Democracy: History, Comparison, and the Predicament of Liberal Democracy in the United States," *Social Science Research Network*, August 29, 2017 (https://papers.ssrn.com/sol3/papers.cfm?abstract_id=3028990).

75 Ibid.

76 Thomas B. Edsall, "President Trump is a Very Political Animal," *New York Times* website, May 24, 2018 (www.nytimes.com/2018/05/24/opinion/trump-animals-immigrants-politics.html?action=click&pgtype=Homepage&clickS ource=story-heading&module=opinion-c-col-left-region&region=opinion-c-col-left-region&WT.nav=opinion-c-col-left-region).

77 Rebecca Sinderbrand, "Murtha Apologizes for Calling Western Pennsylvania 'Racist,'" *Cable News Network* website, October 16, 2008 (www.cnn.com/2008/POLITICS/10/16/murtha.racism.apology/).

78 Jon Meacham, *The Soul of America: The Battle for Our Better Angels* (New York: Random House, 2018).

7 The Nomination Process

Are Party Nomination Contests Too Democratic?

As the 2010 midterms grew near, Democrats seemed in a precarious place. Barack Obama was in the White House and the president's party nearly always loses seats in midterm elections. Even more important, Obama's push for the Affordable Care Act had polarized the nation and mobilized the opposition. The Great Recession continued to cause real pain and stir high anxieties. Republicans generally turn out in higher numbers in midterms, and the so-called enthusiasm gap was huge this time. They had lost the presidency two years earlier, but the GOP stood poised to cripple Obama's agenda of "change" by winning the House and Senate. It was going to be a big year for the GOP.

And it was. Republican gains were historic. Obama called the election a "shellacking." They picked up 63 seats in the House, one of the largest swings since the Great Depression, as well as a whopping 680 state legislative seats – which would become critically important as the congressional redistricting process moved forward. Although they gained six seats in the Senate, their goal of retaking that chamber fell short, nevertheless. What was different about the Senate? How did the Democrats stem the tide in the upper chamber of Congress?

In a way, the explanation stretches back to the Progressive Movement – more than one hundred years earlier. As local party organizations became omnipotent during the second half of the 19th century, savvy political operatives understood that they could control the reins of government by controlling nominations. By hand-picking who would be listed under the party banner during the general election, party bosses could rule the roost. No matter how many citizens turned out to vote or how much pressure they might put on an official once in office, by selecting party nominees local leaders had a stranglehold on public policy. This helps explain why there were so few protections for workers and so few public services during the Industrial Revolution – that is to say, the bosses were in the pockets of the industrialists.

In order to strip party bosses of the ability to control nominations, the direct primary was introduced. Under this system, average party followers go to the polls to select their party's nominee. There were a few controls limiting who might be on the primary election ballot, usually the collection of petition signatures, but anyone could run for the nomination and by appealing to the rank-and-file they could get on the general election ballot. This process – the direct primary system – added a great deal of legitimacy to elections even though the vast majority of nominees received a plurality (and not a majority) of votes cast in these primaries. Most party identifiers were moderate and they picked middle-of-the-road candidates. In other words, general elections rarely boasted extremists on either side because they were weeded out in the primaries.

How things have changed. As will be seen below, primary elections have low turnout, which can allow a small group of highly motivated citizens to control the outcome. In the 2010 primary contests, the 800-pound gorilla was the Tea Party. In several states, Tea Party followers picked controversial, deeply conservative Senate candidates. For example, the Republican nominee in Delaware was Christine O'Donnell. She had run for the seat two years earlier, winning just 35 percent of the vote. She had no real experience in public life, had massive financial problems, had made several campaign finance violations and was even caught on television saying that she had dabbled in witchcraft. One of the most seasoned GOP campaign operatives, Karl Rove, said that she was unelectable. But her Tea Party credentials were impeccable, as was her anti-Obama rhetoric. In the primary, O'Donnell narrowly defeated a popular, nine-term member of the House who most analysts believed had a good chance of winning the general election. O'Donnell lost the general election in a landslide. The same process was played out in several other states.

Jump ahead to 2017. A special election was held in Alabama to fill the Senate seat vacated by Republican Jeff Sessions when he became US Attorney General. Donald Trump had won the state with 62 percent of the vote, so most analysts assumed it would be an easy win for the Republicans. The Democrats picked Doug Jones, a former US Attorney, to be their nominee. He was smart, articulate and well-respected but clearly a long-shot candidate given the partisan leanings of the state. The Republican primary pitted the sitting incumbent, Luther Strange (who was appointed to fill the seat until the election) and Roy Moore, the former Chief Justice of the State Supreme Court. Strange was endorsed by an overwhelming number of Republican leaders in Alabama and in Washington, but Moore was the darling of Evangelical Christians. Years before he was found in contempt for not removing a marble monument of the Ten Commandments from the state courthouse. As the race progressed, several media outlets, led by the *Washington Post*, disclosed that Moore had dated teenage girls when he was in his 30s. One of the girls was just 14 at the time, far below the age of legal consent. Even so, Moore won the nomination. It was too much for Alabama general election voters, and they sent Jones to office – a stunning upset for Republicans.

Beyond winning or losing particular elections, the larger issue in an age of hyper-polarization, sorted communities and lower turnout is if the primary system sends ideological extremists to office. We have said throughout this book that the number of moderates in government has shrunk to record lows, leading to gridlock in Congress and cynicism among the public. Much of this springs from primary elections. Even those in office are loath to upset the ideological wing of their party, given how animated and mobilized they can become and how likely they are to vote on primary day. There is a vanishing number of swing (competitive) general election seats, but that does not mean officials are not worried about losing. The true threat to their hold on power comes during the primary election.

Scholar Robert Boatright penned *Getting Primaried: The Changing Politics of Congressional Primary Challenges* in 2013. Among much else, he finds the reasons incumbents get challenged in primaries has changed. In the not-so-distant-past, the most frequent reason for a strong primary challenge to an incumbent was a scandal or incompetence. In the last two decades, however, the foremost reasons for a primary challenge is ideological purity: "[T]he predominance of ideological challenges is unmistakable ... More than half of current House incumbents have been in office for ten years or less, and their tenure has been marked by a steady increase in the number of ideological challenges, so perhaps it is more natural for them to worry more about being primaried than it would be for longer-serving representatives."[1] Boatright also finds that ideologically driven interest groups have discovered primaries are a good way to advance their cause. "Precisely because congressional primaries are often low-visibility, low-spending affairs, the activities of one group can make far more of a difference than is the case in a general election."[2]

Unlike most democracies across the globe, nominations in the United States are a free-for-all. Party leaders used to be able to exert a level of influence through nomination conventions (where in some states the party's endorsement eliminates or reduces the number of signatures needed to get on the primary ballot), or by tapping into a legion of activists to help particular candidates. There was a modest, but real, gatekeeping function. Today, determined candidates – propelled by a single issue, ideological fervor or a small group of supporters – storm nomination contests and win, often with a plurality. Moderate voters, who often make up a majority in a district, are left choosing the lesser of two evils in the general election.

This chapter deals with another important party function: the mechanism for picking which candidates will appear on the general election ballot under the party's banner; the process of deciding who will be the Democrat and who will be the Republican on the ballot. For voters, party nominations narrow choices on Election Day. Without nominations, they might confront dozens or even hundreds of candidates on the ballot.

In the 2003 California recall election for governor, for example, some 135 candidates appeared on the ballot because party nominations were not used. This was a rare occurrence, but a vivid demonstration of why nominations are necessary. How we might best structure the winnowing process has been a contentious topic in recent years. As will be seen below, the oft-cited solution of simply opening up the process may not be the answer.

Variations in the Nomination Process

The direct primary first emerged in Crawford County, Pennsylvania in 1842. Frustrated by a series of contentious nominating conventions that left their local party divided and out of office, Crawford County Democrats sought a way to nominate candidates who would have public legitimacy and would unite the party behind a single candidate.[3] This approach caught on throughout the rest of the nation. Many urban areas were controlled by corrupt party machines and the direct primary proved a powerful weapon for reformers. The Democratic Party dominated southern politics following the Civil War, and the direct primary was introduced as a way to encourage competition in an otherwise one-party region.[4] The Progressive Party added support for the direct primary to its platform around the turn of the 20th century, arguing that more involvement implied a healthier democracy. By 1920, direct primaries were used in nearly every state and every community across the nation.[5]

Not every state and municipality uses the same primary system, however. On the contrary, the diversity of approaches is significant. "It is probable," wrote William J. Keefe and Marc J. Hetherington, "that no nation has ever experimented as fully or fitfully with mechanisms for making nominations as has the United States."[6] In 2018, 22 states used what is called a closed primary system.[7] This is where only registered party members are allowed to vote in the primary. In some states, the declaration of one's party registration must occur well in advance of the primary election – often 30 days – while in other states it can be done on primary day. The latter is sometimes called a partial- or semi-closed system. Either way, states that rely on this system mandate that only those who have registered with the party can play a role in selecting its nominees. You must be a Republican to pick the Republican nominee, a Democrat to select the Democratic candidate.

Most of the other states use an open primary system, where voters are allowed to participate in the primary election without declaring a party membership. On primary day, voters can simply choose to vote in the Republican primary or the Democratic primary, and no record is kept. But how might non-members choose a party's nominee? The courts have weighed in on this issue. In the 2017 case of *Hawaii v. Nago*, the Supreme Court found that open primaries do not infringe upon the party's freedom of association. The court also agreed with the government's claim that open primaries bolster the democratic process by making voting easier and by being more inclusive.

A few states – California, Washington, Alaska and Nebraska – have explored how open their systems might be. Several years ago "blanket primaries" were introduced. This is where voters are allowed to participate in the primaries of both parties at the same time. For example, an Alaskan might vote in the Republican primary for governor and the Democratic contest for the Senate – in the same election. These states were responding to desires for a less partisan system, but leaders of the major parties were not pleased, as you might expect. For one, they argue crossover voters in blanket primaries could sabotage the opposition by supporting an inferior candidate. There is little hard data to support his claim, sometimes called the "strategic voter," but many party operatives can point to anecdotal evidence of strategic crossover voting. Second, and more to the point, blanket primaries completely strip the nomination process from the party organization, so non-party members, even non-partisan voters, can pick the nominees for a party.

Several parties in California challenged the blanket primary system on the grounds that it was a violation of free association rights under the 1st Amendment of the Constitution. It was a step beyond open primaries, they argued. The Supreme Court case was *California Democratic Party, et al. v. Jones* (2000). The parties argued that they are private organizations, comprised of their own members, and that blanket primaries allow non-members to decide the groups' leaders (candidates). One observer summed it up this way: "I am not a member of the Rotary Club, or the Kiwanis, or Ruritan, or Lions, or any other organization of that kind. And I would not claim to have any right to tell them who their leaders should be. Why should a Democrat or Independent have the right to tell Republicans, for example, who have formed a party, who their leaders should be?"[8] Among other things, this intrusion would have detrimental impacts on the long-term viability of party organizations, a harmful turn for democratic politics, they argued.[9] The Supreme Court agreed. Writing for the majority of the Court, Justice Antonin Scalia stated:

> [California is] forcing political parties to associate with those who do not share their beliefs. And it has done this at the crucial juncture at which party members traditionally find their collective voice and select their spokesman ... The burden [California's primary system] places on [the political parties'] rights of political association is both severe and unnecessary.[10]

Since the court's decision, these states have scrambled to find a system that meets the new judicial muster and satisfies the desire for a truly open primary system. The outcome has been to jettison party-based nominations altogether. In 2004, voters in the state of Washington passed a ballot initiative to create a "top two" nomination process. Here, any number of candidates are allowed to run in an initial contest, but only the top two are placed on the general election ballot. These two candidates might be of a different party, or they might not. Louisiana has had a similar system for many years. In 2010, voters in California made a similar switch. Then Governor Arnold Schwarzenegger, a supporter of California's proposition 14, said, "[A top-two primary] will reduce the power of the political parties and give it back to the people, which is exactly where it belongs."[11] On the other hand, Libertarian Party Chair Mark Hinkle suggested, "This top-two system will shut out all but two voices in our November elections, which are the elections that count. Now more than ever, we need more political voices and broader representation on the November ballot, but this proposition will do just the opposite."[12]

The change has been controversial, to say the least. The far-and-away front runner in the 2018 California gubernatorial primary was Lt. Governor Gavin Newsom, a Democrat. But a second place finisher was uncertain and for a period it looked as if it might go to another Democrat – meaning that the general election would pit two candidates of the same party against each other. In the end, Republican John Cox came in second, averting a shut-out for the Republicans. Many were also paying close attention to several congressional primaries where a crowded field on both sides might have led to members of the same party running against each other. The Democrats were eyeing six House districts held by Republicans but won by Hillary Clinton in 2016. As primary day approached one scholar noted, "It has the feeling of one of those civil wars in the Middle Ages, where the king is fighting against barons and there's multiple alliances that form and collapse. It's a lot less straightforward than just you got your Democrat, you got your Republican. It's sort of organized chaos."[13]

One final model, used in Mississippi and Louisiana, is sometimes called a jungle primary. Here, the primary election occurs on the same day as the general election and there are often a large number of candidates on the ballot. If one candidate receives more than 50 percent of the vote, the election is over. But if no candidate gets more than 50 percent, the top-two participate in a head-to-head runoff election a few weeks later.

The Special Case of Presidential Nominations

Given that our political system began without political parties, and that there were great hopes that parties would not take hold, presidential nominations were deemed unnecessary. It was assumed that several states would advance their favorite son and that men of high intellect and good character would somehow rise to the top. Members of Congress would then suggest a small set of candidates for the Electoral College to consider, and the right leader would emerge. This congressional-based nomination system was used for three decades and was so important in selecting the eventual president that it became known as King Caucus.

Within a few decades the elitism of this system became evident, and many began to push for a different approach to better reflect the will of average voters. The outcome was the national presidential nominating convention. The idea was that delegates from across the nation would convene in one city to discuss the strengths and weaknesses of potential candidates and, after a few days, settle on a candidate – the party's best hope for the general election. It would also be an opportunity to develop a party platform, or list of policies that the party supports, as well as rules for conducting party business. The major parties held their first national conventions in 1832 and have done so every four years since – usually in late summer before the presidential general election.

The birth of the national nominating convention was an important turning point in the history of popular elections in America. Reflecting on this change, a prominent scholar noted, "The destruction of the caucus represented more than a mere change in the method of nomination. Its replacement by the convention was regarded as removal from power self-appointed oligarchies that had usurped the right to nominate … Sharp alterations in the distribution of power were taking place [in the 1830s], and they were paralleled by the shifts in methods of nomination."[14]

This is not to say the early convention model was completely democratic. One of the sticking points was how delegates would be chosen from their communities and the role they would play at the convention. A few states developed mechanisms to let average party members (also called the rank-and-file) select delegates, but most simply allowed state and local party leaders to hand-pick them. Once at the convention, these delegates were obliged to follow the dictates of their local party leader. This often led to high drama, as party bosses used their delegates as negotiation chips, looking to play a central role in nominating the candidate – that is, they used them to play the role of kingmaker. Rules were established to mandate that successful candidates – the eventual nominees – had to receive at least 50 percent of the delegate votes. Given that several candidates were usually under consideration, this process often resulted in numerous ballots and high drama. It took the Democrats 103 ballots in 1924, for instance, to finally decide on John Davis of West Virginia for their nominee. Conventions were about selecting the presidential nominee and making deals. This system, often referred to as the days of smoke-filled rooms, lasted for nearly 140 years.

The strain between party bossism and the role of average party followers came to a head in a fight over the 1968 Democratic presidential nomination. Early that year, most had assumed that the sitting President, Lyndon Johnson, would accept his party's nomination, but there was a groundswell of opposition to Johnson over the escalation of the Vietnam War. He decided to step out of the race after narrowly winning the first primary in the nation, in New Hampshire (a contest that should have been a blowout). A sharp division emerged between the party leaders, who then backed Vice President Hubert Humphrey, and the anti-war Democrats, who supported either Minnesota Senator Eugene McCarthy (not to be confused with Joseph McCarthy of Wisconsin, leader of the anti-communist witch hunts of the 1950s), who had challenged Johnson in New Hampshire, or New York Senator Robert Kennedy. As the nomination season progressed, Kennedy and McCarthy drew wide support, yet the party bosses continued to back Humphrey, who did not enter any of the state primary contests. Kennedy's assassination after winning the California primary added a greater sense of urgency to anti-war Democrats. Faithful to their local party bosses, delegates at the nomination convention in Chicago nominated Humphrey, but thousands of anti-war Democrats filled the streets in protest outside the convention hall. To make matters worse, Mayor Richard Daley of Chicago, one of the nation's top Democratic bosses, ordered his police to break up the protests, and the violence of the clash was broadcast to living rooms across the nation. Although he won the nomination, Humphrey went on to lose the general election against Richard Nixon. The Democratic Party seemed to be in shambles.

A reform panel was established, called the McGovern–Fraser Commission (after its two chairmen, Senator George McGovern of South Dakota and Congressmen Donald Fraser of Minnesota). Their eventual report, *Mandate for Reform*, forever changed the way presidential nominations would be conducted for both parties. The report argued that the nomination process must be "open, timely, and representative." A number of mechanisms were devised to achieve these goals, the most important pertained to the process of selecting delegates. Binding primaries were established in most states. Similar to the direct primary, this is where voters head to the polls to pick delegates who are pledged to support a particular candidate. The winners in each state are sent to the convention, where they vote to nominate a candidate. These delegates are bound to support the candidate that they were pledged to during the primary (at least for the first ballot). Party leaders are removed from the process.

Another way to pick delegates, used in about 15 states, is a nomination caucus. Here average party followers attend a local meeting, share ideas and concerns about particular candidates, and cast a ballot for delegates to attend a state-wide meeting. The same process takes place and the delegates who win at the state level are sent to the national party convention. The key difference between primaries and caucuses is that the former is an election and the latter a series of town-hall-like meetings. The outcome is the same: bound delegates are sent the national convention.

The Republican Party was not obligated to follow any of these reforms made by the Democrats, but the general public soon became convinced that the old system was corrupt. Binding primaries and caucuses seemed to be a fairer, more legitimate process, so the GOP followed suit. There are key differences between the two parties, often in the same state. For example, in Maine, Republicans use a mix of a primary and a caucus, but Democrats rely on a caucus only. Generally speaking, the model proposed by the McGovern–Fraser Commission has become the overarching framework for both parties.

A subsequent Democratic commission recommended the proportional allocation of delegates. This meant that if a candidate netted 25 percent of the vote from a state, he or she should get 25 percent of the delegates. The Republicans, on the other hand, leave it up to the state, where some are proportional and others rely mostly on a winner-takes-all system. If a candidate wins the state, he or she gets all the delegates from that state. For Democrats, this commission also led to the creation of a special category of participants called superdelegates. Here, 15 percent of Democratic convention delegates are chosen by party leaders. The idea was to select elected officials, such as mayors, members of Congress, and state legislators, so they would come to the convention and bond with other party officials. Superdelegates did not have to declare their support for a candidate until the convention. The Republicans never adopted a similar category of delegates.

While many agree that nominations should not be held in smoke-filled rooms, the current system has problems, to be sure. Opening the primaries to the entire population may have helped with transparency, but it is not clear if the primary system has become a true reflection of the electorate. At the top of the list of concerns, primary elections are notorious for low turnout. Even in the record-setting 2008 elections, few states recorded a primary or caucus turnout of greater than 30 percent of the eligible population.[15] In the 2016 presidential nomination contest, also a drawn-out, rough-and-tumble affair, just 26 percent of Americans participated. Gubernatorial and municipal primary elections have turnout rates that rarely break double digits.

A related concern is that the current nomination process might *not* reflect the will of average party members because those who turn out to vote or attend a caucus might be different than average party followers. Scholars have been debating this issue for some time. For example, political scientist John G. Geer has found that primary voters for both parties are less educated and earn less money than regular party followers.[16] On the other hand, several years ago, scholar Alan Abramowitz suggested that on an ideological measure, primary voters and general election voters were very similar.[17] This surely bucks traditional wisdom, which suggests that only the most ideological members of the party turn out to vote in primary elections. There may be party differences, with Republican voters more conservative than the average GOP follower.[18] Evidence from the 2014 House and Senate primary contests suggests the wings of each party are more engaged during these contests than moderates. In nearly a dozen contests, for example, moderate Republicans were knocked off by more conservative, often Tea Party-backed, candidates.

Do delegates to presidential nomination conventions reflect the views of general election voters? In a famous study of delegates attending the 1972 Democratic and Republican conventions, political scientist Jean Kirkpatrick found them to be largely unrepresentative of the American electorate: 56 percent of the Democratic delegates had a college degree or more; 59 percent of the GOP delegates also had college degrees.[19] At the time, only 13 percent of the electorate had a college degree or more.[20] Given this data, it was not surprising that George McGovern, the most liberal Democrat nominated for the presidency since William Jennings Bryan in 1896, received the Democratic nomination in 1972.

In a more recent time-series study conducted by political scientists John Jackson and John Green, the convention delegates were found to be much more polarized on ideology and numerous political issues than the general public. While the Democratic delegates were more liberal than the Republican delegates, the Democrats were spilt – between liberal and moderate factions. Republicans fit rather well under the conservative label. The authors also asked about social welfare, foreign policy, and cultural issues to study the polarization of the parties' elites. The delegates supported their respective party platform and showed that some factions do occur within the party.[21]

It seems clear that those who attend a presidential nomination *caucus* are more ideological than the average party follower. Quite often, for example, the winner of the nation's first caucus, held in Iowa, is more liberal or conservative than most of the other candidates. There is also evidence to suggest rank-and-file party followers understand the limits of caucuses. Using data from the Cooperative Congressional Election Study, scholars Christopher Karpowitz and Jeremy C. Pope find that "compared to primaries, caucuses are seen by many voters as being less fair and more likely to advantage special interests, making them less representative, and more likely to attract more partisan voters. This in turn means that caucuses are more likely to select a more extreme nominee."[22]

The presidential nomination process has become very expensive, time-consuming, and negative. Historically, candidates who can raise the most money (especially those who can do it quickly) have a significant advantage. This money can be used to attack the other candidates – who are all part of the same party, of course. Some of the harshest attacks against presidential candidates occur during the primaries, not in the general election. On top of this, candidates able to garner media attention before and during the primary season do much better – unfairly advantaging well-known candidates. The process is drawn-out, but at the same time puts a premium on winning early primary and caucus contests – which, of course, helps raise money and draw media attention. Many argue that states like New Hampshire and Iowa, which hold their nomination contests early in the process, are given a disproportionate role in selecting the eventual nominee. For the 2020 presidential election, fundraising began two years out. Some observers claim that, barely half a year into Donald Trump's first term, the so-called "invisible primary" had already begun for the Democratic nomination. "The modern process of running for president – 24 months of nonstop fundraising, travel, and relinquished privacy – is so unpleasant and degrading that it requires something like a personality disorder to submit to it."[23]

Much has been made of Bernie Sanders' and Donald Trump's ability to do well without early endorsements and big money donors, but they were exceptions to the rule. Sanders tapped into a groundswell of dissent on the left and used social media to raise a large chest of funds, as will be discussed in a subsequent chapter. Trump used his celebrity and a unique style to flood the airways and fill newspapers. His use of earned media was without precedent, and by some estimates totaled upwards of $5 billion worth of air time.[24] Much of this coverage centered on his recurrent attacks on his Republican rivals.

The current system allows anyone the opportunity to run for office, and while this might seem like a good idea, many believe there should be some sort of screening mechanism. To put it a bit differently, in today's system anyone with a hefty bank account, a degree of celebrity and a team of slick campaign consultants can run for office and do quite well regardless of their knowledge, experience, background, and character. One could argue, for example, that Alabama Governor George Wallace, an outspoken segregationist, might have been able to mount a bid for the White House in 1968 through the Democratic Party if not for the screening function performed by party leaders. As will be discussed in a subsequent chapter, he was widely popular in the South and the upper Midwest, and had a national approval rating of 40 percent. With plurality contests and a multi-candidate field, Wallace might have done surprisingly well. In the conclusion of their book on radical-right politics in the United States, renowned scholars Seymour Martin Lipset and Earl Raab argue that the "chief practical bulwark" against extremist candidates has party leaders performing this screening function.[25] The inability of the Republican establishment to halt the rise of Donald Trump has again brought this issue to the forefront.

The early start of the presidential election process has led to what is called front-loading – moving the state's nomination contest up in the election calendar in order to be relevant to the final outcome. In the 2000 election, for example, by March Texas Governor George W. Bush and Vice

President Al Gore had essentially locked up the Republican and Democratic nominations, respectively, while voters in 33 states had not yet cast their primary ballots.[26] If presidential nominations are essentially over after a few early contests, why not move your state's primary or caucus up in the calendar? Many states have done just that. The 2008 pre-primary season saw an intense leapfrog contest, leading to a dramatic rearrangement of the primary calendar, week after week. Both Iowa and New Hampshire have passed legislation protecting their first-in-the-nation status, and the Democratic National Committee continues to support these states. Democratic National Committee rules stipulated that no state should hold its nomination contest before Iowa and New Hampshire, at the risk of having its delegates barred from the national convention; the DNC went so far as to strip half of the delegates of Michigan and Florida because these states scheduled their events in January (under DNC rules, only Iowa, New Hampshire, South Carolina, and Nevada are allowed a January primary). Despite the many threats and regulations, the 2008 primary leapfrog contest quickly took on aspects of the absurd. One state would schedule its nominating contest earlier, only to be leapfrogged by another state – and in response, the first state would again move up its date.

The results were nothing short of chaos. Commenting on the state of the presidential nomination process in 2008, Anna Quindlen in *Newsweek* suggested the system had become "piecemeal, arbitrary, even downright wacky, turning the nation's most important task into a jerry-built mess."[27] South Carolina, for example, decided to move its contest earlier in order to have the distinction of being the first primary in the South. Nevada made a similar move. But in spring of 2007, Florida changed its primary date to January 29, reasoning, why shouldn't Florida be the first in the South? In response, both South Carolina and Nevada pushed their dates even earlier in order to be ahead of Florida.

Several additional problems sprang from this turbulent leapfrog process. It put even more pressure on the early stages of the nomination process and led to an unprecedented early campaign season. Nearly all candidates in both parties had declared their intentions to run a full 18 months before the general election in 2016. No fewer than eight prominent candidates had dropped out of the race in 2015 – months before a single ballot took place.

One of the greatest shortcomings of the modern nomination process (for both presidential and non-presidential offices) is that it often leads to plurality winners. Just ten states use run-off primaries for state and local offices. Under this system, when all candidates in the race fail to net at least 50 percent of the vote, a follow-up contest, known as a "run-off election," is held between the top two. There is no similar mechanism in the presidential system. Worse yet, the Republicans use a winner-take-all system for plurality winners in nine states, and in another 12, candidates who do particularly well can trigger a winner-takes-all process.[28] In a crowded field, it is possible for a candidate with 25 or 30 percent of the vote to net all of the delegates. This is possible in 21 states.

Conclusion: Are Party Nomination Contests Too Democratic?

Is the current nomination process too demanding on candidates and downright harmful to the electoral process? Many people are beginning to question the utility of the current system and to explore changes. The idea behind the open primary model was to broaden engagement and by doing so reduce the weight of extremists in government. With more voters coming out for primaries, the outcome would be general election candidates who better represent the middle of the ideological spectrum. This has become the panacea for many good-government activists.

There is some evidence to suggest it might work, at least when it comes to higher levels of engagement. Turnout in states with open primaries is roughly 8 percentage points higher than in states with closed systems,[29] mostly because they allow independents to play a role. But many scholars caution against reading too much into these numbers. For example, the states mostly likely to have open primaries are also those with higher numbers of independents. Would a similar increase in turnout be seen in partisan states? If the prerogative of party identifiers to pick their party's candidates is stripped, would they have less interest in turning out to vote in the general election? Also, there is a great deal of variance from state to state based on a host of idiosyncratic factors. Many of the open primary states are also those with the highest turnout in the general election, for instance. Another way to explore this issue is "before and after." Turnout in Hawaii actually dropped from about 70 to 50 percent when the state switched from a closed to open nomination system.[30] At best, the picture is mixed.

There may be some party-based differences, too. According to the nonpartisan United States Election Project, turnout in 2016 open presidential nomination contests was higher for Republicans than for Democrats. This may have been due to a surge in independents and working-class Democrats voting for Donald Trump.[31]

Then there are the issues of whether open primary states yield more competitive general election races and if voters in these states are more satisfied with their general election matchups. Regarding the competitiveness issue, scholars have been unable to find much direct evidence because, frankly, the sample is so small. Out of 435 congressional races, in recent years only about 60 have been competitive, making claims about competitive general elections in open systems tenuous. As to whether voters in open states are more satisfied with general elections matchups, here again, hard evidence is scant. Clearly, more scholarly work needs to be done on these issues.

Do voters from open primary states send more moderate elected officials to Congress or the state legislatures? Recent scholarship suggests there is no discernible difference in the ideological leanings of elected officials in open versus closed primary states. There is also no hard evidence to suggest that voters who turn out to vote in open primary states are more moderate than those who come out of closed primary states.[32] This may be because independents often report having strong preferences for one party or the other, while "pure" independents tend to turn out at lower levels than die-hard partisans.[33] What is more, because primaries in both open and closed states often see a large number of candidates, and usually only require a plurality to win (just ten states require run-off elections, as noted above), victorious candidates tend to be the ones who can corral a bloc of ideologically hard-core supporters. In other words, 20 or 30 percent of the most ideological voters in open state contests can propel their candidate to the general election.

Even if open primaries brought droves of moderate voters to the polls, such a process assumes that they can accurately discern the ideology of different candidates. In research on the impact of California's top-two model, a team of scholars found that voters failed to distinguish moderate and extreme candidates.[34] This would call into question the entire "open systems yield moderate winners" theory.

All told, there is little hard data to support the idea that opening the primary system would lead to more moderate public officials or middle-of-the-road policies. Theoretical notions about the ability of open systems to draw in more voters and to produce more moderate general election candidates abound, but the only clear empirical finding we might hang our hat on, at least at this point, is a modest bump in turnout.

We do know that scorn for the top-two model is one of the few bipartisan issues of our day – at least among elected officials. During the heat of the 2018 California contest, House Minority Leader Nancy Pelosi, a Democrat, said "This is not a reform. It is terrible," and House Majority Leader, Kevin McCarthy, a Republican, commented, "I hate the top-two."[35] Would it really be fair to moderate residents, for example, if the general election pitted one conservative candidate against another conservative? But again, there is a vague sense that open systems can help. Senate Minority Leader Chuck Schumer, a Democrat, was quoted as saying, "While there are no guarantees, it seems likely that a top-two primary system would encourage more participation in primaries and undo tendencies toward default extremism."[36]

It is worth brief mention that a growing number of independents (nonpartisan voters) balk at the creation of open primary systems. If one is truly interested in greater options on Election Day, as many independents hope, then funneling energy and time into a mechanism to enhance the standing of the two major parties would seem misguided. Most open primary systems invite independents to select a Republican and Democratic candidate. If the goal is additional options, perhaps a viable third party would be better. Would open primary systems curtail energy for other big changes? As noted by one observer, "A situation in which all primary elections were open would ... reinforce the notion that meaningful political participation occurs only within the major parties, and it would stymie efforts to build stronger third parties that can break the bipartisan control over not just elections, but over the entire political process."[37]

Regarding the presidential nomination process, all manner of reforms have been suggested, often dealing with the nomination calendar. Despite the official standing of Iowa and New Hampshire in the primary season among both Republicans and Democrats, there is increasing concern that these states have undue influence over the electoral process and that their voters have an unfair advantage over the rest of the country. One approach would be to have a national primary day. Just as with the general election, voters from across the nation would pick their party's nominee on a single day. To all intents and purposes, as front-loading increases, the country seems to be naturally moving in the direction of what amounts to a national primary, so why not formalize this process?[38] Many suggest that this plan would increase turnout because more people would feel that their vote could make a difference (recall that in the current system the nominee is often determined after a few weeks, leaving some states without a say in the process). But others have argued that the retail (meaning intimate, face-to-face) electioneering common in smaller states, particularly New Hampshire and Iowa, would be lost. In its place would be one massive national media campaign.

The so-called Delaware Plan would group four blocks of states according to population to determine the order of primaries. The smallest 13 states would go first, then the next 13, then 12 medium states, followed by the largest 12 states. States would remain free to decide between a primary and caucus and could schedule their event for any time during their appointed period. This plan addresses the problem of front-loading, and supporters argue that it would encourage voter participation and increase grassroots campaign efforts while giving small states – historically not influential – a chance to participate. On the other hand, opponents argue that in this plan money would still play a large role, and instead of a single winner, the plan could produce multiple winners in the many competitions. The main concern is that the four blocks would effectively be four media-centered campaigns.[39] Again, retail campaigning would be lost.

Under a rotating primary model the nation is split into four regions – Northeast, Midwest, West, and South. Each has about the same number of votes in the Electoral College, based on the most recent census. This plan has the same structure as the Delaware Plan; however, the blocks would rotate every presidential election, allowing different regions to be influential each time. The goal is to give all the candidates a fair chance by allowing voters to view them over a longer period of time, and therefore to let a more diverse group choose the frontrunners.

Another approach would be to determine the order of blocks by a lottery, and lead-off states (like New Hampshire and Iowa) would not be allowed. Scholar Larry Sabato argues, "The key to this plan is a lottery will be used to determine the order each region will participate in the nominating process. Because candidates are unable to know more than a few months in advance which region will lead off the calendar, home-steading is eliminated and candidates are forced to focus equally on all areas."[40] Another interesting idea is to order states based on the turnout of the previous presidential election. This would create an incentive for state officials to take steps to ensure higher levels of engagement, but the downside might be the zigzagging of candidates across the country.

One of the criticisms made by the Bernie Sanders campaign in 2016 was that the system was rigged in favor of insiders, like Hillary Clinton. Certainly part of this was the overwhelming number of superdelegates pledged to Clinton. In the wake of the election, several states made changes to open up the process to outsiders, like Sanders. One proposed reform was to bind superdelegates to the candidate that wins their state. As noted by one political scientist, "With reduced insider influence, increased openness to non-traditional voters, and a lack of an obvious next-in-line for the next presidential nomination contest, the Democratic Party may be more internally democratic in 2020 than ever."[41] During the summer gathering in 2018, the DNC greatly reduced the role of superdelegates. Several states have also jettisoned caucuses in favor of primaries.

Also in the wake of the 2016 contest, several ideas have been floated involving the precise role of the party conventions. Could parties use the primaries and caucuses to select a group of well-informed party activists who would go to the conventions to discuss, debate and compromise on the selection of the right candidate? This would reduce the role of money, as smart, experienced, but poorly funded candidates might find favor with some delegates, and it would certainly alter the front-loading element. Scholar Seth Masket of the University of Denver put the matter this way:

> Not too long ago, conventions were where parties actually made nominations. State parties selected delegates to go, but quite a few were either uncommitted or were committed to someone they knew wasn't interested in running and couldn't win. Shouting for different candidates wasn't considered a breach of decorum – it was part of how the convention reached a decision.[42]

It is illustrative, suggests Masket, that several of our greatest presidents, including Abraham Lincoln, were not in the top tier of candidates as their party's convention began. They were consensus candidates who helped bridge the gap between warring factions of the party. Instead of large segments of the party being disgruntled with the nominee, open, delibera-tive conventions allow for compromise, for coming together.

Most agree that the nomination process is not perfect, but does that mean we should go back to the boss-centered system? Most would balk at this, but at the same time there is an acknowledgment that the current system is rife with problems. Citizens are unenthused about their choices during the general election, and once in office, hyper-partisan officials are grinding the system to a halt. Changes designed to make the system more "open, timely and representative" have moved things in the right direction, but have also created a new set of issues. The decline of traditional news outlets and the rise of social media have shattered the parties' historic gatekeeping role. Levitsky and Ziblatt note, "While the rules of the game hardly guaranteed the rise of a Trump-like figure, they could no longer prevent it."[43] Conversely, one has to wonder whether some of our greatest presidents – like Abraham Lincoln, with his odd appearance and his shy demeanor, Franklin D. Roosevelt, bound to a wheelchair at a time when disabilities were less well received, and Ronald Reagan, who refused to see his opponents as the enemy – would have won their party's nomination in today's process?

Notes

1 Robert G. Boatright, *Getting Primaried: The Changing Politics of Congressional Primary Challenges* (Ann Arbor, MI: University of Michigan Press, 2013), 86.
2 Ibid., 55.
3 Essays by Howard Reiter, Robert Kolesar, J. Morgan Kousser, John F. Reynolds, Jon Enriquez, and Thomas Coens, "H-Pol's Online Seminar: The Presidential Nominating Process," *SSHA Politics Network New*, Fall 1996 (www.h-net.org/~pol/ssha/netnews/f96/reynol2.htm).
4 L. Sandy Maisel, *Parties and Elections in America: The Electoral Process*, 3rd Edition (Lanham, MD: Rowman & Littlefield Publishers, Inc., 1999), 193.
5 Ibid.
6 William J. Keefe and Marc J. Hetherington, *Parties, Politics, and Public Policy in America,* 9th Edition (CQ Press: Washington, DC, 2003), 59.
7 "State Primary Election Types," *National Conference of State Legislatures,* July 21, 2016 (www.ncsl.org/research/elections-and-campaigns/primary-types.aspx#Partially%20Closed).
8 Andy Schmookler, "Open Primaries: A Wrong Idea," *HuffPost,* June 15, 2016 (www.huffingtonpost.com/andy-schmookler/open-primaries-a-wrong-id_b_10471396.html).
9 John K. White and Daniel M. Shea, *New Party Politics: From Jefferson and Hamilton to the Information Age,* 2nd Edition (Belmont, CA: Wadsworth, 2003), 218.
10 503 U.S. 567 (2000). See also the Associated Press, "Supreme Court Throws Out California's Blanket Primary," June 26, 2000.
11 Arnold Schwarzenegger, "Press Release: Governor Schwarzenegger Discusses New Era of Government with Passage of Proposition 14," *Office of the Governor,* June 11, 2010.

12 "Libertarian Party Chair Mark Hinkle Opposes Proposition 14," *Independent Political Report,* June 3, 2010 (www.independentpoliticalreport.com/2010/06/libertarian-party-chair-mark-hinkle-opposes-proposition-14/).

13 Andrew Prokop, "California's 'Top Two' Primary Chaos, Explained," *Vox* website, June 5, 2018 (www.vox.com/2018/5/29/17381244/california-elections-2018-top-two-primaries).

14 V.O. Key Jr., *Politics, Parties and Pressure Groups,* 4th Edition (New York: Thomas Y. Crowell, 1958), 373.

15 Drew Desilver, "Turnout was High in the 2016 Primary Season, But Just Short of 2008 Record," Pew Research Center, June 10, 2016 (www.pewresearch.org/fact-tank/2016/06/10/turnout-was-high-in-the-2016-primary-season-but-just-short-of-2008-record/).

16 John G. Geer, "Assessing the Representativeness of Electorates in Presidential Primaries," *American Journal of Political Science* 32 (November 1988), 929–945.

17 Alan Abramowitz, "Don't Blame Primary Voters for Polarization," *The Forum 5,* 2008 (www.themonkeycage.org/Abramowitz.Primary.Voters.pdf).

18 Matt Grossmann and David A. Hopkins, "Why Primary Elections Scare Republican Politicians More than Democrats," *Vox* website, September 14, 2016 (www.vox.com/polyarchy/2016/9/14/12905660/primary-elections-scare- republicans).

19 Jeane J. Kirkpartick, *Dismantling the Parties* (Washington, DC: American Enterprise Institute, 1978).

20 American National Election Studies, "ANES Guide to Public Opinion and Behavior, 1948–2016" (https://electionstudies.org/resources/anes-guide/top-tables/?id=4).

21 John Jackson and John C. Green, "The State of Party Elites: National Convention Delegates 1992–2008" in John C. Green and Daniel J. Coffey, eds., *The State of the Parties: The Changing Role of Contemporary American Parties,* 6th Edition (Lanham, MD: Rowman & Littlefield, 2011).

22 Christopher F. Karpowitz and Jeremy C. Pope, "Compared to Primaries, Caucuses are Less Representative and More Likely to Select an Ideologically Extreme Nominee," *London School of Economics US Centre,* April 27, 2015 (http://blogs.lse.ac.uk/usappblog/2015/04/27/compared-to-primaries-caucuses-are-less-representative-and-more-likely-to-select-an-ideologically-extreme-nominee/).

23 John Frederick Martin, "Our Broken Presidential Nominating System," *The New Republic,* February 24, 2016 (https://newrepublic.com/article/130396/broken-presidential-nominating-system).

24 Philip Bump, "Assessing a Clinton Argument that the Media Helped to Elect Trump," *Washington Post* website, September 12, 2017 (www.washingtonpost.com/news/politics/wp/2017/09/12/assessing-a-clinton-argument-that-the-media-helped-to-elect-trump/?utm_term=.29114cc3794a).

25 As noted in Levitsky and Ziblatt, *How Democracies Die,* 48.

26 "The Report of the National Symposium on Presidential Selection," The Center for Governmental Studies at the University of Virginia, 2001 (www.centerforpolitics.org/downloads/rnsps.pdf).

27 Anna Quindlen, "First Tuesday of Huh?," *Newsweek,* December 24, 2007, 68.

28 Seth Millstein, "Which States Have Winner-Take-All Primaries or Caucuses? Some Big Ones Are on The Horizon," *Bustle*, March 9, 2016 (www.bustle.com/articles/147024-which-states-have-winner-take-all-primaries-or-caucuses-some-big-ones-are-on-the-horizon).

29 United States Election Process, "2016 Presidential Nomination Contests Turnout Rates," 2016 (www.electproject.org/Election-Project-Blog/2016presidentialnominationconteststurnoutrates). "National Primary Turnout Hits New Record Low," *Bipartisan Policy Center*, October 10, 2012 (http://bipartisanpolicy.org/wp-content/uploads/sites/default/files/Summary%20Charts.pdf).

30 Darwin Peng, "Why Hawaii is a One-Party State," *Harvard Political Review* website, April 12, 2017 (http://harvardpolitics.com/united-states/why-hawaii-is-a-one-party-state/).

31 Molly Rockett, "Stark Trends towards Higher Republican Turnout, Lower Democratic Turnout in Open Primaries," *FairVote*, July 22, 2016 (www.fairvote.org/stark_trends_towards_higher_republican_turnout_lower_democratic_turnout_in_open_primaries).

32 Barbara Norrander and Jay Wendland, "Open Versus Closed Primaries and the Ideological Composition of Presidential Primary Electorates," *Electoral Studies* 42 (June 2016).

33 Samantha Smith, "5 Facts about America's Political Independents," Pew Research Center, July 5, 2016 (www.pewresearch.org/fact-tank/2016/07/05/5-facts-about-americas-political-independents/).

34 Douglas J. Ahler, Jack Citrin, and Gabriel S. Lenz, "Do Open Primaries Improve Representation? An Experimental Test of California's 2012 Top-Two Primary," *Legislative Studies Quarterly* 41 (May 2016).

35 Russell Berman, "'This is Not a Reform. It is Terrible,'" *The Atlantic* website, June 1, 2018 (www.theatlantic.com/politics/archive/2018/06/california-top-two-jungle-primary-democrats-republicans/561689/).

36 Ibid.

37 Andrew Gripp, "An Independent's Case against Open Primaries," *The Independent Voter Network*, May 4, 2016 (https://ivn.us/2016/05/04/independents-case-open-primaries/).

38 "The Report of the National Symposium on Presidential Selection," *The Center for Governmental Studies at the University of Virginia*, 2001 (www.centerforpolitics.org/downloads/rnsps.pdf).

39 Ibid.

40 Ibid.

41 Seth Masket, "How to Improve the Primary Process? Make It Less Democratic," *Pacific Standard* website, August 11, 2017 (https://psmag.com/magazine/how-to-improve-the-primary-process).

42 Ibid.

43 Steven Levitsky and Daniel Ziblatt, *How Democracies Die* (New York: Crown Publishing Group, 2018), 56.

8 Minor Parties in the United States
Can a Third Party Save Our Democracy?

The 2016 presidential election was unusual in a number of ways, as noted in the first chapter. Money played a very different role than in the past, one candidate shattered all sorts of rules about acceptable political behavior, social media became a huge factor, new voter coalitions brought a true outsider to office, a foreign government launched a cyberattack and much else. At the top of this list, Donald Trump and Hillary Clinton were probably the least-liked candidates ever to run for the presidency. By the end of the campaign, 52 percent had an unfavorable view of Clinton and 61 percent disliked Trump – the highest unfavorable ratings since polling began in the late 1940s. According to Gallup, "Even the former Alabama governor and proponent of racial segregation, George Wallace, who ran for president as a third-party candidate in 1968, did not earn a lower unfavorability score."[1] A *USA Today*/ Suffolk University Poll conducted in the waning weeks of the campaign found only 27 percent of Clinton supporters and 29 percent of Trump followers would be "excited" by their candidate.[2] It was, for many, a choice of the lesser of two evils.

We also know that while the number of Americans who are intensely partisan has grown in the past two decades, there is still a huge swath of Americans who consider themselves independent – that is, not affiliated with either of the two major parties. According to the Pew Research Center, in 2017 some 37 percent of Americans considered themselves independent, a figure that has grown over the years.[3]

One might imagine, then, that there would be clamoring for additional choices – for a third party or maybe even a full scale multi-party system in the United States. Sure enough, there is. In 2017, Gallup found a whopping six in ten Americans said that a third party is needed in our system. Twenty years ago, this figure was 40 percent. It jumps to 71 percent for those who consider themselves independent, and even half of those who say they are partisan (either Democrat or Republican) want a viable third party.[4]

If we want more choices on Election Day, why do minor parties languish in the American system? Has there ever been a period in

American history when minor parties played a significant role in the electoral process? Most other democratic political systems rely upon a multi-party model, so why does America seem fixed on the two-party approach?

This chapter confronts what we might call the minor party paradox. You will soon read that even though there may be support for a multi-party system, the persistence of a two-party model is likely. Furthermore, while some Americans might wish to shake things up with a third party, a prolonged change in that direction would wreak havoc. It is rather ironic that in their zeal to create a set of checks, balances and shared powers, so that no one individual or entity could have too much power, the constitutional framers propelled a two-party model.

Why Do We Have a Two-Party System?

Most democracies across the globe boast a multi-party model. Many, such as the United Kingdom, have recently been dominated by two major parties, but a multitude of smaller parties exert real influence. In most parliamentary systems a coalition of parties come together to form the "government" (majority party), and likewise others merge to form the "opposition." In the United States, no third-party candidate has ever won the presidency, nor has a third party ever controlled either branch of Congress. For the first two decades in the early part of the 19th century it is fair to say we had a one-party system (also referred to as the Virginia Dynasty after Jefferson, Madison and Monroe), and of course the Solid South was characterized by complete domination by the Democrats for over 100 years. There are a few additional nuances, as will be discussed in detail below, but the underlying reality is that two parties have ruled the roost in the American setting. Why are we different from most democracies across the globe?

Institutional barriers refer to legal components created by statute, court decisions, or the Constitution. The most significant of these is the single-member district, first-past-the-post system used for legislative elections in the United States. That is, legislative districts boast only one legislator – one elected official – and this person is sent to office by simply receiving more votes than any other candidate. They are sent to office with either a majority or a plurality. This process alone propels a two-party model, and here is how: one might imagine, for instance, that in the first election candidates from three parties vie for the office. One candidate nets 45 percent of the vote and the others about 27 percent each. Because the first candidate received more votes than the others, and because only one person can represent the district, that person is sent to Washington (or to the state capital). The losing parties get nothing for their efforts. This process might continue for a few elections, but eventually operatives of the two losing parties will consider joining forces – that is, if they are not too ideologically far apart. After all, their combined strength is greater than the other party's, so by working together they can win. A party might be ideologically pure and refuse to merge with another, but losing again and again gets old and the inclination to join forces with the party closest to them becomes irresistible. This is called Duverger's Law after the famous French sociologist Maurice Duverger who wrote about this phenomenon in the 1950s. In many European systems, legislative districts are multi-member and use proportional representation. This means that if a party receives 30 percent of the district's vote and the district sends three legislators to Parliament, then the party gets one seat. In that system, several parties get a reward for their efforts, but in the American model the losing team gets zip.

An example in contemporary politics would be the Green Party of North America. This left-leaning, environmentally-centered party has been plugging along in American politics for some time with little success at the ballot box. They might continue to slog through elections and build their grassroots organizations, but political groups need occasional wins to keep members. In the 2000 presidential election the Greens nominated consumer rights activist Ralph Nader as their candidate. Nader netted less than 3 percent of the popular vote, which is bad enough, but the real rub was that Nader's support seems to have tipped the scales to the Republican, George W. Bush. Because Al Gore, the Democrat, lost by a fraction of votes in several states, and by a fraction of Electoral College votes overall, it is entirely possible that he would have become President if Nader had withdrawn from the contest. Although Nader did so unintentionally, writes University of Wisconsin professor Barry Burden, he "nonetheless played a pivotal role in determining who would become president following the 2000 election."[5] To put it another way, many suggest that support for Nader helped elect the Republican – the candidate farthest away from the beliefs of the Greens. To be fair, many Greens argue that Gore lost the election for other reasons.

A third-party candidate's vote share has exceeded the winning candidate's margin of victory numerous times in the last century. While analysts disagree on the precise effects of these so-called election spoilers, it is reasonable to suggest that they played roles in shaping the outcome in many contests – often tilting things to the side least favorable to the minor-party voters. In the 2016 election, for instance, it is likely that the two leading minor-party candidates, Jill Stein of the Green Party and Gary Johnson of the Libertarian Party, may have shaped the outcome in several key states. Neither netted any significant numbers, but in several states Trump defeated Clinton by a whisker. For example, Stein and Johnson got a combined total of 220,400 votes in Michigan. Trump beat Clinton in that state by fewer than 16,000 votes. In Florida, Stein and Johnson received just under 300,000 votes – twice the margin of Trump's victory over Clinton.[6]

Another institutional barrier is the Electoral College. While the Constitution is vague on this point, 48 states have decided to allocate their electoral votes as a block – a "winner-takes-all" system. This is also referred to as the unit rule. The two states that do not are Maine and Nebraska, which allocate electors at the congressional district level, with the winner of the state-wide popular vote receiving an extra two electors. In order to have a chance of winning the presidency, a candidate has to win states outright; nothing is gained by running a strong second. A perfect example here would be Ross Perot in 1992, who netted 19 percent of the popular vote but not a single Electoral College vote because he did not win any state outright or any congressional districts in Maine or Nebraska. "Like the single-member district system, the winner-take-all feature of the Electoral College means that third parties have little chance of winning any state's electoral votes, let alone carry a sufficient number of states to elect a president."[7] Third-party candidates have won Electoral College votes only four times in the 20th century: in 1912 Theodore Roosevelt netted 88; in 1924 Robert La Follette got 13; in 1948 Strom Thurmond received 39; and in 1968 George Wallace picked up 46. One should bear in mind that 270 electoral votes are needed to win.

A third powerful institutional barrier to minor-party success is the public funding of presidential elections. Ever since the early 1970s, candidates for the presidency can receive federal funds for both their primary and general election campaigns, but not every candidate gets the same amount. Major party candidates, defined as those whose party received at least 25 percent of the popular vote in the previous election, are entitled to "full funding." Candidates from minor parties receive a much smaller amount and must have crossed a 5 percent threshold in the previous election to receive any help whatsoever. This creates a powerful self-fulfilling prophecy: without the money, minor-party candidates languish and generally fail to cross the 5 percent threshold, which, of course, bars them from getting federal funds for their next effort. It is very rare that minor parties receive federal funds. This has only occurred three times since the public financing system took effect: John Anderson, 1980; Ross Perot, 1996; and Pat Buchanan, 2000.[8]

While less recognized, the direct primary system has a powerful impact on maintaining the two-party model, too. It has been said that primary elections create a safety valve for the major parties. When a partisan voter gets upset with her party's candidates, she can vent her frustration in the primary by supporting someone quite different – but within the same party. Without primaries, upset voters would look elsewhere – that is, to minor-party candidates. As noted by a team of scholars, primaries are a "uniquely American institution" that "channel dissent into the two major parties."[9] A clear example would be Bernie Sanders, who has always labeled himself an independent, choosing to run for president in 2016 as a Democrat instead of a Democratic-Socialist or Progressive.

Finally, the two-party system is maintained by myriad state ballot access laws. States have an interest in limiting the number of candidates on a general election ballot. Would we really want voters to choose between 40 or 50, or perhaps even 100 candidates? Probably not, but what should be the restrictions for ballot access? Beginning at the turn of the 20th century, states devised schemes to limit the number of candidates, and at the same time make things easier for the major parties. After all, the regulations were being written by members of the two major parties. Generally speaking, parties whose candidates receive 25 percent in the previous election are automatically given a place on the ballot. Other parties have to gather petition signatures to be allowed a spot. In Pennsylvania, for example, minor-party presidential candidates must collect nearly 100,000 signatures in a 14-week period to be placed on the November ballot.[10] This is a time-consuming, difficult, and expensive chore that minor parties have to undertake but major parties do not. Writing in the *New Republic*, Micah Sifry suggests, "Today, third parties can't mount their own presidential bids after they learn whom the two major parties have nominated – there simply isn't enough time between the end of primary season and the general election to gain meaningful ballot access in enough states to win an Electoral College victory."[11]

Institutional barriers are not the only hurdles to minor-party success in America. The momentum of history is a powerful force, also. There has never been a prolonged period when the United States has had a multi-party model. Minor parties seem odd – the exception rather than the rule. It is more than simply a tautology to suggest that America has a two-party model because we have always had a two-party model. Much related, a powerful element in our political culture has generally been the acceptance of compromise and incremental change (although this may be changing). Americans do not expect dramatic changes in public policy, and there is evidence to suggest that we favor slow shifts and middle-of-the-road policies. This makes support for alternative parties, often thought of as more radical, less likely. Moreover, the United States has historically had a large middle class, at least in a comparative light. Many scholars believe that this mitigates against radical, class-based minor parties common in other countries.

Perhaps the greatest attitudinal snag is called the wasted-vote syndrome. Americans seem anxious to have their vote count – to make an actual difference in selecting who will serve in office. The media tells us that minor-party candidates usually stand little real chance of victory and, as a result, most Americans are reluctant to waste their vote. It is revealing that support for minor-party candidates often peaks several weeks before the election. As the day approaches, voters abandon the minor-party candidate, hoping to add their voice to the contest between the "real" candidates. This would also explain why so many Americans will tell pollsters that they want more parties, but at the same time minor-party candidates languish on Election Day. Both Stein and Johnson were polling near double digits in October of 2016, but on Election Day neither crossed the 5 percent mark. There is much to frustrate minor-party candidates and activists, but the wasted vote syndrome surely tops their list.

In summary, minor parties confront a hostile environment in the American setting. There are numerous laws and regulations that limit their chances for success, as well as deep-seated attitudinal factors that make matters worse. If support for additional choices remains high, it is conceivable that significant changes might occur, but chances are high that the United States will remain a two-party system.

Minor Parties in American History

This is not to suggest that minor parties play no role in the American system. Minor parties have sprouted up throughout American history and have changed the political landscape. This section takes a brief look at several of the more significant minor parties.

The Anti-Masons: Due in large measure to the Corrupt Deal between John Quincy Adams and Henry Clay, by the late 1820s, there was a wide-spread reaction against elite politics. This mood translated into, among other things, a potent minor-party movement and the development of the Anti-Masons. In nearly every community in the United States, there was a Masonic Lodge or Freemason organization. These were secretive clubs, boasting members from the social, economic, legal, and political elite of each area. Many prominent politicians were Freemasons, including George Washington, Henry Clay, and Andrew Jackson. Members were bound to secrecy concerning the goings-on of the group, which included their many rituals. In 1826, the backlash against these secretive, elite groups led to the creation of a political party.

By the 1830s, the Anti-Masons had organizations throughout the nation, but especially in New York and throughout New England. Their candidate in the 1832 presidential race, William Wirt, netted 8 percent of the popular vote and seven Electoral College votes (all from Vermont). Their efforts at the state level were more successful, however, as they won gubernatorial contests in Vermont and Pennsylvania, and numerous state legislative posts in New England. By the end of the 1830s, the party began to fade, due to the popularity of Democrat Andrew Jackson, who endorsed many of the Anti-Mason policies. The most lasting impact of the party came from its use of conventions to nominate presidential candidates.

The Free Soil Party: A number of abolitionist groups burst onto the scene in the years leading up to the Civil War. The most significant of these was the Free Soil Party, founded in 1848. That year, nearly 20,000 delegates converged at the party's nominating convention in Buffalo, New York. They nominated ex-president Martin Van Buren as their candidate and set off to spread the word, but on Election Day they garnered just 10 percent of the popular vote, nearly all from northern states. This did not translate into a single Electoral College vote, but in the next presidential election a new party, the Republicans, captured the support of many abolitionists. The Free Soil Party faded into the history books.

The American (Know Nothing) Party: Slavery was not the only major issue in the pre-Civil War period. Another burning concern, especially for urban blue-collar workers, was the influx of immigrants (mostly Irish Catholic). Jobs were scarce, and these newly arrived Americans were desperate enough to work for pennies. The American Party emerged as an openly bigoted group aimed at limiting the role of immigrants in economic and political life. Among other things, the party called for a 20-year residency requirement to earn the right to vote, and they wanted to bar immigrants from ever holding public office. The party's nickname became the Know Nothings after a reporter asked an operative about the goings-on of a meeting, who told him that he "knew nothing."

What is even more startling than the mean-spiritedness of this party is the level of success it achieved. In 1854, the American Party won scores of congressional and state legislative seats, mostly in the Northeast. In Massachusetts, for example, they won 347 of 350 state house seats, all of the state senate and congressional contests, and even the governorship.[12] A similar level of success was seen in New York, Rhode Island, New Hampshire, and Connecticut.[13] In the 1856 presidential election, the American Party netted a whopping 21 percent of the popular vote and eight Electoral College votes. Four years later, the party was split over the slavery issue and soon disappeared from the national scene. The popularity of the Know Nothing Party is one of the uglier tales of American electoral history.[14]

The Populist Party: Within a few decades after the Civil War, an agricultural depression gripped the nation. Farmers in the upper Midwest were especially hard hit. This was occurring at nearly the same time as the Industrial Revolution. Business owners, the so-called robber barons, were making fortunes in the burgeoning cities, often at the expense of the working class. Hardships and growing concerns about staggering inequities in wealth distribution led to the formation of several economic-based political parties, most notably the Populists.

The Populists, sometimes referred to as the People's Party, emerged in 1891. Their platform called for, among other things, the public regulation of railroads (given that commodities were shipped back east on railroads), the free coinage of silver (as a means to increase the amount of money in circulation), and the implementation of a graduated income tax. They nominated James Weaver as their presidential candidate in 1892, and he went on to capture 8 percent of the popular vote and

22 electoral votes, nearly all from Midwestern states. After that election the party's strength grew; by 1896 the Populists had become a force to be reckoned with. Its leaders realized, however, that their chance of picking up many congressional seats was small, and their hopes for capturing the White House just as distant. They opted to merge with the Democrats by endorsing William Jennings Bryan. After all, Bryan had endorsed much of the Populist agenda, and by working together the chances of victory in November were good.

The strategy did not work as Bryan was defeated by Republican William McKinley in a hard fought, close race. The Populist Party faded from the political scene. Many of their proposals were picked up by both the Democrats and the Republicans and were eventually adopted into law. Commenting on the role of parties like the Populists, political scientist Clinton Rossiter noted, "One of the persistent qualities of the American two-party system is the way in which one of the major parties moves almost instinctively to absorb (and thus be somewhat reshaped by) the most challenging third party of the time."[15]

The Progressives: On three occasions, a Progressive Party candidate had an impact on the electoral–political process. The first time was in the early part of the 20th century. The progressive movement had captured public attention and numerous reforms were being undertaken. But there was no party-based movement until Theodore Roosevelt was denied his own party's nomination in 1912. Four years earlier, Roosevelt, then the sitting president, decided to step aside and champion the nomination of his friend and Secretary of War, William Howard Taft. Taft was nominated by the Republicans and was sent to the White House. But Roosevelt became disappointed in Taft's failure to push the progressive agenda. He told his fellow Republicans that a mistake had been made and that he should receive the nomination in 1912. But parties are quite reluctant to deny a sitting president re-nomination, so despite Roosevelt's objections Republican bosses kept Taft on the ticket. Roosevelt and a group of his supporters stormed out of the GOP nominating convention and started a new party – the Progressive Party. Roosevelt was chosen as their nominee, of course. Declaring himself ready for the challenge, Roosevelt likened himself to a bull moose. The party quickly picked up the nickname of the Bull Moose Party.

Republican voters divided their support between Roosevelt and Taft. Roosevelt picked up 27 percent of the popular vote (88 Electoral College votes) and Taft 23 percent of the vote (eight electoral votes). Democrat Woodrow Wilson netted 42 percent of the vote and a whopping 435 electoral votes (due in large measure to the unit rule). Roosevelt's candidacy had, in effect, given the election to the Democrat; he played the role of the spoiler. The Bull Moose Party faded from the scene because of the loss, and Wilson picked up many of the progressive causes and was reelected rather easily four years later.

By the 1920s, progressive issues had once again captured the public's attention, and the party experienced a bit of a resurrection. In 1924, they held a presidential nominating convention and emerged with Robert La Follette, Sr., a firebrand reformer from Wisconsin, as their nominee. La Follette was a tireless campaigner and a splendid orator, but on Election Day he netted just 16 percent of the popular vote. The only state that he won was his own. Once again, the Progressive Party faded.

Finally, in 1948 the Progressive Party was again dusted off for a run at the presidency. That year a group of liberal Democrats came into conflict with their party's leader, President Harry Truman, and his "get tough" policy with the Soviet Union. Former Democratic Vice President Henry Wallace was picked as the Progressive candidate. His platform included, among other things, anti-lynching laws, scrapping the Electoral College, and a system of national health care insurance. Wallace drew large crowds and seemed to have a message that resonated with many Democratic voters. Yet on Election Day, he received just 2 percent of the popular vote, which nearly gave the election to the Republican, Thomas Dewey. The race between Truman and Dewey was extremely close in three states – New York, Maryland, and Michigan – and went to Dewey by a whisker. But for Wallace, Truman would have won these states and the Electoral College count rather handily. The same scenario played out in California, but in that case Truman was able to edge out Dewey and win reelection. The Progressive Party disappeared, this time, it would seem, for good.

The Segregation Parties: After World War II, two parties emerged in the South focused on the civil rights movement and the desire to maintain the status quo of racial segregation. The first, in 1948, was the States' Rights Party, also known as the Dixiecrats. Their nominee for the presidency was J. Strom Thurmond, then governor of South Carolina. He netted just 2.5 percent of the overall vote, but was able to win five southern states for an Electoral College total of 38. The party folded after the election. Thurmond switched his affiliation to Republican and went on to serve for nearly five decades in the US Senate.

Most assumed that the stir over the Dixiecrat Party was long gone, but in the fall of 2002 it returned to the front page. At Thurmond's retirement celebration, the sitting Majority Leader of the Senate, Republican Trent Lott of Mississippi, commented:

> I want to say this about my state. When Strom Thurmond ran for president, we voted for him. We're proud of it. If the rest of the country had followed our lead, we wouldn't have had all these problems over all these years, either.[16]

Given that Thurmond's candidacy was based on maintaining segregationist policies, Lott's comments seemed insensitive to most and outrageous to many. In the end, Lott was forced to resign his post as Majority Leader of the Senate.

The second segregationist party emerged in the 1968 election. George Wallace, then governor of Alabama, had flirted with a run for the White House as a Democrat four years earlier, but realized the chances of wrestling the nomination from Lyndon Johnson were slim. In 1968, he again saw the chances of a Democratic nomination as far-fetched, so he decided to organize a new party, calling it the American Independent Party. Wallace's proclamation of "segregation now, segregation tomorrow, segregation forever," made several years earlier, became the rallying point of his presidential bid. He also stressed a "law and order" platform, which echoed Nixon's "southern strategy," discussed in Chapter 6. On Election Day, Wallace won nearly 10 million votes nationwide, some 13.5 percent, and 46 Electoral College votes (all of which came from the Deep South). Wallace fell short of winning the election, but he did shape the outcome of the contest: By taking southern states out of the Democratic base, Wallace ensured the election of Republican Richard Nixon. The South could no longer be taken for granted by the Democrats, and, in fact, the 1968 election marked the end of Democratic presidential dominance in the region.

The American Independent Party dissolved after the election. Wallace threw his hat into the ring again in 1972, but this time as a Democratic candidate. Shortly after entering the race he was shot and paralyzed from the waist down. Wallace withdrew from the race and spent the rest of his life in a wheelchair. Before his death, in 1998, he accepted integration and recognized the profound injustices of his earlier segregationist policies.

As a parting note on George Wallace, it would be a mistake to assume his support was confined to the South. Numerous studies have revealed that he was quite popular in all regions of the country.[17] One account notes that his national approval rating in 1968 was 40 percent.[18] His backing was particularly strong among white ethnic groups in the industrial Midwest, places hard-hit by factory closures. As noted by *New York Times* journalist B. Drummond Ayers Jr., who covered the South for decades, "Wallace understood that there were people who were hurting, struggling, losing jobs. He tapped into that and appealed to that, because folks that are struggling often feel put upon."[19] Many have drawn a parallel to Donald Trump's appeal to votes in the same regions of the country: "The two men fired up crowds in similar fashion. Both appealed to 'forgotten' Americans, stoking fear and loathing of 'the other' – blacks in Mr. Wallace's case, immigrants in Mr. Trump's ... The message from both was that a nefarious other, enabled by a bumbling government, was stealing work and wealth from upright Americans."[20]

John B. Anderson and the 1980 Election: Often, minor-party efforts center on a particular candidate, such as with Teddy Roosevelt in 1912.

The same thing occurred in 1980 when a higher than average share of the vote went to a third-party and independent candidate. John Anderson netted 6.6 percent, the most since Wallace's 1968 run. Concerned and angry about the country's direction, many voters rejected Jimmy Carter, whom they saw as ineffective. Anderson, a moderate Republican congressman from Illinois, had initially sought the Republican nomination and had polled well in early primaries. But after Reagan secured the nomination, Anderson organized an independent bid for the presidency. He courted voters disillusioned with Carter but unwilling to embrace Reagan's conservatism; Anderson mainly appealed to moderate "Rockefeller Republicans" and independents in the Northeast, West, and near his home state of Illinois. Although he polled as high as 25 percent early in the contest,[21] Anderson – in keeping with the pattern followed by most third-party candidates – saw his numbers drop consistently until Election Day.[22]

The Reform Party: Another significant third effort in presidential politics was the Reform Party. In 1992, many Americans seemed unsure about the two major party candidates, sitting President George H.W. Bush and Arkansas Governor Bill Clinton. Rumors began to spread of a third potential candidate, Texas billionaire H. Ross Perot. Excitement grew and Perot soon announced that he would enter the race if volunteers would secure his name on the ballot in all 50 states. This was soon done and Perot entered the fray. Although polls showed the Texan doing well, and in fact leading the pack at points throughout the early summer, Perot withdrew his candidacy by August. In yet another surprise move, he reentered the race in October. By then Perot's popularity had waned and on Election Day he netted 19 percent of the popular vote, which did not translate into a single Electoral College vote. Most analysts agree that his support had little effect on the outcome of the race and that the second choice of Perot voters divided equally between Clinton and Bush.

Perot's political star seemed to keep a bit of its luster after the election, unlike many minor-party candidates. Instead of fading from the scene, Perot decided to put his efforts into creating a viable third party – the Reform Party. Two issues lay at the heart of the Reform Party: cleaning up the electoral system (removing big money from the process) and reducing the federal deficit. Perot entered the 1996 presidential contest and, of course, received his own party's nomination. This time he netted just 8.4 percent of the vote – and again not a single electoral vote. The party struggled after the election, due mostly to the absorption of their issues by the two major parties. Jesse Ventura, a former professional wrestler, shocked the political establishment with his successful run for the Minnesota governorship as a Reform Party candidate, but he broke ties with the party shortly after he was elected. The party nominated a candidate in the 2000 election, but he received just 1 percent of the popular vote. The Reform Party has since withered away.

The Tea "Party" or "Tea Party Movement": Not long after the election of Barack Obama, conservative activists across the country began to organize. By the summer of 2009, a new group had been formed – dubbed Tea Party Activists. The "tea party" was a reference to the Boston Tea Party in 1773, when the Sons of Liberty stormed merchant ships docked in the Boston Harbor and threw tons of imported tea over the side as a way to protest the newly imposed "tea tax." The 2009 group set their sights on what they perceived to be the growing scope of the federal government under Democratic control, particularly the economic stimulus bill and the proposed health care reform initiative. The group's membership list swelled, as did its coffers. By February of 2010, the group held its first convention, with their keynote speaker being none other than former Alaska Governor Sarah Palin. The event was widely covered by the media.

There was no doubt that the Tea Party had a dramatic impact in the 2010 election. They moved quickly to organize local chapters, raise money, and endorse conservative candidates in Republican primaries. Roughly half of the Tea Party – endorsed candidates were successful in these GOP primaries that year, most notably US Senate candidates Christine O'Donnell of Delaware, Joe Miller of Alaska, and Sharron Angle of Nevada. Yet many of these candidates, including O'Donnell, Miller and Angle, lost the general election. By most accounts, the results of the 2010 election were mixed for the Tea Party. The question of whether this group would shift toward the development of a third party or remain a movement within the Republican Party seemed unclear. Many, including Palin, argued that they should remain Republicans, but others argued a clean break was needed. By 2016, most Tea Party activists had fallen in line with the GOP nominee, Donald Trump.

Minor Parties at the Local Level

Although most studies on the viability of minor parties have focused on national party organizations, few have attempted to chart local minor-party dynamics. There are many state-based case studies, such as those dealing with Bernie Sanders of Vermont, Angus King of Maine, Jesse Ventura of Minnesota, and Joe Lieberman of Connecticut, but it is difficult to make general assessments from these few works.

The problem with using the nation as the unit of analysis is that it is likely that local, state, or regional nuances tend to be lost. While it is true that minor parties and third-party candidates face an uphill battle everywhere in the United States, they clearly do better in some states and in some communities than in others. We might take, for example, Ross Perot's election results in 1992. Perot ran a nationwide campaign. There is little evidence to suggest that this targeted particular states or regions. Given his widespread use of earned and paid network television (his oft-cited "infomercials"), one would be hard pressed to discern a particular geographic focus. Nationwide, Perot received 19 percent. When we look at his state-level returns, a great deal of variance emerges. In some states, his share of the vote languished far below the national average: Arkansas (10%), Georgia (13%), Louisiana (12%), Mississippi (9%), Tennessee (10%), and so on. But in other states, Perot's percentage was much larger than the national average: Alaska (28%), Idaho (27%), Kansas (27%), Maine (31%), Nevada (26%), Oregon (24%), Washington (24%), and Vermont (23%), among others. Some of this variation was likely due to Perot himself, but it seems likely that a good bit was centered on differences in voter receptivity to minor-party candidates in local political cultures.

It is revealing that the correlation between Perot's state-by-state vote share in 1992 and Ralph Nader's share of the vote as a Green Party candidate in 2000 and in 2004 is rather high. Perhaps both candidates were reformers of sorts; the similarities are limited beyond this. But in most respects, they were very different candidates, appealing to different constituencies, pushing a unique set of issues. What would explain this surprisingly high state-based correlation?

Several years ago, two scholars, C. Dan Myers, of the University of Minnesota, and the author of this text, created an "index of minor party support" based upon three important factors:

Major Party Dynamics: Likely one of the most important forces shaping minor-party success is the overall party culture. A host of studies detail significant differences in state and local party dynamics. On the most basic level, certain states have a tradition of aggressive party activity while others do not. Local party organizations in some communities are vastly more "present" than in other communities. The degree to which the major parties claim the allegiance of average voters (i.e., the number of hard-core partisans) is also an important part of local electoral culture. Furthermore, in some communities voters are accustomed to highly competitive elections, where Democratic and Republican candidates stand on an equal footing. Here we would expect the wasted vote syndrome to be *more* significant. In other communities, one party dominates.

Institutional Factors: As noted above, institutional factors are key to maintaining the two-party system throughout America. Yet not all of these factors are the same in every state. The first-past-the-post, single-member-districts system and the Electoral College (setting aside Maine and Nebraska) are universal, but other laws and regulations are state-specific. As noted in a previous chapter, the direct primary system allows anyone to run in a primary with or without the blessing of party leaders. As scholars John Bibby and L. Sandy Maisel write, "The direct primary system makes American parties particularly porous and susceptible to external influences and in the process reduces the incentive to create additional parties."[23] Of course, the key aspect of direct primaries for our concerns is that while every state uses direct primaries to pick party candidates, regulations vary greatly. In some states, the system is vastly more "open" than in other states.

A second state-level institutional variable is ballot access. Once again, ballot access is often pointed to as one of the many legal barriers that minor parties confront nationwide. But there is significant state-by-state variance; access to the general election ballot is easier in some states than in others. For instance, it requires roughly 50 times the number of voter signatures for minor parties to list their presidential candidate in Florida than it does for minor parties in Minnesota. Other stipulations, such as the requirement that signatures be collected in a set amount of time or from people registered as members of a minor party, produce even more variance.

A final institutional issue is fusion. In a small number of states, candidates are allowed to run on numerous party lines in the general election. The results of each line are added up to one total. In New York, for example, Democratic candidates will often try to run on the Working Families Party line as well, and Republican candidates will sometimes try for the Right to Life Party or Conservative Party endorsement. In the 19th century, fusion was quite common, most notably the joint endorsement by the Populists and the Democrats in many Midwestern states. There was a backlash against such moves, leading to laws banning the practice. Minnesota's Democratic-Farmer-Labor Party (essentially the Democratic Party) is a vestige of a merger to overcome an anti-fusion law. There was also a Supreme Court case on whether states had to accept fusion: *Timmons v. Twin Cities Area New Party* (1997). The court ruled that fusion can be rejected by the state. "The decision foreclosed a rare avenue of tangible minor-party inroads into the two-party duopoly," noted scholar David Ryden.[24] Today, only nine states allow party nomination fusion – California, Connecticut, Delaware, Idaho, Mississippi, New York, Oregon, South Carolina and Vermont.

Demographics: Studies of political behavior have long noted the importance of demographic factors. They have been key to our understanding of modes of participation, voter choice, trust, efficacy, attitudes toward partisanship and the party system more generally, and much else. In *American Voter*, an immensely important book on numerous aspects of individual voting behavior written in 1961, as noted in a previous chapter, the authors spend a great deal of time exploring the relationship between a host of demographic factors and levels of party identification.[25] More recently, Martin Wattenberg[26] explored demographic trends and the rise of non-affiliated voters. In short, several factors such as race, income and level of education appear to have a bearing on one's willingness to support minor-party candidates.

These elements were pulled into a composite score for each state. Given these three factors, how receptive is each state for minor-party candidates? The following table lists the results. One is immediately struck by the variation. "Most supportive" states are as widely different as Alaska and Maine; and they are geographically disparate, including California, Hawaii, New York, and Oklahoma. Interestingly – with the exception of Oklahoma – no Southern states are classified as "most supportive." Kansas ranks as "somewhat supportive"; the remainder are "unsupportive." This is probably due to the generally more restrictive ballot access laws and traditionally uncompetitive elections in the South. In brief, it seems clear that local and state variation in minor-party performance is significant. Minor-party candidates are more accepted – and thus do better – in some parts of the country than others. It is difficult to break these reasons down comprehensively, but they have much to do with the wide variances in state laws and voter attitudes.

Ranking of minor-candidate support by state[27]

State	Index score
Most Supportive	
Alaska	12.07
Arizona	6.53
California	4.86
Connecticut	9.10
Hawaii	6.42
Maine	10.05
Minnesota	6.50
Nevada	4.64
New York	12.49
Oklahoma	4.47
Utah	5.32
Vermont	23.33
Somewhat Supportive	
Colorado	2.73
Kansas	2.45
Massachusetts	3.26
Montana	2.64
New Hampshire	3.06
New Jersey	2.47
Ohio	2.62
Oregon	3.74
Pennsylvania	2.84
Rhode Island	2.41
Wyoming	2.12
Unsupportive	
Alabama	1.31
Arkansas	0.33
Delaware	1.24
Florida	0.43
Georgia	0.91
Iowa	1.29

State	Index score
Idaho	1.78
Illinois	1.41
Indiana	1.27
Kentucky	1.81
Maryland	0.11
Michigan	1.69
Missouri	1.96
Mississippi	1.46
North Carolina	1.27
North Dakota	1.26
Nebraska	1.13
New Mexico	1.88
South Carolina	1.43
South Dakota	1.75
Tennessee	1.89
Texas	1.45
Virginia	1.33
Washington	1.25
Wisconsin	1.77
West Virginia	1.24

Conclusion: Can a Third Party Save Our Democracy?

Given the challenges that minor parties confront in the American system and the limited success they have had at the polls, one might be tempted to conclude that they are a waste of time; that they play no role in changing the course of government. But nothing could be farther from the truth. Minor parties have played a significant role in shaping public policy by drawing attention to particular issues and by threatening to divert support from parties and candidates. Indeed, it has often been minor parties' success that has led to their downfall: once a new party draws attention to an issue, and thus gains popularity, one or both of the major parties pick up the issue and the voters will fall back in line. The minor-party falters, but the issue has new life. One might even go so far as to say established parties rarely develop ideas or present new issues on their own. The major parties are reinvigorated precisely because minor parties nip at the edges of the process, pushing the "big guys" to innovate. It is not a coincidence that minor parties have generally been most active before realigning elections.

Minor parties have historically played a significant role in bringing more citizens into the political process, too. Voters often begin to feel distrustful of the major parties – or at the very least poorly represented by them. They slowly withdraw from the process altogether, only to be drawn back in by the energy and excitement of minor-party activity. When minor parties are most active, the number of people heading to the polls increases. While not a "party" per se, one clear example would be the Tea Party; much of the Republican Party's success in recent years has been due to the robust mobilization of these voters.

As noted in this chapter's introduction, support for minor parties appears to be on the rise. Survey after survey suggests that Americans are ready for more alternatives on Election Day, and other data tell us that the number of minor-party candidates at the local level may also be increasing. Is it time to finally move into a genuine multi-party system? Consider the writings of John Burtka of the *American Conservative*:

> Enter the 2018 election cycle where ... state legislatures are even more polarized than the US Congress. Followers of Bernie Sanders feel that the Democratic Party cheated them out of their voice – some even defected to the Trump camp. Many well-intentioned Trump supporters, although in lockstep with some of his agenda, are disgusted by his personal antics. The Democrats have suffered from an inability to recruit interesting new candidates and the Republicans have failed to bring fresh blood into many of their races ... This is the perfect recipe for the emergence of a viable third party.[28]

Republican operative Juleanna Glover put it this way: "All kinds of previously unimaginable possibilities make a new kind of sense. A third-party presidency in 2020 is no less likely today than the prospect of Donald Trump's election appeared to be two years ago."[29]

Distraught over the ascent of Donald Trump, *New York Times* columnist, book author, and conservative icon David Brooks expounded on the need for a third party in the spring of 2018. According to Brooks, many of the conditions necessary for the emergence of a new party are present. The list includes a renaissance of interesting, important people thinking about proper governance; a large pool of partisans unable to support their party's leader (Trump); a warrior mentality where the right pulverizes the left, and the left feels the need to pulverize back; and a growing generational imperative. He writes, "Decent liberals and conservatives will eventually decide they need to break from it structurally. They will realize it's time to start something new."[30]

It seems that the strongest call for a new party in the post-Trump election is coming, perhaps ironically, from those on the ideological right – the camp that won the election. There is some hope that perhaps a business type, wealthy enough to finance his or her own campaign, will save the day. This group longs for a traditional conservative who believes in limited government, free markets and free trade, and who is pro-immigration.

Could a third party from *any* ideological mold better represent Americans? Setting aside whether this could happen given the myriad hurdles noted earlier in this chapter, would a third party be the panacea to our electoral ills? The answer is no. The framers of our system were concerned, first and foremost, with the prospects of tyranny. They hoped to create a long-term, stable government where ambition would be made to counteract ambition. The breadth of "constitutional obstruction," the cure for tyranny, is staggering. Not only is the federal government divided into three branches, but the legislature is bifurcated and critical powers, like going to war and regulating commerce, are split between the branches. The second part of Madison's so-called "double security" is federalism, where vast elements of governance are relegated to state and local officials – where we also find similar checks and balances. The framers were more worried about corruption and tyranny than they were about efficiency. And that's the rub when it comes to additional parties.

To the framers' astonishment, the only element that has been able to bridge constitutional obstruction has been political parties. During most of American history, one party at a time has been in charge; the government was unified and that was when big change occurred. When Jefferson displaced Adams, he brought with him a Republican-controlled Congress. The powers behind Andrew Jackson were his Democratic colleagues in the House and Senate. It was McKinley and the Republicans who stoked the fires of the Industrial Revolution, and of course the speed and breadth of Roosevelt's New Deal was possible only because his party held a huge majority in Congress. The same can be said about Lyndon Johnson's Great Society. A Republican in the White House would never have been able to push civil rights legislation through the Democratically controlled Congress in the 1960s.

Some Republican presidents, like Dwight Eisenhower, Richard Nixon and Ronald Reagan, confronted a divided government and were successful in advancing many of their policy initiatives. But that happened because conservative Democrats in Congress, mostly from the South, crossed over on occasion. Ronald Reagan's historic tax cuts in the early 1980s were possible because an overwhelming percentage of Boll Weevils backed the move. Likewise, Nixon's law and order agenda was supported by conservative Democrats, and Truman was able to nudge civil rights forward because he got help from a few liberal Republicans.

That's changed. Record high party unity scores in Congress in recent decades underscore the necessity of unified government. Barack Obama's Affordable Care Act and Donald Trump's tax reform bills both passed by a whisker, and only because their partisan colleagues in Congress stayed in line. Help from the other side was virtually non-existent. Rigid party loyalty is a reality and it has changed our politics. The days of the crossover legislators are gone.

The prospects of divided government, perhaps an exceptionally divided government, where a different party controls the presidency, the House and the Senate, would be enhanced by the introduction of an additional party. Unlike in parliamentary systems, where competing parties merge to form a government and the opposition, and where the chief executive springs from the majority in the legislature, in the American setting, with distinct branches, the outcome would be hyper-gridlock. This is even more likely given trends in party identification – where there is little overlap on policy positions and where each side views the other as dangerous. Again, there is little incentive to find the middle ground when each side sees the other side as crazy.

There is a recent case study that makes this point. Maine has a history of support for minor-party candidates – as noted in the table above. One of the state's US Senators in 2018 was Angus King, an independent, who also served as an independent governor. In the 2010 race for governor, three viable candidates were on the general election ballot and each netted about one-third of the vote. The winner, with 38 percent, was conservative firebrand Paul LePage. Running as a Republican, LePage narrowly edged past a field of candidates in the primaries. Once in office, LePage pursued a far-right, Tea Party – like agenda that was at odds with many of the Republicans in the legislature. Soon, the government began to split into three parties, of sorts: LePage's far right group, traditional Republicans (many of whom were leaders in the House and Senate) and the Democrats. To say that governance was acrimonious during LePage's tenure would be a grand understatement. He shattered the all-time record for vetoes in short order (well over 500 bills), even though the Republicans controlled at least one branch of the legislature during all of his time in office. By most accounts, the Maine government ground to a halt. As noted by one commentator, "While Mainers were more accustomed to political leaders who emphasized consensus building, Mr. LePage sees governing as digging in and bringing the system to a halt if necessary."[31] Even when the voters of the state passed ballot initiatives to legalize pot, expand Medicaid and introduce ranked-choice voting, LePage somehow found an avenue to create roadblocks. One of the most notorious feuds during this period occurred between factions of the Republican Party.[32] Maine's latest foray into minor-party politics proved to be such a disaster that voters in Maine not only became the first state to approve a ranked-choice process in 2016, but they also voted to reinstate the process in 2018, once its implementation was stopped by LePage. (This model will be discussed in the concluding chapter, but the idea is to eliminate plurality winners – like LePage.)

While it is true that roughly 38 percent of Americans consider themselves independent (non-partisan), a few points should be raised. First, studies have shown that independents who lean toward one party or another (which would be a majority), tend to consistently vote for that party. They might say they are moderate, willing to move back and forth, but their voting behavior suggests otherwise. In fact, there is new data to suggest independent voters who lean to one party also "fear and loath" members of the other party just as strong partisans now do.[33] Perhaps more importantly, while the overall American electorate might be normally distributed when it comes to ideology, this is certainly not true at the state, district and community level. Voters in highly sorted districts compel their representatives to hold the line. Moderation and compromise are out of the question. Would they somehow give their members license to find a middle ground with an additional party in the mix? Again, the outcome would be stalemate and ever-increasing hostility toward the other sides.

The introduction of a viable third party would likely wreak havoc with the Electoral College, given the unit rule. The prospects of one candidate not receiving a majority of the Electoral College votes would increase greatly, as would the prospects of elections being settled by the House of Representatives where each state has a single vote. The smallest 25 states make up just 19 percent of the population – a percentage that will dramatically *drop* in the years ahead. One might wish for reforms, such as the National Popular Vote Plan, but why would rural states dominated by Republicans cede their power? If a future presidential contest is resolved in the House, it is entirely likely that the men and women who represent a fraction of the American public would put their person in power.

At all levels, the prospects of plurality winners would increase with the introduction of a third party. The snag here, unlike what happens in parliamentary systems, is our single-member-district, first-past-the-post system. The person sent to office might net only a fraction of the overall vote, leaving any final vestiges of legitimacy in the election process shattered.

Finally, it is worth noting that while a majority of Americans say they would like more choices on Election Day, this is not a new development. If they yearn for a third party, why do minor-party candidates of all stripes fare so poorly? Like it or not, the two-party model is ingrained in the American psyche.

There are certainly a host of reforms that could compel major party candidates to better reflect the interests of voters in the ideological middle, several of which will be discussed in the concluding chapter. Likely the most viable avenue for change would be in the nomination process, where candidates on the ideological fringes make their way to the general election ballot, thus leaving moderates cold. All is not lost, but looking to a third party to solve our election woes will lead to disappointment, even higher levels of frustration and anger, and a crisis of legitimacy.

Notes

1 Laura Saad, "Trump and Clinton Finish with Historically Low Images," *Gallup* website, November 8, 2016 (http://news.gallup.com/poll/197231/trump-clinton-finish-historically-poor-images.aspx).

2 Brittany De Lea, "Two-Party System Killing Democracy?," *Fox Business* website, September 8, 2016 (www.foxbusiness.com/politics/two-party-system-killing-democracy).

3 Pew Research Center, "Party Identification Trends, 1992–2017," March 20, 2018 (www.people-press.org/2018/03/20/party-identification-trends-1992-2017/).

4 Laura Saad, "Perceived Need for Third Major Party Remains High in U.S.," *Gallup* website, September 27, 2017 (http://news.gallup.com/poll/219953/perceived-need-third-major-party-remains-high.aspx).

5 Barry C. Burden, "Ralph Nader's Campaign Strategy in the 2000 US Presidential Election," *American Politics Research* 33 (2005), 672–699.

6 Alexandra Jaffe, "By the Numbers: Third-Party Candidates Had an Outsize Impact on Election," *NBC News* website, November 8, 2016 (www.nbcnews.com/storyline/2016-election-day/third-party-candidates-having-outsize-impact-election-n680921).

7 John F. Bibby and L. Sandy Maisel, *Two Parties or More? The American Party System,* 2nd Edition (Boulder, CO: Westview, 2003), 62.

8 Federal Election Commission, "Public Funds of Presidential Elections," (www.fec.gov/introduction-campaign-finance/understanding-ways-support-federal-candidates/presidential-elections/public-funding-presidential-elections/).

9 Ibid.

10 Ibid., 70.

11 Micah L. Sifry, "Why America Is Stuck with Only Two Parties," *The New Republic,* February 2, 2018 (https://newrepublic.com/article/146884/america-stuck-two-parties).

12 "The American Party (the Know-Nothing Party) Comes to Power in Massachusetts in 1955," *The Massachusetts Historical Society,* January 2005 (www.masshist.org/objects/2005january.cfm).

13 John K. White and Daniel M. Shea, *New Party Politics: From Jefferson and Hamilton to the Information Age* (Boston, MA: Bedford/St. Martin's, 2000), 283.

14 Ibid.

15 Clinton Rossiter, *Political Parties in America* (Ithaca, NY: Cornell University Press, 1997), 73.

16 Jay Rosen, "The Legend of Trent Lott and the Weblogs," *Press Think: Ghost of Democracy in the Media Machine,* March 15, 2004 (http://archive.pressthink.org/2004/03/15/lott_case.html).

17 See, for example, Michael Ross et al., "Patterns of Support for George Wallace: Implications for Racial Change," *Journal of Social Issues,* Vol. 36, No. 2, 1976.

18 As noted in Levitsky and Ziblatt, *How Democracies Die*, 47.

19 As cited in Clyde Haberman, "George Wallace Tapped into Racial Fear. Decades Later, Its Force Remains Potent," *New York Times*, April 1, 2018.

20 Ibid.

21 Mark Bisnow, *Diary of a Dark Horse: The 1980 Anderson Presidential Campaign* (Carbondale, IL: Southern Illinois University Press, 1983), 214.

22 US Election Atlas, "1980 Presidential General Election Results" (http://uselectionatlas.org/RESULTS/national.php?year=1980&off=)&f=1).

23 John F. Bibby and L. Sandy Maisel, *Two Parties – Or More? The American Party System* (Boulder, Co.: Westview, 1998).

24 David K. Ryden, "The Good, the Bad, and the Ugly: Judicial Shaping of Party Activities," in John C. Green and Daniel M. Shea, *The State of the Parties*, 3rd Edition (Lanham, MD: Rowman and Littlefield, 1999).

25 Angus Campbell, Philip Converse, Warren Miller, and Donald Stokes, *The American Voter* (Hoboken, NJ: John Wiley and Sons, 1961).

26 Martin P. Wattenberg, *The Decline of American Party Politics, 1952–1980* (Cambridge, MA: Harvard University Press, 1998).

27 C. Daniel Myers and Daniel Shea, "Local Political Culture and Support for Minor Parties." Paper presented at the Midwest Political Science Association, April 17, 2004.

28 John Burtka III, "Will 2018 Be a Breakout Year For a Viable Third Party?," *The American Conservative* website, January 10, 2018 (www.theamericanconservative.com/articles/will-2018-be-a-breakout-year-for-a-viable-third-party/).

29 Juleanna Glover, "Are Republicans Ready to Join a Third Party?," *New York Times* website, January 29, 2018 (www.nytimes.com/2018/01/29/opinion/republicans-third-party-.html).

30 David Brooks, "The End of the Two-Party System," *New York Times* website, February 12, 2018 (www.nytimes.com/2018/02/12/opinion/trump-republicans-scarcity.html).

31 Jennifer Levitz, "Maine Gov. LePage Ending His Two-Term Tenure with More Vetoes," *Wall Street Journal* website, May 1, 2018 (www.wsj.com/articles/maine-gov-lepage-ending-his-two-term-tenure-with-more-vetoes-1525176000).

32 Steve Mistler, "Republican Party Strife Threatens Maine Governance," *Portland Press Herald* website, November 2, 2015 (www.pressherald.com/2015/11/02/lepages-divorce-from-maine-legislature-now-threatens-governance/).

33 Philip Bump, "Independent Leaners Hate the Other Party More than They Like the One They Vote For," *Washington Post* website, September 13, 2017 (www.washingtonpost.com/news/politics/wp/2017/09/13/independent-leaners-hate-the-other-party-more-than-they-like-the-one-they-vote-for/?utm_term=.856e4d679ffd).

9 Campaign Finance
Is Too Much Money Really the Problem?

Earlier in this book a story was told of how, in 2015, Virginia Governor Terry McAuliffe made a bold move to restore the voting rights of felons who had served their sentences and were no longer on probation. Over 200,000 Virginians were being denied their right to vote – a majority of whom were African Americans – and the state law allowed the governor to grant clemency on a case-by-case basis. In an unprecedented move, McAuliffe, a Democrat, issued an executive order granting *all* former convicts the right to vote.[1] Following a lawsuit, the Virginia Supreme Court sided with the Republicans, saying the governor had overstepped his bounds, so the governor responded by pardoning 155,221 convicts on an individual basis by the summer of 2017.[2] "Expanding democracy in Virginia has been my proudest achievement during my time as Governor," said McAuliffe.[3]

Those concerned with the health of our democracy lament low turnout and scorn laws limiting who can vote. Can we really have a vibrant democracy when so many citizens are stuck on the sidelines? Others also bemoan the scourge of big money. The system is awash in cash, we hear, and the wealthy are able to shift election outcomes, steer public policy by lobbying and, more recently, pouring huge sums into the creation and maintenance of grassroots organizations. Our democracy is undermined by too few voters and too much money!

The irony in this instance is that McAuliffe likely won his election in 2015 because one billionaire liberal activist, Tom Steyer of California, dumped some $8 million into his race. This was a staggering amount for a Virginia gubernatorial campaign, and it was used to fund television commercials, online ads, door-to-door advertising and much else. Steyer's main priority was environmental protection, and in Virginia his NextGen focused on areas of the state vulnerable to sea level rise from climate change. The money was not given directly to McAuliffe, in accordance with campaign finance laws, but there is little doubt that it was key in helping the Democrat win a tough race. In particular, the funds were critical for a massive get-out-the-vote drive in many of the state's college towns.

So a governor who reformers might applaud for enriching the demo-cratic character of his state was brought to power by a massive influx of funds – from one individual. Or was he? One of the many riddles of money in politics is the cause-and-effect relationships, which can move in a number of directions. For example, there is little question that candidates who raise the most money usually win. But does that imply the money created the win? Perhaps some candidates are better able to raise money because they are, well, more popular. And because they are more popular, they win. What, exactly, does money buy? We know that money can buy more ads and create better organizations, but how effective are they? As noted earlier in the book, the "minimal effects" argument is buoyed by a legion of scholars. Elections, they argue, are not won or lost by slick ads and skillful debates, but rather broader systemic forces like the state of the economy. Steyer's funds were aimed at college towns, mostly on the coast, but McAuliffe actually did worse in these communities than Barack Obama did in 2012.

And what about the buying of votes after the election – the ability of money to sway officials to back certain policies as a payoff to contributors? The causal link is very hard to pin down. Does, for instance, the money lead or follow? That is, does it lead an official to back a particular policy, or does it follow a candidate who has already pledged to support a par-ticular set of policies? McAuliffe was a well-known environmentalist long before Steyer decided to jump in the race; Steyer would never have supported McAuliffe if he was not *already* a committed environmentalist.

Many are frustrated by the slow pace of change when it comes to gun control. Why can't Congress do something to reduce the mass shootings in America? One of the most forceful voices for gun control in contem-porary politics is former New York City Mayor Michael Bloomberg. Bloomberg is a billionaire who spent upward of $110 million of his own money in 2009 to win reelection – a staggering sum for a mayoral race.[4] And what is his current strategy for shifting gun laws in America? Sending hundreds of millions to fund pro-reform candidates in the 2018 election. Do progressive, reform-minded Americans balk at the notion of a few individuals funding conservative groups and causes, but somehow forget that many of the key players on their side are also fat cats?

In the summer of 2018, Americans learned of how the Trump Administration's zero tolerance policy at the American–Mexico border led to the separation of children from their parents. The image of hundreds of children behind fences, crying for their mothers and fathers, was gut-wrenching. But how could an average citizen help change this policy? In short order, massive sums of money streamed into immigrant legal defense operations and advocacy groups. Along with recurrent news accounts, the public became aware of the crisis through these groups. Donald Trump soon changed the policy. In a very real sense, thousands of big and small checks shifted what many thought was a cruel policy. At the same time, it should be noted that ongoing congressional struggles to reform immigration policy have been circumscribed by the expenditures of hundreds of millions of dollars, most from a small number of wealthy individuals.

Finally, even if there might be a clear link between money and outcome, what's wrong with that? Are candidates not charged with rallying support, and does support not come in different ways? What if one candidate was able to recruit more volunteers than another? Are campaigns *only* about voting? Do we want to restrict a particular form of engagement at the same time we are trying to broaden involvement? Is big money okay when it helps build local organizations, but not okay when it funds television ads or lobbying efforts? Or do huge piles of money in elections discourage engagement by fueling cynicism and lowering a sense of efficacy? Did we say that the money–elections–democracy nexus is complicated?

The headlines can be explosive and even jarring. In 2016, candidates for all federal offices spent a staggering $6.4 billion on their campaigns, and another $3.2 billion was spent by lobbyists in an attempt to influence government. These figures have doubled since 2000.[5] Even the sleepiest race of the House of Representatives in an inexpensive media market can spill into the millions. By one estimate, some legislators expecting a tough reelection will spend upwards of five hours a day fundraising – time that might be better spent serving constituents.[6] Even at the local level, the cost of running for office has skyrocketed. One scholar has suggested that local campaigning has become an "arms race."[7] This money has to come from somewhere – increasingly from special interest groups, labor unions, corporations, and wealthy individuals.

While the sums have grown by leaps and bounds, and although there are new ways to spend it, concerns about a system awash in cash is an old tune in politics. Do campaign contributions skew the policy process toward the will of the donors, rather than the will of the people? Can candidates really buy their way into office? Do wealthy donors and interest groups control elected officials with their campaign contributions? Does big money in elections lead to growing voter cynicism and distrust of our political institutions? Fewer and fewer Americans seem interested in politics these days, but is big money really part of the problem? Isn't contributing money to a candidate a form of advocacy, akin to political speech? If so, is it not protected by the 1st Amendment of the Constitution? This chapter will take a look at the nuanced, complicated link between electoral democracy and money.

The History of Money in Elections

Many would be surprised to hear that money has *not* always played a central role in the election process. During the early days, there was simply less to spend money on. Candidates would often "treat" voters, meaning that they would sponsor lavish picnics and barbeques. George Washington, for example, was said to have purchased a quart of rum, wine, beer, and hard cider for every voter in the district when he ran for the Virginia House of Burgesses in 1751 (there were only 391 voters). In 1795, one would-be Delaware officeholder roasted a steer and half a dozen sheep for his friends and another candidate gave a "fish feast."[8]

Four decades later, Ferdinand Bayard, a Frenchman traveling the United States, commented that "candidates offer drunkenness openly to anyone who is willing to give them his vote."[9] A candidate might also spend a good bit on newspapers – either buying space or perhaps starting or buying his own to push his candidacy. Indeed, the most heated campaigns of the century were conducted through battling newspapers. Quite often when a wealthy individual was anxious to aid a particular candidate he would simply create a newspaper. Money was rather secondary, however, given that the principal means of connecting with voters was interpersonal: word of mouth spread by local party activists. Even Abraham Lincoln secretly purchased a small newspaper in Illinois in 1860.[10] On the whole, however, money simply did not play a pivotal role in elections because there were few ways to spend it.

Things began to change in the election of 1896. For one, William McKinley's closest advisor, Mark Hanna – considered to be the first campaign consultant – believed that the Republican could win by spending unprecedented sums on newspapers, pamphlets, buttons, billboards, parades, and speakers to travel across the nation. Indeed, some 200 million pamphlets were mailed from a headquarters that housed over 100 full-time clerks. More significantly, for the first time in American history, corporations made contributions directly from their company treasuries. A massive sum was raised and spent – likely in the range of $7 million. The strategy worked, as McKinley narrowly defeated the popular Democrat William Jennings Bryant.

As technology changed throughout the 20th century, so too did the cost of elections. Money became critical by the late 1950s. It seemed that the cost of running for office, at every level of government, was rising out of control.

Several factors accentuated the increase in the importance of money by the midpoint of the century. For starters, there was a decline in local party organizations. Given that these structures had, in the past, been responsible for connecting with voters, candidates needed new ways of reaching out. These new means for connecting – direct mail, and radio and television ads – were costly. Along with the decline of party organizations, fewer voters displayed steadfast loyalty to any political party. The number of "independent" voters grew during this period, leading to, among other things, greater uncertainty at election time. Split-ticket voting reached record highs. What is more, control of

Congress was often razor thin and most presidential races were close. Nervous candidates and their sponsors spent as much money as possible, given the new electoral context.

A hugely important factor was the rise of television. In the early 1950s, only a small percentage of homes boasted a television; by the early 1960s they had become nearly universal. Television transformed much of American life and it changed the way campaigns were run. Airing television advertisements requires huge sums of money, but these ads are now critical to success. Coupled with the growing importance of television were the professionals hired to create the commercials. Professional campaign consultants burst on to the political scene in the 1960s, bringing with them many other sophisticated technologies, such as direct mail and survey research. These techniques proved effective, of course, but they came with a hefty price tag.

Given these changes and others, the cost of running for the presidency increased by leaps and bounds. One observer noted, "Even when adjusted for inflation, the amount of money it takes to become president has increased more than 250-fold from Abraham Lincoln to Barack Obama. Even more striking, the trajectory has steepened, suggesting not only campaign spending itself but the growth rate in campaign spending is accelerating rapidly."[11] In all, the 2016 presidential election, which includes the nomination phase, cost $6.4 billion.[12]

As you would expect, the same trend can be seen in congressional elections. The average winning US Senate candidate spent roughly three times more in 2016 than in 1990 (around $10 million compared to $3.8 million). The average winning House candidate spent four times as much (about $1.6 million compared to $400,000).[13] Even when adjusted for inflation, the growth has been significant.

The Center for Responsive Politics, which also goes by the name Open Secrets, has tallied the total cost for federal elections, both candidate and outside group spending, for the last two decades. In the 2000 election between Al Gore and George W. Bush, some $3 billion was spent – by historic standards a staggering sum. That figure had jumped to well over $6 billion in the contest between Trump and Clinton.[14] A team of analysts put it this way: "Since the mid-1980s, the amount dumped on elections by campaigns and outside groups, as measured by the Federal Election Commission, has grown 555 percent – faster than even the alarming increases in the costs of health care and private college tuition."[15]

When it comes to running for local office, the amounts have also skyrocketed. As noted by one observer, "It's less visible, but this accelerated spending is happening at the micro-level, too. Politicos coveting the keys to America's major cities are pounding through the historical ceilings of campaign contributions."[16] In short, running for office in America has been become very, very expensive.

The Rage for Reform

Efforts to control the flow of money in elections stretch back to the Progressive Era. The federal government and many states adopted laws that barred businesses and labor unions from giving money directly to candidates. The rationale behind these changes was to limit the likelihood of a quid-pro-quo relationship – that an elected official would feel obligated to pay back their campaign contributors with favored policies. Representatives were expected to look out for all citizens, not just the ones that flooded their campaign war chest with contributions. Given that the very politicians enacting these laws were dependent upon big contributions to get reelected, it is not surprising that these laws had little real impact. The early reforms were filled with loopholes large enough to drive a truck through – or should we say an armored truck!

Real reform came in the early 1970s, as members of Congress began to worry about being thrown from office by wealthy candidates, perhaps political novices, who could simply spend more. The self-interest that inhibited meaningful reform during the Progressive period led to draconian changes in the 1970s. The Federal Election Campaign Act (FECA) was signed into law in 1971. Three years later, a series of amendments were passed to make the law even more restrictive. Among much else, FECA limited the amount of money candidates for federal office could spend; limited the amount any individual or group could give to federal office candidates; restricted the amount a federal office candidate could spend of his or her own money on their own campaign; and set caps on the spending by independent groups (groups not connected to a candidate or campaign). It also established the Federal Election Commission to oversee campaign fundraising and spending in federal office campaigns, and to enforce election finance statutes, and set in place public funding for presidential elections.

Few disputed that the provisions were real or that they would have a significant bearing on the way elections were conducted. Yet, shortly after the amendments took effect, James Buckley, a conservative senator from New York, along with a group of politicians from both sides of the political aisle, challenged the constitutionality of the law in the federal courts. Buckley and his colleagues argued that spending campaign money was akin to free speech, so any limits would be an abridgement of 1st Amendment protections.

The case of *Buckley v. Valeo* (1976) was the most significant election-centered court decision in American history. The Supreme Court sided with Buckley, for the most part. It struck down provisions related to limits on overall spending, spending by the candidate, and spending by independent groups. The court upheld public funding of presidential elections so long as it was voluntary, but surprisingly allowed limits on how much an individual or a group might give to a candidate. The majority opinion stated: "The quantity of communication by the contributor does not increase perceptibly with the size of this contribution, since the expression rests solely on the undifferentiated, symbolic act of contributing."[17] In other words, when people give money to a candidate, they are expressing their support regardless of the size of the gift. Therefore, reasonable restrictions, designed to level the playing field somewhat, are fine. Finally, the decision noted that political parties were special, given their role in the democratic process, and that few restrictions should be placed on their activities.

It is hard to overstate the ramifications of *Buckley*. More than any other force, this case has shaped the nature of elections ever since. The decision pushes candidates to raise money from numerous smaller sources, rather than from a small group of large donors. While this was certainly not the intent of the law, candidates now spend much of their time – perhaps most of their time – chasing donors. Not only has this made running for office less appealing, but it has also greatly lengthened the time needed to invest in a campaign. Also, an entire industry was born overnight: fundraising consultants. Few candidates today head into the trenches without the aid of a high-priced fundraising expert.

The role of political parties in elections was radically transformed by *Buckley* and the subsequent court decision. Candidates found that they could reach voters without the help of party workers, but because of FECA regulations and the special status afforded parties in the decision, state and national party organizations were reinserted into the process. Indeed, parties were placed at the center of the fundraising process. In an effort to outdo the opposing party, new methods of stretching the legal system were devised in each election. The most significant of these loopholes was dubbed soft money. Although individuals and groups were limited in the amount they could contribute to a candidate by FECA, there were no restrictions when it came to giving money to a political party. Immense contributions were filtered through the parties to support particular candidates. To many Americans, the soft-money loophole was little more than a money-laundering scam. Writing of this process in the late 1990s, Colby College scholar Anthony Corrado suggested that "An illness that has plagued previous elections has developed into an epidemic."[18]

Another spin-off of FECA and *Buckley* was the proliferation of political action committees (PACs). Labor unions and corporations were barred from giving money to federal candidates by earlier acts of Congress. PACs were devised in the 1940s as a means to get around these restrictions. Here, none of the monies used to support a candidate can come directly from a union or corporation, but instead from their independent political arms. Because FECA limits the amount that candidates may raise from an individual, they were forced to solicit help from a broad range of sources. The contribution limit for PACs was also five times higher ($5,000), so their importance mushroomed. The number of these groups exploded: in 1974, there were roughly 600 PACs, and following the 2016 election there were 8,666.[19]

Political action committees give money to candidates because they want to shape public policy. Business groups, for example, want policies that help them make a profit, environmental PACs want policies that protect the natural world, and labor PACs seek policies that help working Americans. But do these groups buy policies with their contributions? This is a hotly debated issue. Some suggest the connection between contributions and policy is direct – that contributors are rational and not inclined to spend their money without a direct payback. This is the alarm raised by most good government or watchdog organizations. For example, the Center for Responsive Politics tracks the flow of money in elections and the development of public policy. Their website boasts detailed information on who gives and who receives campaign money. On one of their pages, called "Influence and Lobbying," users can explore who receives campaign contributions from particular groups and how these donations might shape policy outcomes.[20] Once again, the assumption is that money can buy policies.

Most observers suggest the link between contributions and policies is a bit less direct, however. Election officials often point to the difference between lead and follow, as noted in the introduction to this chapter. Public perception is that money leads elected officials in a particular policy direction, perhaps a direction they would not likely take if not for the money. The reality, most officials argue, is that money follows; contributions are essentially rewards for supporting a policy choice. Put a bit differently, contributions often come *after* the candidate has supported a policy or, at the very least, he or she has proclaimed a clear policy preference. PACs support candidates who agree with them. Instances where one contribution or a host of contributions changed a member's vote are rare, they argue.

Another perspective, perhaps the most likely, is that campaign contributions buy access. Elected officials are busy and have to make tough choices about how to spend their time. A major hurdle for those interested in persuading the elected official to support their cause is to gain an audience – a meeting. Campaign contributions help open the door to give the contributor a few minutes with the elected official. As noted by one PAC officer, "[Contributions] give you access. It makes you a player." Another way of thinking about access is to imagine two groups each wanting a moment of a legislator's time. The first group contributed $5,000 in the last election and the second provided nothing but lip service. Which of the two groups would likely get their meeting?

When it comes to fundraising, there are important differences between the three types of candidates (incumbents, challengers, and open-seat candidates). Political action committees and wealthy donors hope that their money will advance their policy goals, which means they hope their money will be given to the candidate who will be the eventual winner (how can a losing candidate shape public policy?). Accordingly, they prefer to send their funds to incumbents, because those already in office have a head-start when it comes to reelection, what scholars call the incumbent advantage. By sending their money to incumbents, PACs increase the incumbent advantage. "The biggest thing I learned," commented Republican Wendy Long after her unsuccessful bid for the US Senate in 2012, "was the power of incumbency and the power of money. I guess I was a little idealistic and thought if you are honest and you're well-qualified and capable of waging a good fight, you can raise money. And what I learned is that our campaign finance laws are really a great big incumbent protection act."[21]

In most elections in the last few decades, the percentage of successful US House reelection campaigns extends well beyond 90 percent. In 2018 this figure stood at 91 percent. This occurs even though many Americans seem frustrated with "business as usual politics" and seem anxious to "throw the bums out." Incumbents have always had an advantage, but recent changes have made this advantage even stronger. Yale University scholar David Mayhew was one of the first to draw our attention to the problem.[22] In his seminal book *Congress: The Electoral Connection*, Mayhew argues that nearly all legislative activity is now geared toward securing the next reelection. These efforts fall within three categories: *credit claiming*, which is receiving praise for bringing money and federal projects back to the district; *position taking*, which is positioning on the popular side of issues; and *advertising*, which includes constituent outreach through mailings (when paid for by the government, this is called franking) and other means. Others have pointed to additional sources of incumbent support, such as ongoing, frequent media attention – which challengers rarely get. Most agree that things have gotten out of control and that the advantages now given to incumbents are exceptional.

But can anything be done about the incumbent advantage? Numerous reforms have been suggested in the past few decades. One proposal that jumped to the forefront was term limits. Simply put, if we are worried about an unfair advantage given to those already in office, why not mandate more open-seat contests? Limiting the number of times legislators can be reelected, as we do with the presidency, would guarantee turnover – a stream of new faces, energy, and ideas. Representatives should know the concerns of average citizens; what better way of ensuring this connection than by forcing entrenched legislators to step aside after a fixed period? Opponents of term limits argue that the legislative process is complex, especially these days, and that it takes time to become familiar with even the most basic elements. Term limits remove experienced legislators and replace them with green ones. Moreover, term limits deny voters an option that many of them would likely choose – the option of reelecting their current representative.

By the early 1990s, roughly half of the states had adopted term limits for state legislators *and* for federal office candidates. The issue came to a head in the Supreme Court case of *US Term Limits, Inc. v. Thornton* (1995). In a five-to-four decision, the majority stated that "allowing individual states to craft their own qualifications for Congress would thus erode the structure envisioned by the framers, a structure that was designed, in the words of the Preamble to our Constitution, to form a 'more perfect Union.'"[23] Today, 15 states have some form of term limits for the state legislature. It is fair to say that the experiment in limiting the terms for state and local office has been a mixed bag. Some applaud the turnover, while others bemoan loss of experts in government.

21st-Century Finance Reforms

As the 20th century drew to a close, Americans had grown cynical about the election process. A 1994 survey found that 75 percent agreed (39 percent agreeing "strongly") that "our present system of government is democratic in name only. In fact, special interests run things."[24] Another poll, conducted in 2001, found that 80 percent of Americans felt that politicians often "did special favors for people or groups who gave them campaign contributions."[25] Something needed to be done; the reforms of the early 1970s had done little to halt the flow of big money and, if anything, had made matters worse by giving the impression that money was limited, when in fact the loopholes were both numerous and gaping.

Any time legislators are called upon to reform the system that put them in office the process of change is slow, rife with problems. The benefits of reform must be weighed against other issues, namely potential partisan advantages. Would one side gain an advantage with more restrictive campaign finance rules? There did not seem to be a clear answer to this question, so, while calls for reform echoed across America, measures in the legislature stalled. By the start of the 21st century, many state and local governments moved to restrict the flow of big campaign money, but at the federal level the prospects of real change seem grim.

Leading the call for reform were Senators John McCain, a Republican from Arizona (and later the 2008 Republican presidential nominee), and Russ Feingold, a Democrat from Wisconsin. Both were significant players in national politics, but it was McCain who drew the most attention. He had run for the presidency in 2000 and, while he was defeated for the Republican nomination by George W. Bush, McCain had become the darling of the media and the leader of a growing number of reformers across the nation. As McCain spoke frequently and passionately about the growing corruption in the election process, more and more Americans began demanding change. Campaign finance became a big issue in many of the congressional elections in 2000, and most of the successful candidates had pledged to do something about the problem. After much debate and maneuvering by both parties, the Bipartisan Campaign Reform Act (BCRA) was passed and signed into law by George W. Bush in February of 2002. Here again, the ramifications have been huge.

In brief, BCRA prohibited national political party committees from raising or spending any funds not subject to federal limits, even for state and local races, and banned group-sponsored advertisements 30 days before primary elections and 60 days before general elections. Most observers agree that these limits were dramatic. Yet the law also raised the contribution limits to $2,000 for individuals and $10,000 for groups, and left open the ability for wealthy individuals to donate soft money to state and local party organizations. The new restrictions did not apply to political action committees, which were still free to raise unlimited amounts of money.

The law took effect the day after the 2002 midterm election and had a controversial beginning. The very same day that BCRA was signed into law, Senator Mitch McConnell (Republican from Kentucky), a strong opponent of campaign finance restrictions, and a host of other legislators, interest groups, and minor parties, sought to nullify the measure by taking it to the federal courts. The core of their argument was that the changes represent an assault on free speech. Those in support of the new law argued that contributions may be regulated without being a burden on the 1st Amendment because contributions are indirect, rather than direct, speech.

McConnell v. The Federal Election Commission was heard in the Supreme Court in the fall of 2003. A decision was handed down on December 10, 2003. In a five-to-four decision, the court upheld the most important elements of the law. It was, according to a *New York Times* account, a "stunning victory for political reform."[26] The court reasoned that Congress has a "fully legitimate interest in … preventing corruption of the federal electoral process through the means it has chosen." Moreover, the majority suggested that the problem with big, unregulated contributions was preferential access and the influence that comes with it. It was, they noted, not simply an issue of the appearance of corruption, but there were, rather, volumes of data strongly suggesting the existence of real problems. In short, where the majority of justices in the *Buckley* case seemed anxious to protect individual rights (i.e., treating money as akin to free speech), the majority in *McConnell* appeared anxious to protect the dignity of our electoral system.

Since *McConnell*, there have been several other legal challenges to the law. In June 2007, the US Supreme Court ruled that provisions in

BCRA that banned ads funded by corporations or labor unions from being broadcast within 60 days of a general election and 30 days of a primary were unconstitutional if applied to ads that could reasonably be interpreted in ways other than directing a vote for one candidate or against another. The Supreme Court also overturned what was called the Millionaire's Amendment to the law, which increased contribution limits for candidates in races where an opponent spends a large amount of personal funds. Finally, in 2009, the Supreme Court heard a case on whether documentary films with clear political messages could be considered an ad, and thus be subject to BCRA limits. The case stemmed from a documentary that a nonprofit organization attempted to air during the 2008 primary season.

This issue culminated into yet another critically important decision handed down by the Supreme Court on January 21, 2010. It was *Citizens United v. Federal Election Commission,* and it dealt with a provision of BCRA that outlawed explicit campaigning by non-partisan groups within 60 days of a general election and 30 days prior to a primary election. Citizens United, a conservative nonprofit corporation, produced a 90-minute documentary called *Hillary: The Movie,* which was highly critical of the then-New York Senator. They were anxious to distribute it throughout the fall of 2007 and spring of 2008, even though Clinton was running in primaries and caucuses for the Democratic nomination for the presidency. Because they were barred from doing so, and because they thought this was a violation of their 1st Amendment rights, Citizens United took the issue to the federal courts.

When the case was first heard by the Supreme Court, the issue seemed to center on the prohibitions stipulated in BCRA. But when the justices heard arguments a second time (a rather unusual move) the concern appeared to be much broader: whether prohibitions on direct spending by corporations and unions during campaigns, established a half-century before and upheld in several prior cases, were constitutional.

In yet another five-to-four decision, the Court ruled that unions and corporations were entitled to spend money from their general treasuries (without the use of PACs) on federal elections. They could not give directly to candidates, but they were free to spend lavishly on their behalf. This might imply, for example, that a large multinational corporation could spend $100 million, only a fraction of its budget, toward the election of a handful of members of Congress. Unions could do likewise.

The decision sent shockwaves across the political system. What would this mean? One commentator, writing for the National Review Online, suggested, "The ruling represents a tremendous victory for free speech ... The ruling in Citizens United is a straightforward application of basic First Amendment principles."[27] But, others feared that the decision would let loose a flood of money and lead to greater corruption. The *New York Times* editorialized, "With a single, disastrous five-to-four ruling, the Supreme Court has thrust politics back to the robber-baron era of the 19th century."[28]

Additionally, another court case, *SpeechNow.org v. FEC,* occurred in the wake of the *Citizens United* decision. In February 2008, SpeechNow.org filed a suit in the US District Court of the District of Columbia that challenged the legality of federal contribution limits and disclosure requirements for political committees that only make independent expenditures. Independent expenditures are any campaign communications that advocate the election or defeat of a political candidate but are *not* made in conjunction with a candidate, his or her campaign committees, or a political party. An ad that advocated for the election of Hillary Clinton in 2016, for example, but was created and paid for by an outside group unaffiliated with Clinton or the Democratic Party would be an independent expenditure.

In its ruling in March 2010, just two months following the *Citizens United* decision, the district court struck down the federal contribution limits that applied to committees that only made independent expenditures, therefore siding with SpeechNow.org. However, the court ruled that the disclosure requirements for such groups were legal.[29] Given that the *Citizens United* decision eliminated the prohibition on corporations making independent expenditures during an election, the combination of these two rulings meant that corporations would be able to make unlimited contributions to committees that only make independent expenditures. The two landmark court cases have led to a massive proliferation of these independent-expenditure-only committees, which have become not-so-affectionately known as "Super PACs."

While many expected corporations to play a significant role in campaign funding following *Citizens United* and *SpeechNow.org,* the main donors to Super PACs have actually been individuals, particularly, as one would expect, wealthy individuals.[30] Since Super PACs are typically established to aid candidates of a certain political ideology and because their donors still have to be disclosed, corporations have not participated nearly as much as they could, perhaps to avoid disappointing or angering consumers who would disagree with the ideology or positions of the candidates benefiting from the corporation's donations. Nevertheless, individuals do not face this problem, and the growth of Super PACs has allowed the wealthiest Americans to contribute even more money and, consequently, increase their impact on our elections. For example, in 2012, conservative billionaire business magnate Sheldon Adelson donated a total of $20 million to Super PACs that supported Republican presidential candidate Newt Gingrich. This money allowed Gingrich to stay in the GOP race longer than his general support and campaign committee fundraising otherwise would have.[31]

While Super PACs cannot coordinate with candidates in any way (remember that they can only make independent expenditures), nearly all Super PACs so far have been created to help a single presidential candidate or a host of congressional candidates of a single party running in competitive districts. On the presidential side, it seems imperative for legitimate presidential candidates to have at least one Super PAC aligned with him or her in order to be competitive. (Nevertheless, in 2016, Bernie Sanders proved that a viable primary campaign could be run without the help of Super PACs.) In June 2016, at the end of primary season, all presidential candidates, except for Sanders, who had raised at least the small sum of $1 million had a Super PAC supporting them.[32]

One may wonder how a supposedly "independent" committee could be so closely aligned with a particular candidate. The short explanation is that campaigns and Super PACs have mastered the practice of working around the rules that bar coordination to, essentially, work together. Journalist Adam Wollner, during the early days of the 2016 election, detailed a number of methods presidential campaigns used to coordinate with their aligned Super PACs without technically violating the rules. For example, Republican candidate John Kasich's Super PAC, New Day for America, ran ads that included Kasich speaking directly into the camera – seemingly a clear example of coordination. However, Kasich filmed these ads before he officially became a presidential candidate, so there was no presidential campaign for the Super PAC to coordinate with at the time. Wollner also noted that some Super PACs associated with GOP candidates have utilized social media to share information with aligned campaigns. For instance, some Super PACs have been known to run polls for candidate, and post the results on public Twitter accounts.[33] The information is technically open to the public, but only someone who knows where to look (the candidates?) will be able to access the data.

Overall, Super PACs have greatly increased the amount of money spent in American elections. In 2010, the year that Super PACs burst onto the scene, they spent a combined total of over $62 million. This figure would prove to be minuscule. In the following midterm election Super PACs spent nearly $340 million. Even that number, while perhaps still astonishing, is small in comparison to Super PAC spending in presidential years. During the 2012 election, the first presidential election following these landmark court cases, Super PACs spent over $600 million. In 2016 this number jumped to nearly $1.1 *billion*![34] Super PACs supporting Hillary Clinton raised $217.5 million, and those helping Donald Trump raised $82.3 million.[35] The Super PAC money raised in support of Trump is considered to be rather low; the lack of money was likely due to Trump being a very atypical candidate. Some conservative Super PACs, for example, chose not to act in support of Trump and focused all of their efforts on congressional races instead. This also means that Super PAC spending in future presidential campaigns that feature more conventional candidates will likely grow by leaps and bounds beyond the 2016 figures.

As expected, the 2018 midterm elections were awash with campaign money. There was a great deal of enthusiasm on the Democratic side, leading to early money, hefty contributions and an array of dark money and Super PAC support. For example, one unit, called the Hub Project, channeled more than $30 million to a handful of targeted races.[36] But Republicans certainly benefited from similar groups. In all, it appears that upwards of $1 billion was spent by independent groups alone in the midterm – a sizeable increase from the previous midterm election.[37]

In sum, the impact of the *Citizens United* and *SpeechNow.org* rulings on the amount of money spent during American elections has been significant. While many expected (or, in some cases, feared) that corporations would begin to dominate the campaign finance scene, this has not been the case. During the 2014 and 2016 election cycles, corporations contributed less than 1 percent of the money raised by Super PACs.[38] The real effect of these court cases has been the increased impact of individual wealthy donors, and, subsequently, the drastic increase in independent expenditures. Given the patterns of Super PAC spending in their brief history, we should expect that these committees will continue to spend more and more in future elections, augmenting their impact on American politics.

Conclusion: Is Too Much Money Really the Problem?

The role of big money in elections is troublesome to many Americans. The process seems to give some candidates an unfair advantage and it spills past Election Day into the policy process. A survey conducted by the Pew Research Center in 2018 found that a large majority of Americans (77 percent) believe there should be limits on the amount of money spent in politics.[39] A smaller majority (65 percent) said they thought new laws should be written to reduce the role of money. Surely contributors to campaigns expect something for their investment, right? Would they be content with mere access? Three-quarters of respondents in the Pew poll said large donors have more say in government than they do. (Interestingly, those who had contributed money to a political candidate or group in the past year were much more likely than those who had not to say that their representative in Congress would help them if they had a problem.) The idea of shifting control of the policy process toward those who can give – and give big – is contrary to the egalitarian part of elections, outlined in Chapter 2. It is one of the many ironies of an open political process: individuals and groups are encouraged to vigorously support political candidates, but in doing so their efforts create an unlevel playing field. In a way, the freedom to participate creates a lopsided system – often leading to less engagement.

Shortly after the 2012 election, an analysis was done using every congressional race in the nation to help pin down the impact of campaign money on election outcomes.[40] The data was based on information collected by the Center for Responsive Politics. Many of their findings were what we would expect. For example, there appears to be a strong, positive correlation between the amount of money spent and the likelihood of success, and this was especially true in tight races. Incumbents also raise more than challengers. It is only fair to say that these findings, and a host of similar studies, only confirm what we know: money plays a powerful role in today's electoral system. A late California politician accurately proclaimed that "money is the mother's milk of politics."[41]

But we also know that in every election a few candidates run for office on shoestring budgets, overcome the odds, and are sent into public life. In the 2016 presidential contest, Donald Trump spent much less than Hillary Clinton, and Bernie Sanders gave Clinton a run for her money, so to speak, with a smaller war chest – the vast bulk of which was raised through small contributions. We relish stories in which candidates with guts, determination, and grassroots support bring down the overconfident, wealthy Goliath. Maybe it is not money that wins elections but ideas and character. Viewed optimistically, perhaps fundraising is simply a measure of public sentiment – that is, some candidates raise more than others because they are more popular and thus more likely to win on Election Day. Sanders was wildly popular with the progressive wing of the Democratic Party. Moreover, we might applaud the flow of money into campaigns as a form of speech. In a democracy, the more political speech the better, right?

And yet, many Americans are convinced that limiting money, or at least getting our arms around the growing volume of money, will enhance our democracy. The system would be more egalitarian if the finance playing field was leveled, they argue. Average citizens would have more faith in the process, too. As noted by a *New York Times* columnist, "The tide of money swelling around the American political system continues to rise … Sums [in 2016 were] twice those of 2000 levels. So, what does all that money buy? No one seriously thinks that the quality of American representative democracy has doubled in value. Has it instead become doubly corrupt?"[42] To others, the drive to limit or even rid the system of money has become one of the great red herrings of our day.

Either way, while the federal courts might one day backtrack on some of their recent decisions that have broadened the flow of money – particularly with regard to corporations and unions – it is unlikely that they will change course on the core part of *Buckley*. In other words, the courts will continue to see campaign contributions and spending as expressions of advocacy, protected by the 1st Amendment. Many other nations limit the amount of money in elections and even curtail advertisements and the length of campaigns. Those wishing for a more European-centered approach in the United States will be disappointed.

One of the most frequently cited approaches to minimizing the weight of money in elections is to level the playing field. This usually means some form of public financing of campaigns. There is no federal program for House and Senate candidates, but FECA introduced an optional public funding model for presidential candidates. Setting aside myriad rules and regulations, the overall idea is that to qualify for these funds a candidate must agree to limit their overall fundraising and spending. In the nomination phase, a matching formula is used once the candidate demonstrates a level of viability (such as raising $5,000 in 20 states), and in the general election candidates are given a lump sum if they agree not to solicit additional funds or to spend more than $50,000 of their own money. In 1976, each major party nominee received $21.8 million, but the figures are adjusted for inflation, so in 2016 the general election grant was $96.14 million. We might also note that there does not seem to be any appetite for enhancing the current system – that is, in giving candidates even larger amounts.

Through the years it worked rather well, but no major party general election candidate has accepted public funds since 2008. Changes have made the program ineffective in recent elections. Fundamentally, top-tier candidates can simply raise much higher sums; they are increasingly likely to turn down the public money because they believe they would be at a relative disadvantage. Additionally, outside groups are now spending massive amounts independent of the candidates. In fact, one could argue that most of the action in presidential campaign spending is today not candidate expenditures, but rather the huge sums dished out by numerous outside groups. Olympia Snow, a former member of the Senate from Maine, put the matter bluntly: "Unfortunately, money in politics is an insidious thing – and a loophole in our campaign finance system was taken advantage of with money going to existing or new groups with the sole purpose of influencing the election."[43]

Public financing of elections can be found at the state level. According to the National Conference of State Legislatures, in 2018 some 14 states had some form of public financing. Most of these states (12) provide money for gubernatorial contests, with only a handful (five) giving public aid for state legislative candidates. In each, accepting public money is optional, with the great majority of candidates, particularly for the legislature, accepting. In exchange, candidates must agree to limit the size of contributions and the overall amount they can raise and spend. One can imagine a growing number of states moving in this direction, especially if the grant amounts are big enough.

Are there other reform options, given the parameters laid out in *Buckley*? A forest of trees has been sacrificed by scholars and activists in the pursuit of effective legal reforms. One of the most obvious, easily achievable, and important ideas is to tighten reporting and disclosure requirements. In other words, create more transparency by ridding the system of "dark money."

Dark money is a fairly new term in the vernacular of American elections and it refers to the expenditure of funds by individuals and organizations whose identity is unknown. A growing number of commercials are aired, billboards are put up, robo-calls are made, and ads are posted on social media by unknown sources. Money given directly to candidates or parties has to be disclosed by law, meaning the source of the funds has to be reported. But since *Buckley*, funds given to non-profit organizations, unions, trade associations, and other groups to influence the outcome of an election do not have to be disclosed. In other words, huge sums can be given to groups in secrecy, which can then be used to influence the outcome of an election. The expression of support by the initial donor, the so-called free speech, is made without voters knowing who it is. (In all fairness, many organizations voluntarily disclose the sources of their funds, but they are not compelled to do so.) According to the Center for Responsive Politics, the amount of dark money has mushroomed in recent years – quadrupling between 2010 and 2016.

It is important to note that a great deal of this secretive money is also being spent on lobbying for certain policies and to boost "grassroots" citizen groups. Dark money is common on both sides of the political fence, too. One of the most detailed looks at the breadth and significance of this practice was conducted by journalist Jane Mayer. Her book, *Dark Money*, sent shockwaves through the system. Mayer painstakingly investigated the role of the Koch brothers in secretly funding conservative groups and candidates over four decades. Charles and David Koch control Koch Industries, one of the largest privately owned businesses in the United States. They are outspoken defenders of fossil fuels and have railed against efforts to confront climate change. Mayer's eye-opening book reveals the breadth of their political involvement, from funding think tanks and local conservative groups, to helping particular candidates. Mayer believes that the Koch brothers and a small number of allied plutocrats have essentially hijacked American democracy, using their money not just to compete with their political adversaries, but to drown them out.[44]

We could say, then, that while it might be a constitutionally protected right for wealthy individuals, and maybe even corporations and unions (which is highly debatable), to spend money on politics, should citizens have the right to know the source of these funds? It is likely that comprehensive disclosure requirements would be upheld by the courts. In *Citizens United*, the Supreme Court recognized that providing the electorate with information about the sources of election-related spending helps to "make informed choices in the political marketplace." Or, as noted by researchers at the Sunlight Foundation, "Transparency in government means that the government provides information that allows the public to see critical decisions and transactions. Understanding both the processes and outcomes of government action lets us know whether we have the right policies, and right political leaders, in place."[45]

It would take an act of Congress for greater disclosure for federal office candidates. While there are grumblings about tightening these laws, it is also a system that helped bring these men and women to power. If we know anything about the motivations of legislators it is that their first priority is often self-preservation.

It is worth noting that many states are moving quickly to ensure complete transparency in elections; disclosure laws are being introduced across the nation. In 2016, some 16 states made or tightened existing disclosure laws. Maine, for example, has one of the nation's tightest requirements. In 2017, the voters of the state were asked in a ballot referendum whether or not they wanted to approve the construction of a $200 million casino in the southwest corner of the state. The push for the project entailed two years and nearly $9 million – a staggering sum for a ballot question in Maine. Opponents of the plan, on the other hand, had few resources and were clearly losing the paid media battle. Commercials in favor of the scheme were nearly constant. Early in the contest the source of the funds for the pro-casino side was unknown, but through strict disclosure rules and good journalism it was later revealed that nearly all of it came from Shawn Scott, the owner of a Nevada-based casino corporation. To many Mainers, it seemed that Scott and his family were trying to buy a policy change. On election, the plan was rejected by 83 percent of the voters. After two years and $9 million, Scott and his partners netted just 17 percent of the vote. Many pointed to the importance of the state's disclosure rules for helping voters make an informed choice. The voters understood where the money was coming from – and they did not like it.

Notes

1 Laura Vozzella, "Va. Gov. McAuliffe Says He Has Broken U.S. Record for Restoring Voting Rights," *Washington Post* website, April 27, 2017 (www.washingtonpost.com/local/virginia-politics/va-gov-mcauliffe-says-he-has-broken-us-record-for-restoring-voting-rights/2017/04/27/55b5591a-2b8b-11e7-be51-b3fc6ff7faee_story.html?utm_term=.d534f0578098).

2 Ibid.

3 Ibid.

4 John Metcalfe, "The Skyrocketing Costs of Running for Mayor of a Major U.S. City," *Citylab*, November 6, 2012 (www.citylab.com/equity/2012/11/skyrocketing-costs-running-mayor-major-us-city/3814/).
5 Celestine Bohlen, "American Democracy is Drowning in Money," *New York Times* website, September 20, 2017 (www.nytimes.com/2017/09/20/opinion/democracy-drowning-cash.html).
6 Ibid.
7 J. Cherie Strachan, *High-Tech Grass Roots: The Professionalization of Local Elections* (Lanham, MD: Rowman & Littlefield, 2003), 72.
8 John Kenneth White and Daniel M. Shea, *New Party Politics: From Jefferson and Hamilton to the Information Age* (Boston MA: Bedford/St. Martin's, 2000), 210.
9 Robert Dinkin, *Campaigning in America: A History of Election Practices* (Westport, CT: Greenwood, 1989), 8.
10 R.J. Brown, HistoryBuff.com – A Nonprofit Organization (www.historybuff.com/library/refrailsplit.html).
11 Investopedia, "How Much Does it Cost to Become President?," October 24, 2017 (www.investopedia.com/insights/cost-of-becoming-president/).
12 Christopher Ingraham, "Somebody Just Put a Price Tag on the 2016 Election. It's a Doozy," *Washington Post* website, April 14, 2017 (www.washingtonpost.com/news/wonk/wp/2017/04/14/somebody-just-put-a-price-tag-on-the-2016-election-its-a-doozy/?utm_term=.4b40492cb711).
13 Soo Rin Kim, "The Price of Winning Just Got Higher, Especially in the Senate," *Open Secrets*, November 9, 2016 (www.opensecrets.org/news/2016/11/the-price-of-winning-just-got-higher-especially-in-the-senate/).
14 Center for Responsive Politics, "Cost of Elections" (www.opensecrets.org/overview/cost.php).
15 Michael Scherer, "The Incredible Rise of Campaign Spending," *Time*, October 23, 2014.
16 John Metcalfe, "The Skyrocketing Costs of Running for Mayor of a Major U.S. City," *Citylab*, November 6, 2012 (www.citylab.com/equity/2012/11/skyrocketing-costs-running-mayor-major-us-city/3814/).
17 *Buckley v. Valeo*, 424 U.S. I, 44.
18 Anthony Corrado, "Financing the 1996 Elections," *The Election of 1996: Reports and Interpretations*, Gerald M. Pomper, ed. (Chatham, NJ: Chatham House, 1997), 151.
19 "Number of Federal PACs Increases," *Federal Election Commission News Release*, March 9, 2009 (www.fec.gov/updates/number-of-federal-pacs-increases/).
20 OpenSecrets, "Influence and Lobbying," (www.opensecrets.org/).
21 Brian Tumulty, "Wendy Long Announces Run against Schumer," Press Connects.Com, March 3, 2016.
22 There has been a great deal written on the incumbent advantage. The work that kicked it all off, however, was penned by David Mayhew in 1974. See David Mayhew, *Congress: The Electoral Connection* (New Haven, CT: Yale University Press, 1974).
23 *US Term Limits, Inc., et al. v. Thornton et al.*, 63 U.S. Law Week 4413, 4432, May 22, 1995.

24 Roper Center for Public Opinion Research, 1994, as cited in the Center for Responsive Politics, *The Myths about Money in Politics* (Washington, DC: Center for Responsive Politics, 1995), 19.

25 Bloomberg News Poll, conducted by Princeton Survey Research Associates, July 31–August 5, 2001.

26 Editorial Desk, "A Campaign Finance Triumph," *New York Times*, December 11, 2003, 42.

27 Paul Sherman, "Citizens United Decision Means More Free Speech," *National Review Online*, January 21, 2010 (www.nationalreview.com/bench-memos/citizens-united-decision-means-more-free-speech-paul-sherman/).

28 Editorial, "The Court's Blow to Democracy," *New York Times*, January 21, 2010, A30.

29 "SpeechNow.org v. FEC," *Campaign Legal Center,* June 25, 2015 (https://campaignlegal.org/cases-actions/speechnoworg-v-fec).

30 David B. Magleby, "Super PACs and 501(c) Groups in the 2016 Election," paper presented at the State of the Parties: 2016 and Beyond, Ray C. Bliss Institute of Applied Politics, University of Akron, November 9–10, 2017, 2.

31 Abby Phillip and Dave Levinthal, "Adelson Tally to Gingrich: $20M," *Politico* website, April 20, 2012 (www.politico.com/story/2012/04/gingrich-camp-mired-in-debt-075418).

32 *New York Times,* "Which Presidential Candidates Are Winning the Money Race," June 22, 2016 (www.nytimes.com/interactive/2016/us/elections/election-2016-campaign-money-race.html).

33 Adam Wollner, "10 Ways Super PACs and Campaigns Coordinate, Even Though They're Not Allowed To," *The Atlantic* website, September 27, 2015 (www.theatlantic.com/politics/archive/2015/09/10-ways-super-pacs-and-campaigns-coordinate-even-though-theyre-not-allowed-to/436866/).

34 David B. Magleby, "Super PACs and 501(c) Groups in the 2016 Election," paper presented at the State of the Parties: 2016 and Beyond, Ray C. Bliss Institute of Applied Politics, University of Akron, November 9–10, 2017, 5.

35 Bill Allison, Mira Rojanasakul, Brittany Harris, and Cedric Sam, "Tracking the 2016 Presidential Money Race," *Bloomberg* website, December 9, 2016 (www.bloomberg.com/politics/graphics/2016-presidential-campaign-fundraising/).

36 Alexander Burns, "With $30 Million, Obscure Democratic Group Floods the Zone in House Races," *New York Times*, October 31, 2018.

37 Campaign Finance Institute, "Independent Spending in General Election to Surpass $ 1 Billion," November 5, 2018.

38 David B. Magleby, "Super PACs and 501(c) Groups in the 2016 Election," paper presented at the State of the Parties: 2016 and Beyond, Ray C. Bliss Institute of Applied Politics, University of Akron, November 9–10, 2017, 6.

39 Pew Research Center, "Most Americans Want to Limit Campaign Spending, Say Big Donors Have Greater Political Influence," May 8, 2018.

40 Philip Bump, "Does More Campaign Money Actually Buy More Votes: An Investigation," *The Atlantic* website, November 11, 2013 (www.theatlantic.com/politics/archive/2013/11/does-more-campaign-money-actually-buy-more-votes-investigation/355154/).

41 This remark was made by California State Treasurer Jesse Unruh. See John Kenneth White and Daniel M. Shea, *New Party Politics: From Jefferson*

and Hamilton to the Information Age (Boston MA: Bedford/St. Martin's, 2000), 95.

42 Celestine Bohlen, "American Democracy is Drowning in Money," *New York Times* website, September 20, 2017 (www.nytimes.com/2017/09/20/opinion/democracy-drowning-cash.html).

43 John Avlon, "How Partisan Politics Drove Olympia Snowe Away," CNN, March 3, 2012.

44 Alan Ehrenhalt, "'Dark Money,' by Jane Mayer," *New York Times* website, January 19, 2016 (www.nytimes.com/2016/01/24/books/review/dark-money-by-jane-mayer.html).

45 Emily Shaw, "Change for the Better in State-Level Campaign Finance Disclosure," *Sunlight Foundation,* December 9, 2016 (https://sunlightfoundation.com/2016/12/09/change-for-the-better-in-state-level-campaign-finance-disclosure/).

10 New Media and Russian Interference

Are Objective Assessments Possible in the 21st Century?

With Carlo Macomber

It was not surprising that Barack Obama would ask his main rival for the Democratic nomination in 2008, Hillary Clinton, to be his Secretary of State, and most knew that she would attack the job with vigor. She was smart, experienced and by all accounts one of the hardest working politicians in Washington. She had received high praise for her work in the Senate from both Democrats and Republicans, and in her new job Clinton traveled to 112 nations, shattering previous records. There were some bumps in the road, but when Clinton left her post in 2012 her national approval rating was at 65 percent, an exceptionally high figure for any politician in such a highly partisan era.[1] Flatly stated, she was one of the most well-liked public officials in America. She seemed a shoo-in for the 2016 Democratic nomination, and many thought her chances of moving back into the White House were good.

As the presidential contest began, Clinton's approval ratings remained modestly high, even as the race tightened. But then things changed – drastically – in the spring of 2016. Some of the rapid decline had to do with close media scrutiny, to be sure. Clinton had problems regarding her role in fundraising for the Clinton Foundation, incredibly high speaking fees which made her seem elitist, and of course her use of a private email server for official government business, which led to an FBI investigation. All this and other issues were brought up by her primary opponent, Bernie Sanders, and attacks by Republicans were relentless. On one level, her drop was predictable; politicians always take a beating when they run for higher office.

As her race for the Democratic nomination came to a close, polling found that Clinton had a 54 percent *negative* rating and a mere 41 percent approval. Other than Donald Trump, no other public official had a lower approval rating than Clinton. And it was not just that voters were moving away from Clinton and lining up behind Trump because of big policy differences. Rather, there was a growing hatred of Clinton – a raw, visceral abhorrence. She was now loathed by a wide segment of the population. Even seasoned observers were stunned at how so many Americans had come to despise Clinton so quickly. Why was she such a villain? At Trump rallies, and even at the Republican National Convention later in the summer, a standard crowd chant was "lock her up."

Again, Clinton had baggage – she was far from a perfect candidate. And yet, it was later revealed that a number of fictitious news stories were spread on social media, many of which were insidious. One story, dubbed Pizzagate, is illustrative and worth recounting. A few months prior to the election, Wikileaks released emails hacked from the account of John Podesta, Clinton's campaign chair. Social media users on popular conservative message boards, such as Reddit's forum dedicated to Trump and 4chan's far-right board, sorted through the hacked emails and claimed to find a link between the Clinton campaign, other Democratic officials, and a child sex ring at a Washington DC pizzeria. One 4chan user drew a connection between the phrase "cheese pizza" (which was included in a hacked email about dinner plans) and "child pornography" because, as this user noted, pedophiles on message boards often use "c.p." as code for child pornography.[2] Comet Ping Pong, a pizzeria in DC, became embroiled in discussions on far-right message boards when a user discovered emails sent by the restaurant's owner, James Alefantis, to Podesta (Alefantis had allowed Democratic operatives to use his restaurant for fundraising events).

Pizzagate spread throughout more popular social media platforms, such as Facebook and Twitter. Articles were posted about the scandal that were meant to look real. Attempts to debunk Pizzagate by the mainstream media only added fuel to the fire. For example, shortly after the publication of an article debunking Pizzagate, a tweet from a fake Representative (named Steven Smith), from a fake congressional district (Georgia's 15th), stated that the story was actually coming from the mainstream media. This tweet, which had a veneer of legitimacy, was retweeted over and over.[3]

While the Pizzagate conspiracy may seem quite ridiculous and difficult to believe, many took it seriously. In December of 2016, a heavily armed man from North Carolina drove more than six hours to the pizzeria where he believed children were in danger. He stormed the restaurant and fired several shots, but fortunately no one was hurt. The man surrendered after realizing that no children were in peril.[4]

A poll conducted days after the shooting found that 9 percent of Americans believed Hillary Clinton was connected to a child sex ring at a DC restaurant, and another 19 percent were unsure. Of those who voted for Donald Trump, 14 percent thought Clinton was connected to a child sex ring and 32 percent were unsure. Just 54 percent were confident enough to say that she was not.[5] This deserves repeating: nearly half of Trump supporters were unsure if the former First Lady, United States Senator and Secretary of State was complicit in a child sex trafficking ring run out of a neighborhood pizzeria.

It is a given that public officials who decide to run for the presidency see their approval rating drop, and Hillary Clinton clearly had some issues. But her fall from one of the most well-liked politicians to one loathed and mistrusted was remarkable. Arguably, no candidate for the White House has ever had a longer résumé – a more robust record of accomplishments. But as the social media bots got to work and incendiary fake news stories spread from one screen to the next, all of that vanished. The essence of Clinton, her experience, persona, and skills, evaporated into the ether.

Technological innovation has always had an impact on American campaigns. Looking for a competitive edge, campaign strategists embrace new technology in the hope that it will make the difference between a victory celebration and a concession speech. The railroad, for instance, initiated whistle-stop tours, allowing candidates to cover more territory and see more voters than ever before. Radio and television ads allowed candidates to enter millions of homes in the blink of an eye. Celebrities and well-known political figures leave messages on millions of answering machines each election cycle. Mass mailings allow campaigns to target tightly defined groups of voters, and satellites can place candidates in front of local news anchors at a rate of up to 20–30 interviews per day. Full 3D-holograms of candidates and surrogates are beamed to Wolf Blitzer's CNN Situation Room. Technology is constantly changing how we access and evaluate candidates.

But the internet is qualitatively different. It has revolutionized nearly every aspect of our lives, from how we communicate and correspond, how we organize our day and create relationships, and how the world conducts commerce. In an article charting the "36 Ways the Internet Has Changed Us," *Washington Post* journalist Caitlin Dewey writes, "With more than four billion indexed Web pages, thousands imploding and starting up by the day, any thorough accounting of the Web's impact would be impossible."[6] Another observer calls the web a sort of secular, modern-day Shiva: "god of creation, god of destruction."[7] Computer company executive and author Eric Schmidt put the matter this way: "The internet is the first thing that humanity has built that humanity doesn't understand, the largest experiment in anarchy that we have ever had."[8]

Naturally – inevitably – the web has transformed elections. It has become a permanent, significant resource in contemporary campaigns, and it makes for interesting analysis and discussion. But it has also ushered in a potentially insidious dynamic: the ability to define what voters perceive as news. The ability to filter and sort information in ways that reinforce existing beliefs and jettison contradictory messages is redefining the evaluation process. Of course the cherry on top is the ability of foreign actors, like the Russian Government, to infiltrate campaigns, hijack emails and campaign data, and potentially corrupt the tallying of results.

Few think the 2016 election was an aberration, but rather a harbinger of untold potential pitfalls. This chapter will explore the evolution of the media in campaigns, with a sharp focus on Russian meddling in the 2016 presidential race.

The Partisan Press

When former friends Thomas Jefferson and John Adams squared off against each other for the second time in a quest for the presidency in 1800, both were assailed in newspapers. It was one of the most negative, hard-hitting electoral contests in American history. Jefferson's supporters called Adams a "hideous hermaphroditical character, which has neither the force and firmness of a man, nor the gentleness and sensibility of a woman," and in return, Adams' men called Jefferson "a mean-spirited, low-lived fellow, the son of a half-breed Indian squaw, sired by a Virginia mulatto father."[9] And that was just the beginning. Some of these attacks were made through pamphlets, and each side had a legion of speakers who would move from community to community. For the most part, however, the negative campaign was conducted through newspapers, where each side sponsored (financially supported) their own editors and papers. After the election, things calmed down.

By the 1830s, partisan loyalties were increasing once again, and several factors came together to further heighten the importance of the media in elections. Literacy rates were on the rise, leading to more voters who were able to read newspapers and pamphlets. The cost of printing declined due to technological changes related to the production of paper and the process of setting type and, even more significantly, local party organizations burst on the scene and local newspapers fueled the partisan engine. Soon every community boasted several partisan newspapers.

The partisan press lasted about 60 years. During this time, candidates for all offices relied on supportive papers to carry their message and to assail the opposition. Indeed, some of the most aggressive attacks on candidates came from newspapers. It was critical for presidential candidates to have sympathetic newspapers in key states. Much of Abraham Lincoln's behind-the-scenes wrangling during his run for the presidency in 1860 centered on funding supportive newspapers in critical states. Once in office, presidents and other elected officials would often hire editors to work for the government. And while the precise cause-and-effect relationship is unclear, it is not surprising that party identification during this period became ironclad. That is to say, we are not entirely clear whether intense partisanship led to the development of the partisan press, or if these papers further solidified partisan allegiances. Either way, the party spirit ran high during much of the 19th century and newspapers were a key element.

The Progressive Movement, discussed at various points in this book, centered on getting rid of corrupt party organizations, and in this wave of reform, the partisan press also began to fade. Being highly partisan was simply out of vogue. More importantly, during the Industrial Revolution newspapers were used to sell products, so limiting the readership to the backers of one party or the other did not make economic sense. Advertising revenue mushroomed by the turn of the century, predicated on more and more readers. Why cut the potential audience in half? It was soon realized that fortunes could be made in the newspaper business. In place of the partisan press came yellow journalism, where the focus was on sensationalism. Other media outlets moved toward objective news reporting, partly due to the advent of national wire services.

There were certainly a few news outlets that leaned toward one ideological side or the other, but since World War II mainstream newspaper, radio and later television news was professed to be non-partisan. It was considered a violation of journalistic ethics to side with one party or with a particular candidate. This, of course, did not stop candidates from crying foul, arguing that the media was out to get them. It was recurrent news coverage that made Richard Nixon a household name when he was a member of the House in the early 1950s, later leading to his selection as Eisenhower's vice president. Nixon was a staunch anti-communist and his role on the House Un-American Activities Committee was widely covered. But when he ran for the presidency in 1960, and later in 1968 and throughout his presidency, Nixon claimed that he was the target of relentless, unfair attacks by the media. Even so, the standards of objectivity and fairness were the guiding principle of news reporting. Biased reporters or outlets were spurned.

Things have changed, of course. As the number of news outlets grew rapidly with the rise of the internet and cable television, many found a formula for profitability was to maintain a smaller, but stable audience. One route to do this was to jettison the non-partisan approach and vigorously attack one party, while making every policy dispute a crisis. Conservative radio talk show host Rush Limbaugh led the way with this model in the early 1990s. His assaults on Democrats, and Bill and Hillary Clinton in particular, were relentless – and his audience grew. Many credited Limbaugh with fueling the Republican surge in 1994, and later the rise of the Tea Party movement. Soon a host of other conservative radio and television commentators burst on the scene, each driving their ratings upward by throwing red meat to listeners/viewers.

To be fair, many conservatives argue that the popularity of these outlets sprang from a liberal bias in traditional news outlets; many of the conservative outlets offered news and perspectives missing in other stations, they argue. These outlets serve as a counterweight to the liberal, "lamestream" media. This may help explain why so few liberal radio talk shows have been able to follow suit; there is no left-leaning counterpart to Limbaugh, for instance.

It is hard to overstate the importance of Fox News in contemporary electoral politics. It was launched in 1996 as a competitor to CNN, but placed at the helm was the former Republican strategist, Roger Ailes. Ailes had a long list of Republican clients and was a key player in Ronald Reagan's two presidential elections. In its early years, Fox News had a slight, but discernible tilt toward the right, but in the last decade the station has become the go-to source of conservative news. According to a 2017 study done by the Pew Research Center, nearly 50 percent of Trump voters relied on Fox News as their primary source of information. For Clinton supporters there was an array of outlets, with no single source netting more than 20 percent.[10] Beyond the news programming, Fox also carries several popular conservative commentators, including Laura Ingraham, Tucker Carlson and Sean Hannity. Like Limbaugh, without the constraints of objectivity, each night these personalities hammer away at progressive politicians. Hannity even traveled with Donald Trump in the final days of the 2018 midterm election to appear and speak at rallies.

The impact of Fox News has been nothing short of titanic. For many conservatives the scope of their news gathering has narrowed to one outlet and its commentators. Other sources of information are dismissed as biased and rejected as "fake news." The conservative news echo chamber, or bubble, has become formidable. According to a 2017 study conducted by two Emory University political scientists, watching Fox News directly causes a substantial rightward shift in viewers' attitudes, which translates into a significantly greater willingness to vote for Republican candidates. Their data also suggest Fox News has become even more conservative in the last few years.[11] As you might expect, regular Fox viewers have a very low regard for other news outlets.

The echo chamber is not only comprised of conservatives, to be sure. Many scholars point to the role of online sources and, to a lesser extent, MSNBC in shaping the attitudes of left-leaning Americans. There does not appear to be a single, omnipotent source of news for liberals, like Fox for conservatives, but an array of sources certainly reinforces existing beliefs and attitudes. Liberals wear news blinders, too.

Nevertheless, it would be a mistake to assume that the narrowing of information has happened equally on both sides. For whatever reason, conservatives are much more likely to get their information from a single source than are liberals. Not only do Fox News, Rush Limbaugh, Sean Hannity and other sources shape the outlook of conservative voters, but it seems that some Republican officials adopt positions first presented on the network. In other words, some Republican officials seem to be taking their cues from Fox. Many scholars and pundits have noted, for instance, a high degree of consistency between the theories offered by Fox News commentators, particularly Sean Hannity, and Donald Trump's talking points (which often show up in tweets). As noted by one observer, "Fox News may be the most important news organization in America right now simply because it has a devoted audience inside the Oval Office of one."[12]

Have we once again moved into a partisan press era? Not exactly. There are more partisan outlets than in the not-so-distant past, but most news outlets strive to be objective. This is particularly true at the local level. One key difference, however, is that a growing number of Americans believe the press is biased. Some of this has to do with overtly ideological programs, like Fox News and MSNBC, but it also springs from hyper-polarization. A growing number of Americans of all stripes reject information contrary to their core beliefs – a topic taken up at the conclusion of this chapter.

Online Videos and YouTube

In 1960, television exploded onto the presidential campaign scene with the televised Kennedy–Nixon debates. During the 2008 elections, YouTube demonstrated a similar flood of interest with the publication of video streaming from nearly all campaigns. The mention of YouTube as a prominent component of the 2008 campaign is in itself rather remarkable. The online video sharing website started in 2005. The 2008 election was the first presidential election ever to be held with YouTube in existence – and some have called it the "YouTube Election,"[13] implying that the site had a *decisive* role in the outcome.

But this was surely not the first election influenced by YouTube, given the role it played in the historic 2006 election season. During the election, several Republican seats were in jeopardy, with Democrats experiencing a general popularity upswing in response to George W. Bush's falling polling numbers. One of the very tight races was the contest for the Virginia US Senate seat. Incumbent Republican George Allen was running for reelection and in the early stages had a commanding lead over Jim Webb, the Democratic challenger. This lead held steady until one day on the campaign trail when Allen was dramatically tripped up by this new media technology. Allen was at a Republican event in rural Virginia when he noticed a volunteer, a dark-skinned young man of Indian descent, from the Webb campaign filming his speech (this is common; they are called "trackers"). The GOP candidate lost his cool and began disparaging his opponent and the campaign worker. He called the young man a "macaca," twice. This is a racial slur, derived from the macaque, a species of monkey. And, of course, it was caught on tape and immediately posted to YouTube. The post had over one million views in the following week and soon

Allen was apologizing on national television and fending off charges that he had uttered similar racial slurs in the past. Webb closed the gap and ultimately defeated Allen. In previous elections, Allen's comment might have been missed by the media or noted in a sidebar story. Posting the video on YouTube clearly altered the course of the election. Republicans would later send their own trackers into the field hoping to record Democratic blunders.

Early in the 2008 presidential contest, it became clear that candidates and their consultants were thinking formally about how to best utilize the burgeoning power of YouTube. Democratic candidate John Edwards announced his candidacy on the site. YouTube efforts were generally successful because they often heightened an otherwise less-exciting story – the formal announcement of a candidate that had been running for years, for example. When Barack Obama announced he was running for president, the announcement on YouTube itself was newsworthy.

Beyond official candidacy announcements, candidates routinely produce content for YouTube. Nearly all political ads are now posted on the site, many of which never actually run on network or cable television. Many ads are typically played to a specific television market via regional airwaves and then made available to everyone via YouTube. This has allowed campaigns to extend their reach, especially if an ad becomes viral. It has also given journalists an easier way to monitor political advertisements.

One of the most extraordinary uses of YouTube occurred on July 23, 2007. On that date, CNN sponsored a Democratic presidential primary debate in South Carolina where questions were presented by average citizens over YouTube.[14] (The Republican presidential primary CNN/YouTube debate was held on September 14, 2007 in Florida.) The ground-up nature of the event, with average citizens asking questions, gave the debate a greater sense of democratic authenticity.

The use of YouTube on the campaign trail underscores an important relationship between online information and the establishment media. As more and more citizens post videos of campaign events on YouTube, we learn new information about candidates, which is often unflattering.

YouTube continued to have a great impact during the 2016 election season. Campaigns spent about $300 million on online ads during the cycle, which is considerably more than what was spent on radio and newspaper ads.[15] A greater number of political ads were made specifically for YouTube and online viewers, as well. These ads were often more humorous and satirical, such as Republican candidate Ted Cruz's "Invasion" ad, which reached YouTube's most watched list in January 2016. The most popular YouTube ad of the overall campaign, with over four million views, was Bernie Sanders' heartwarming "America" ad, which featured Sanders visiting places throughout America's heartland.

While YouTube proved to be important in 2008, it was considered vital in 2016. Chris Wilson, an operative for the Ted Cruz campaign, said of YouTube, "This is the first cycle where if you're not doing it, you're going to lose."[16] However, it is not known if the website's importance will eventually taper off in favor of another service. Perhaps the 2020 election will be dubbed the "Snapchat election." If so, campaign consultants will find themselves trying to adapt again. In the ever-changing world of the internet and social media, we will just have to wait to find out.

The Rise of Online News

Voters are moving away from traditional newspapers and toward online news sources for campaign information. As noted by Darrell West of the Brookings Institution, "Checking for news online – whether through Google, Twitter, Facebook, major newspapers, or local media websites – has become ubiquitous, and smartphone alerts and mobile applications bring the latest developments to people instantaneously around the world."[17] This began in the mid-1990s, when independent websites emerged to present campaign information. At the time, these sites were interesting because they were not developed or supported by traditional news providers like CNN or ABC. They were often the work of fringe groups with no other publishing outlet, or early internet adopters who found the medium to be an interesting information source. One of the most prominent early endeavors was Web White and Blue (WWB). WWB was an online knowledge network that was university-based. At one point, 17 charters at various colleges and universities contributed information to the network. It was similar in concept to a wiki environment where independent writers submit content.

As general internet usage in the United States swelled, especially among older Americans, traditional news sources began repurposing their content to online sites. As CNN.com, MSNBC.com, CBSNews.com (and more) began to establish their online resources, they soon overwhelmed the nonprofit and independent websites with their content and general information capacity.

The presence of comprehensive and immediate online news sources and the development of news-aggregating engines (e.g., Google News, Real Clear Politics) have caused a shift in the electorate that was identified as early as 2000. In conducting a survey of Web White and Blue users, one scholar found that the group had in general "*substituted* the internet for newspapers as one of its two main election news sources."[18] He found that TV was the most common news source, followed by the internet. This supports more general findings from the Pew Research Center's study of Americans' political news consumption leading up to the 2016 election. Their report found that around 30 percent of US citizens noted an internet source as the "most helpful" medium for obtaining election news. For Americans under the age of 30, this number was 55 percent.[19] According to another 2016 Pew Research Center survey, about 40 percent of Americans now depend on the internet as their primary source of news, significantly higher than newspapers' share, which stood at 20 percent. Furthermore, this percentage is even higher among people under 30, with 50 percent of this demographic "often" getting its news from the internet, nearly double the next closest medium.[20]

Online Fundraising

The late Senator John McCain surprised many when he raised a modest sum online during his 2000 bid for the Republican nomination. But it did not become a significant and widely recognized fundraising medium until 2004, when Howard Dean's presidential campaign and groups like MoveOn.org demonstrated that online fundraising could generate vast amounts of money. In many respects, Dean and his team rewrote the playbook on how to organize, finance, and mold a presidential campaign.[21] After Dean's success with internet fundraising, both John Kerry and George W. Bush followed suit – each raising tens of millions of dollars online.

The success of online fundraising in 2004 startled many observers, but throughout the 2008 campaign such systems were commonplace. And while online contributions remain subject to all campaign contribution guidelines enforced by the Federal Election Commission, they have opened up new strategic territory for the ongoing fundraising needs of politicians. The pace of collecting funds also caught many by surprise. In one month alone – January of 2008 – Barack Obama's campaign collected $36 million, an unprecedented feat at that time for a single month in American politics, especially given that it was powered by small online gifts.[22] "The architects and builders of the Obama field campaign ... have undogmatically mixed timeless traditions and discipline of good organizing with new technologies of decentralization and self-organization."[23]

In subsequent election cycles, online fundraising has, as expected, continued to grow. In the age of online shopping, PayPal, GoFundMe and Venmo, Americans are used to spending and donating money online with the click of a mouse or a tap on their cellphones. In 2016, no candidate was better at exploiting this phenomenon than Bernie Sanders. While many Democrats, including Barack Obama and Hillary Clinton, claim to be against the influence of corporate money and Super PACs in elections, they nevertheless embraced this source of money during their campaigns for the White House. Sanders, however, rebelled completely against corporate money, refusing to accept their donations or to have a Super PAC, instead relying mostly on small donations from individuals. Following his win in the New Hampshire primary, Sanders asked his supporters to go to his website and donate any amount that they could. A day later, his campaign had raised $8 million through online donations. Heading into Super Tuesday, the Sanders campaign had a goal of raising $40 million during the month of February, which it surpassed with ease.[24] Anthony Corrado, one of the nation's leading campaign finance scholars, noted at the time, "Small-dollar donations have become the bedrock of [Sanders'] campaign, and he has been able to motivate more donors more quickly to raise more money from small amounts than was the case for [Barack] Obama or [Howard] Dean."[25] Of course, Sanders did not end up winning the Democratic nomination, but his run against Hillary Clinton was closer than expected. This may have been due to his unprecedented online fundraising abilities. The average donation to his campaign, as he repeated time and time again, was just $27.

Social Media and Russian Interference

During the past three election cycles, candidates have increasingly used social media to communicate directly with voters, spread news about campaign events, identify their positions on critical issues, and fundraise. While Facebook allows candidates to post longer, more official statements, and Instagram allows candidates to post photos from events, Twitter has emerged as a leading platform.

On April 29, 2007, then Senator Barack Obama published the first tweet by a candidate for president. It read: "Thinking we're only one signature away from ending the war in Iraq" and included a link to his campaign website.[26] Considering Obama's relative youth during the 2008 campaign (as well as the age of John McCain, the Republican nominee), it was savvy for him to take advantage of what Twitter (and social media in general) had to offer. In the end, Obama received overwhelming support from younger voters – the very age groups most likely to use social media. Many point to these efforts as Obama's "net-root" campaign.

As a result of Obama's early Twitter use, "political Twitter" was a mostly liberal platform through the early years. Following Obama's victory, Michael Patrick Leahy, a member of the Tea Party movement, started the #TCOT (Top Conservatives on Twitter) hashtag. Leahy created a list of the best accounts for conservatives to follow. His list started in late 2008 with about 30 members, and quickly increased to over 3,500, many of whom participated in weekly conference calls, by the beginning of 2009. The #TCOT movement gained enough political clout that it was able to organize and respond to events quickly. Ultimately, members of the #TCOT list launched the Tea Party in early 2009, and by April of that year, there were over a dozen Tea Party chapters across the country.[27] Learning from Obama's social media success, Leahy was able to use the technology to invigorate and expand the conservative movement. Leahy's work saw considerable early success during the 2010 midterm elections as Tea Party candidates were elected at all levels of government, and the movement culminated into a powerful response to Obama's agenda.

Following Obama's success with social media and the #TCOT response, it was clear that the technology would be a part of future campaigns. The question moved to what the best use of social media would be for candidates. In a sense, Obama had a significant advantage in 2008 just by using the service. How he used it was less important since there was minimal online competition. This has not been the case in subsequent elections as Twitter accounts, in particular, have become ubiquitous for candidates.

In fact, a team of scholars from Sam Houston State University attempted to decipher 2012 House candidates' Twitter styles (which was a spin on scholar Richard Fenno's oft-cited 1978 book, *Homestyle*, about how legislators act in their district). The researchers analyzed every tweet by US House candidates in the two months leading up to the 2012 election (67,119 tweets from 1,119 candidates). Each tweet was coded into one of several categories: attack, campaigning, mobilization, issues, media, and user interaction. It was also noted if tweets pertained to President Obama or his Republican challenger Mitt Romney. They found Republican candidates (the out-of-power party) were more likely to post attack tweets or tweets about Obama than their Democratic counterparts. Further, women were more likely than men to attack their opponents, tweet about issues, and encourage mobilization. Challengers were also more likely to issue attack, mobilization, and user interaction tweets than incumbents.[28] Ultimately, the study provided some key information regarding candidate Twitter style in the first election cycle in which Twitter played a significant role for all candidates.

Donald Trump's use of Twitter during his campaign was exceptional. According to an analysis conducted by the *Wall Street Journal*, Trump had 33 million followers. He sent out about 35,000 tweets, with an average of 11 per day. On one day alone, he sent out 87 tweets to his supporters. Clinton had half as many followers and sent one quarter of that number of tweets.[29] As we all know, President Trump has continued to use Twitter and, like during the campaign, his tweets have been the source of much controversy.

Beyond Trump's use of Twitter, another key piece of the social media puzzle in the 2016 election was the proliferation of fake news, hoaxes and misinformation. Hundreds of fictitious news stories from bogus websites and nebulous sources appeared – and were widely shared – on

Facebook and Twitter. For example, one dubious site published stories that Trump had been endorsed by Pope Francis and another that Clinton had pledged to sell weapons to ISIS if elected. Those two pieces garnered some two million Facebook "engagements" in the months leading up to the election. "To put that figure into perspective, during the same period, the top performing Facebook story for the *New York Times* racked up just over 370,000 engagements."[30] Another fake story said Clinton was determined to implement Islamic Law in Florida. According to BuzzFeed, several of the top fake news stories during the campaign each netted nearly one million engagements. The list of stories includes "Donald Trump sent his own plane to transport 200 stranded Marines," "Ireland is now officially accepting Trump refugees from America," "WikiLeaks confirms Hillary sold weapons to ISIS," "FBI agent suspected in Hillary email leaks found dead in apartment murder-suicide," "FBI director received millions from Clinton Foundation, his brother's law firm does Clinton's taxes," "ISIS leader calls for American Muslim voters to support Hillary Clinton," and "RuPaul claims Trump touched him inappropriately in the 90s."

Some of the fictitious stories during the election were aimed at helping Clinton, but as the headlines suggest, the vast majority were created in support of Donald Trump – by a five-to-one ratio according to one estimate.[31] The spread of fake news typically began with a story being shared by a social media account that appeared to belong to an average American. But these accounts were not run by real people, but rather they were automated accounts – also known as bots.

We now know that a large number of the social media bots were linked to Russia's efforts to influence the 2016 election. In the months leading up to the election, it was common for these automated accounts to post fake news stories into a Facebook group that was most likely to believe (or want to believe) the story. For example, Facebook groups consisting of supporters of Trump and/or opponents of Hillary Clinton would see posts from a bot (who appeared to be just another like-minded group member) linking to a false story damaging to Clinton. This strategy relied on the real members of these groups to take the story at face value and share it widely on their personal pages. The Pizzagate conspiracy, as noted in the introduction to this chapter, ultimately spread through Facebook and Twitter (and had an extensive reach). "So that way whenever [the Russians were] trying to socially engineer them and convince them that the information is true, it's much more simple because you see somebody and they look exactly like you, even down to the pictures," noted former FBI agent Clinton Watts when he testified before a Senate Committee in 2017.[32]

According to a research team at the University of Southern California, one in five election-centered tweets in 2016 were likely sent by Russian bots. These scholars found that bots were just as effective at spreading messages as human-controlled accounts.[33] A cybersecurity research firm, FireEye, determined that possibly thousands of Twitter accounts that campaigned against Hillary Clinton were probably controlled by Russian interests, including many automated by bots. By the spring of 2018, more and more details of Russian efforts to shape the outcome of the presidential campaign came to light. Executives from Twitter, for example, told the Senate Judiciary Committee that Russian bots retweeted posts over half a million times in the waning weeks of the campaign.[34] Much of this material was directed at voters in swing states like Michigan, Wisconsin and Pennsylvania.

We also learned that bots were not the only tool used by the Russians. Computers at Hillary Clinton's campaign office, the Democratic National Committee and the Democratic Congressional Campaign Committee were hacked, sensitive strategic information and upwards of 50,000 emails were stolen. "They harvested everything, including email passwords, opposition research, staff communication, personal banking information of staffers, and a folder about the Benghazi investigation."[35] The process of releasing the information to the public was a bit complex. By one account,

> In June 2016, the Russians first released the information using the website DCLeaks.com and associated social media accounts. When the DNC said it was hacked by Russians, a person going by the moniker "Guccifer 2.0" claimed credit for the leaks, saying he was a lone Romanian hacker … Using this persona, the hackers were in contact with US reporters, people close to the Trump campaign, and WikiLeaks. WikiLeaks told Guccifer 2.0 to send "any new material" so they can ensure it will "have a much higher impact than what you are doing." Then WikiLeaks said it would be best to release the leaks during the Democratic National Convention, in hopes of discord between Clinton and Bernie Sanders supporters. In July 2016, WikiLeaks began publishing the leaks.[36]

In the summer of 2018, 12 Russians were identified by the Department of Justice and indicted for their interference in the 2016 election.

As Americans learned more about Russian meddling in the presidential campaign, federal intelligence officials warned of similar attacks in the 2018 election. In July of that year, Tom Burt, a Microsoft security official, revealed that Russian hackers had registered a fake Microsoft website. It was a phishing website, and unspecified metadata indicated it was set up to target three candidates for the 2018 midterms.[37] A few weeks later, Dan Coats, National Intelligence Director, warned that America was under attack from "a pervasive campaign" by Russia to interfere in the midterm elections.[38] Also at the press conference was Kirstjen Nielsen, Secretary of Homeland Security. Her comments were even more pointed:

"Our democracy itself is in the crosshairs. Free and fair elections are the cornerstone of our democracy, and it has become clear that they are the target of our adversaries, who seek, as the DNI [Coats] just said, to sow discord and undermine our way of life."[39]

It is difficult to determine the precise impact that fake news, bot posts on social media, and the leaked information had on the election. We do know, for instance, that over 40 percent of the visits to 65 different fake news websites came from social media links (conversely only 10 percent of the visits to the top 690 US news sites come from social media). A study also indicated that the more time Americans spent on Facebook, the more fake news they consumed leading up to the election.[40] Researchers found that one group of Twitter bots sent out the hashtag #WarAgainstDemocrats more than 1,700 times on Election Day alone.[41] But whether or not all this changed a single vote, or could have shifted a few states away from Clinton, will remain speculation. A comprehensive analysis of this issue was conducted by Nate Silver of FiveThirtyEight, a research unit with ABC News. Silver is considered by many to be one of the nation's experts on election data analysis. He concludes with the following:

> My view on the effects of Russian interference is fairly agnostic. I tend to focus more on factors such as Clinton's email scandal or the Comey letter (and the media's handling of those stories) ... Clinton's Electoral College strategy ... was pretty stupid. But if it's hard to prove anything about Russian interference, it's equally hard to *disprove* anything: The interference campaign could easily have had chronic, insidious effects that could be mistaken for background noise but which in the aggregate were enough to swing the election by 0.8 percentage points toward Trump – not a high hurdle to clear because 0.8 points isn't much at all.[42]

For their part, after much outrage, Facebook and Twitter officials have begun working to eliminate bots and fake accounts on their platforms and to create stronger protections in order to prevent foreign nations and others from using their services to try to influence future American elections. But the success of social media sites is measured in the eyes of shareholders through the number of "monthly active users," so these companies have a disincentive to police the number of bots on their sites too closely. While it is unknown how many of Twitter's 328 million users and Facebook's nearly two billion users are bots, the two companies are wary of lowering these numbers too far and typically only eliminate bots as a result of serious complaints.[43]

It was a unique and surprisingly potent form of sabotage – and Nielsen was right. Without ever firing a shot, Russia struck a blow to the American psyche. The creation and spread of salacious stories was a stain on the 2016 election – and the ability to steal sensitive information and thousands of emails in an effort to shift the outcome of a race left Americans feeling vulnerable.

Perhaps more than anything, the attack created even deeper divisions in America. Worried that an admission of Russian interference might somehow delegitimize his victory, President Trump continued to call the interference a hoax, and the investigation into meddling a witch hunt. Even though the attack was verified by all five of the US intelligence agencies and was widely reported in the media (see above), just 32 percent of Republicans agreed that Russian hacking took place by the summer of 2018.[44] Reports to the contrary were dubbed fake news by the media opposed to Donald Trump and his agenda. As has been detailed in previous chapters, Americans are incredibly polarized. The proliferation of fake news, it could be said, has contributed to the strongest partisans becoming more set in their ways and even less accepting of the "other side," and this could exacerbate the inability of our democracy to function as it was intended. Fake news is not going to encourage pragmatism, compromise, and a willingness to work with the opposing party. So, while many are concerned that false news stories have had (and can continue to have) impacts on our elections – and this is certainly a great concern – it can also lead to gridlock.

As a final note in this section on social media, it is worth briefly discussing the Cambridge Analytica–Facebook scandal. In 2014, a research firm called Cambridge Analytica began collecting information from nearly 90 million Facebook users. Their plan was to use a survey to create profiles, which would later be used in research. The identity of each respondent was to remain confidential – that is, unless a consent voucher was signed.

In 2018, it was revealed that the Trump campaign hired the firm to help with their voter targeting operations, and that upwards of 50 million voter profiles were created and used. But only about 300,000 of the Facebook users had consented to have their information made public. Put a bit differently, the private information of millions of Americans, pulled from Facebook, was used in a campaign without their consent. Outrage over the breach of privacy was significant and soon Mark Zuckerberg was called before a Senate committee. He apologized and made vague assurances that it would not happen again.

The scandal brought to light a host of issues regarding the ethical standards of social media companies and political campaigns. Who owns data like this and how can it be used? Consumer advocates called for greater regulation, especially more clearly defined privacy rules. Perhaps the government should step in. It is interesting to note, however, that polls conducted after the scandal, and in light of several similar high-tech privacy breaches, suggest Americans did not appear overly concerned. Perhaps we live in a more open world, where all sorts of personal information is shared on social media sites. It is telling that perceptions regarding internet privacy vary by age. In one poll, 53 percent of those 65 and older were greatly concerned over the safety of their personal data, compared to 33 percent of respondents 18 to 29.[45]

Conclusion: Are Objective Assessments Possible in the 21st Century?

Election-centered democracies rely on what we might call vertical accountability. Voters hold public officials' feet to the fire. If they have done a good job, they are returned to office, but if not, they are sent packing and a new group is brought to power. Often these accountability judgments are candidate-specific, but at times they are party-based. In a previous chapter, we talked about realignments, the process of bringing a new party to power for a prolonged period. Either way, the idea is that the voters – the sovereign – use accountability judgments to reward or punish politicians on Election Day.

The question we confront today, and it is rather new, is whether this essential process can take place in today's media environment. The model implies sorting through information – that is, getting down to the hard facts in an objective way. This is why the constitutional framers put such faith in a free press. Partisanship has always served as a cognitive filter, but today's information environment is much different. What happens when we seek out only the news and opinions that confirm our existing positions, and reject outright anything that goes against our views? How do we know when stories are being created and circulated by nefarious actors? Adding to the mix, during the 2016 campaign and in the early months of the Trump Administration, we were also introduced to a new concept: alternative facts. This is the aggressive spinning of policies and arguments regardless of contrary verifiable information.

The barrier for objective evidence has evaporated and overtly partisan, emotion-rich information is used to draw more viewers, readers and listeners. If we add the continual drive for fresh news, the costs of traditional journalism, and the prospects of meddling by hostile foreign nations, we are left with a crisis of consensus and authority. One commentator put it this way:

> For years, technologists and other utopians have argued that online news would be a boon to democracy. That has not been the case. More than a decade ago, as a young reporter covering the intersection of technology and politics, I noticed the opposite. The internet was filled with 9/11 truthers, and partisans who believed against all evidence that George W. Bush stole the 2004 election from John Kerry, or that Barack Obama was a foreign-born Muslim.[46]

Again, citizens (voters) are called upon to judge those in power. Elections make the governors accountable to the governed. There must be an objective standard for the assessment, but with fake news and alternative facts, your side has *always* done a good job and the other party has *always* failed. There is no way to convince hard-core Republicans that Barack Obama saved the economy, and there is little chance of convincing die-hard Democrats that George Bush kept us safe after 9/11. The key ingredient in the accountability process – objectivity – has disappeared and the core rationale for elections has evaporated.

On July 17, 2018, in Helsinki, Finland, President Donald Trump held a one-on-one meeting with Russian President Vladimir Putin. It was a long conversation, lasting two hours, the content of which remains a mystery. One of the topics on everyone's mind was Russian interference in the 2016 election. All five of the US intelligence agencies had issued unambiguous reports that Russia had indeed conducted cyber-attacks against the United States during the campaign. Surely this would be an occasion to call out Putin for these egregious acts. Had the president raised the issue?

After the meeting, at a joint press conference, Trump downplayed his own intelligence agency reports: "I have great confidence in my intelligence people, but I will tell you that President Putin was extremely strong and powerful in his denial today … My people came to me, Dan Coats [Director of National Intelligence] came to me and some others, they said they think it's Russia. I have President Putin; he just said it's not Russia. I will say this: I don't see any reason why it would be." He went on to talk about the tensions between the two nations: "I hold both countries responsible. I think that the United States has been foolish. I think we've all been foolish … And I think we're all to blame." The president's message to the world was clear: The entire Russian meddling in the US campaign was nothing serious, that even if there was interference all would be forgiven, and that both nations share the blame for bad relations.

It was an incredible pronouncement. Russia was to be let off the hook. Condemnation from all sides of the political spectrum was swift, clear and recurrent. Had the president sold out his nation? Some even suggested his acts were treasonous. Fox News commentators, nearly always supportive of the president, vented their disapproval: "Trump is unable to see past himself," tweeted Brit Hume, a senior political analyst on the network. "There is an avalanche of you-know-what rolling downhill at warp speed toward @realDonaldTrump over this summit. Republicans – even the DNI are throwing bucketsful at him," tweeted Fox's chief White House correspondent John Roberts.

The president and his team worked desperately in the following days to minimize the damage. He had not meant to say "would," but instead "wouldn't" said his spokespeople the next day. But there was broad consensus that it was one of the low points of the first two years of his presidency. On the world stage, the president had flopped.

Or had he? One of the most stunning and revealing aspects about contemporary American politics is the percentage of Republicans who are willing to ride through Trump's missteps. The percentage of self-identified Republicans who believed Trump did a *good* job in Helsinki? According to a CBS News poll it is upwards of 70 percent. When Donald Trump was running for the White House he said that he could "stand in the middle of Fifth Avenue and shoot somebody and not lose any voters." Was he right?

When voters have access to an array of information consistent with their beliefs, all transgressions can be ignored or forgiven. And when we add to the mix false stories circulated on social media, stories often laden with conspiracy theories and outlandish claims, and hard-core ideological pundits that know their popularity rests on certainty and ideological purity, it seems fair to wonder if our new media environment has crippled the election-accountability process? Was the Russian assault particularly effective because it struck at an existing vulnerability? If so many Americans doubt the findings of the security agencies, why wouldn't nefarious actors try it again?

Notes

1 Pew Research Center, "Hillary Clinton's Approval Rating Over Time," March 19, 2015 (www.people-press.org/2015/05/19/hillary-clinton-approval-timeline/).
2 Gregor Aisch, Jon Huang, and Cecilia Kang, "Dissecting the #PizzaGate Conspiracy Theories," *New York Times* website, December 10, 2016 (www.nytimes.com/interactive/2016/12/10/business/media/pizzagate.html?mtrref=en.wikipedia.org&mtrref=undefined).
3 Cecilia Kang and Adam Goldman, "In Washington Pizzeria Attack, Fake News Brought Real Guns," *New York Times* website, December 5, 2016 (www.nytimes.com/2016/12/05/business/media/comet-ping-pong-pizza-shooting-fake-news-consequences.html).
4 Ibid.
5 Public Policy Polling, "Trump Remains Unpopular; Voters Prefer Obama on SCOTUS Pick," December 9, 2016 (www.publicpolicypolling.com/wp-content/uploads/2017/09/PPP_Release_National_120916.pdf).
6 Caitlin Dewey, "36 Ways the Web Has Changed Us," *Washington Post*, March 12, 2014.
7 Ibid.
8 This comment was made at the Internet World Trade Show, New York, November, 1999.
9 Mental Floss, "The Election of 1800: The Birth of Negative Campaigning in the U.S." September 23, 2008 (http://mentalfloss.com/article/19668/election-1800-birth-negative-campaigning-us).

10 Jeffrey Gottfried, Michael Barthel, and Amy Mitchell, "Trump, Clinton Voters Divided in Their Main Source for Election News," Pew Research Center website, January 18, 2017 (www.journalism.org/2017/01/18/trump-clinton-voters-divided-in-their-main-source-for-election-news/).

11 Gregory J. Martin and Ali Yurukoglu, "Bias in Cable News: Persuasion and Polarization," *American Economic Review* 107 (2017), 2565–2599.

12 National Public Radio, "Fox News Is President Trump's Favorite TV Channel," April 8, 2018.

13 Beth Kowitt, "The YouTube Election: The Obama Campaign is Taking its Message Directly to the Internet's Huge Audience," *CNN Money.com*, July 18, 2008 (http://money.cnn.com/2008/07/18/magazines/fortune/kowitt_obamavideo.fortune/).

14 "The Skinny on CNN, YouTube's Presidential Debates," *CNN Political Ticker,* June 14, 2007 (http://politicalticker.blogs.cnn.com/2007/06/14/the-skinny-on-cnn-youtubes-presidential-debates/?fbid=2HSoaN0kf8j).

15 Drew Harwell, "How YouTube is Shaping the 2016 Election," *Washington Post* website, March 25, 2016 (www.washingtonpost.com/news/the-switch/wp/2016/03/25/inside-youtubes-explosive-transformation-of-american-politics/?utm_term=.9c53e232b741).

16 Ibid.

17 Darrell West, "How to Combat Fake News and Misinformation," Brookings Institution Report, December 18, 2017.

18 Arthur Lupia and Zoë Baird, "Can Web Sites Change Citizens? Implications of Web, White, and Blue 2000," *Political Science and Politics* 36 (January 2003), 77–82.

19 Jeffrey Gottfried, Michael Barthel, Elisa Shearer, and Amy Mitchell, "The 2016 Presidential Campaign – A News Event That's Hard to Miss," Pew Research Center website, February 4, 2016 (www.journalism.org/2016/02/04/the-2016-presidential-campaign-a-news-event-thats-hard-to-miss/).

20 Amy Mitchell, Jeffrey Gottfried, Michael Barthel, and Elisa Shearer, "The Modern News Consumer," Pew Research Center website, July 7, 2016 (www.journalism.org/2016/07/07/pathways-to-news/).

21 Jim Drinkard and Jill Lawrence, "Online, Off and Running: Web A New Campaign Front," *USA Today* website, July 14, 2003 (www.usatoday.com/news/politicselections/2003-07-14-online-cover-usat_x.htm).

22 Michael Luo, "Small Online Contributions Add Up to Huge Edge for Obama," *New York Times* website, February 20, 2008 (www.nytimes.com/2008/02/20/us/politics/20obama.html).

23 Zach Exley, "The New Organizers, What's Really Behind Obama's Ground Game," *The Huffington Post,* October 8, 2008 (www.huffingtonpost.com/zack-exley/the-new-organizers-part-1_b_132782.html).

24 Bernie Sanders, "You crushed our goal of raising $40 million for the month. Help us reach $45 million. https://berniesanders.com/FEC-Deadline," February 29, 2016, 6:09 PM, tweet (https://twitter.com/BernieSanders/status/704488587589500931).

25 Clare Foran, "Bernie Sanders's Big Money," *The Atlantic* website, March 1, 2016 (www.theatlantic.com/politics/archive/2016/03/bernie-sanders-fundraising/471648/).

26 Barack Obama, "Thinking we're only one signature away from ending the war in Iraq. Learn more at www.barackobama.com," April 19, 2007, 12:04 PM, tweet (https://twitter.com/barackobama/status/44240662?lang=en).

27 Vann R. Newkirk II, "The American Idea in 140 Characters," *The Atlantic* website, March 24, 2016 (www.theatlantic.com/politics/archive/2016/03/twitter-politics-last-decade/475131/).

28 Heather K. Evans, Victoria Cordova, and Savannah Sipole, "Twitter Style: An Analysis of How House Candidates Used Twitter in Their 2012 Campaigns," *American Political Science Association* 47 (April 2014), 454–462.

29 Jon Keegan, "Trump v. Clinton: How they Used Twitter," *Wall Street Journal*, July 10, 2017.

30 Hannah Richie, "Read All About It: The Biggest Fake News Stories of 2016," CNBC, December 30, 2016 (www.cnbc.com/2016/12/30/read-all-about-it-the-biggest-fake-news-stories-of-2016.html).

31 Gideon Resnick, "How Pro-Trump Twitter Bots Spread Fake News," *The Daily Beast*, November 17, 2016 (www.thedailybeast.com/how-pro-trump-twitter-bots-spread-fake-news).

32 National Public Radio, "How Russian Twitter Bots Pumped Out Fake News during the 2016 Election," April 3, 2017.

33 As noted in Denis Clifton, "Twitter Bots Distorted the 2016 Election – Including Many Likely from Russia," *Mother Jones*, October 12, 2017.

34 Donie O'Sullivan, "Russian Bots Retweet Trump Nearly 500,000 Times in the Final Weeks of the 2016 Campaign," CNN, January 27, 2018.

35 Avlin Chang, "How Russian Hackers Stole Information from Democrats," *Vox*, July 16, 2018.

36 Ibid.

37 Thomas Fox-Brewster, "Microsoft: Russian Hackers are Targeting Midterms," *Forbes*, July 20, 2018.

38 "US still Under Attack from 'Pervasive Campaign' by Russia, Officials Warn," *The Guardian*, August 2, 2018 (www.theguardian.com/us-news/2018/aug/03/us-russia-election-meddling-latest-dan-coats).

39 Ibid.

40 Danielle Kurtzleben, "Did Fake News On Facebook Help Elect Trump? Here's What We Know," *NPR* website, April 11, 2018 (www.npr.org/2018/04/11/601323233/6-facts-we-know-about-fake-news-in-the-2016-election).

41 Scott Shane, "The Fake Americans Russia Created to Influence the Election," *New York Times* website, September 7, 2017 (www.nytimes.com/2017/09/07/us/politics/russia-facebook-twitter-election.html).

42 Nate Silver, "How Much Did Russian Interference Affect the 2016 Election?" FiveThirtyEight, *New York Times*, February 16, 2018.

43 Ibid.

44 Jen Kirby, "Poll: Only 32 Percent of Republicans Think Russia Interfered in the 2016 Election," *Vox*, July 19, 2018.

45 Echelon Insights, "New National Poll: Privacy, Facebook and Cambridge Analytics," April 10, 2018 (https://medium.com/echelon-indicators/new-national-poll-privacy-facebook-and-cambridge-analytica-1b2c975799ea).

46 Farhad Manjoo, "How the Internet Is Loosening Our Grip on the Truth," *New York Times* website, November 2, 2016 (www.nytimes.com/2016/11/03/technology/how-the-internet-is-loosening-our-grip-on-the-truth.html).

Conclusion
Are There Pathways for Renewal?

Would a book of this sort or any of the numerous recent critiques of our democracy have been written if Hillary Clinton had won the presidency in 2016? Do the concerns about the stability of our system spring from, well, sour grapes? Are they the mere venting of liberal academic types who cannot fathom the idea of Donald Trump, the former reality TV star, as president? If this guy can be given the keys to the White House, surely there is something deeply wrong with our politics, right? Is our electoral system in danger – or is it just the Democratic position in that system?

Point well taken. There might be some validity to the argument, especially given the turbulence of the election and how Trump has conducted himself in office. There is no doubt that Donald Trump's rise to the most important position in the world has, for some, cast doubt on the wisdom of votes and the value of the entire process. Trump's approach during the campaign was jarring, as he jettisoned one norm of behavior after another. To assail the looks of an opponent, mock the physical disability of a reporter, attack the wives of rivals and Gold Star Medal parents, and show so little knowledge or interest in key policy questions and still win was mind blowing. For a candidate to be caught on camera bragging about assaulting women and grabbing them by their genitals without their consent, and suffer no real consequence with voters, was unfathomable. Voters across the country were looking for a change, for a true break from the establishment. That makes sense. Hillary Clinton was not particularly well liked, and she ran a poor campaign, and one could imagine her losing to any number of Republicans. But to Donald Trump?

So there is probably more than a grain of truth to the argument that the rash of alerts about the viability of our election system stems from the rise of Donald Trump. A few months before the election, the author of this book penned an op-ed in the *Boston Globe* saying, essentially, that we need not worry because the voters would not elect Donald Trump; the voters, he wrote, will act "responsibly" when all is said and done. If he had been right, would this book have been written? Perhaps not.

On the other hand, many of the problems discussed throughout the book have been evident for some time. The rise of hyper-partisanship, for example, predates the 2016 election, and moves to limit voting rights in many states date to shortly after the election of Barack Obama. Parts of the media took a partisan turn decades ago; recall that Rush Limbaugh was instrumental in the Republican sweep in 1994. Trust in government and the perceived efficacy of elections has been on a downward trend for decades, and big money has been an ongoing issue for even longer. The nasty turn in the tone of our politics dates back to the early 1990s.

The election of 2016 and the ascent of Donald Trump brought many of these problems into a glaring light, but they existed before anyone took his candidacy seriously. We might say that while he did not create these conditions, Trump's candidacy and presidency perfectly fit the tenor of the times. As noted by a team of scholars, "Many of the trends that led to Trump's election have been with us for years; he has created a crisis by pushing them to their alarming endpoints."[1]

It is also fitting that in any democracy citizens should take a good look at the conduct of politics from time to time. Regardless of any particular candidate or election, how are things going? Do average citizens play a meaningful role in the system? If not, how might the system be changed? Are there trends or mounting forces that threaten some of the gains made by previous generations? One of the most dramatic systemic recalibrations occurred in the 1960s, ushering in broad range of egalitarian elements. Maybe it is only proper that citizens in a democracy take stock of the conduct of their nation's politics every few decades – and seek needed changes.

So let us step beyond Donald Trump. Given what we now know about the contemporary election process in the United States, how are things going? What is the state of our election-centered democracy? A frank verdict would be, at best, that things are going poorly. There are a few upbeat changes, but also a dizzying number of disturbing trends.

On the positive side, levels of engagement for a number of election-centered activities are higher than in previous decades. We might not be turning out to vote more than in the not-too-distant past, but we clearly talk about politics and tune into political news. Americans are certainly paying attention. Giving money to candidates is a form of engagement and we're doing more of that, too. Increasing numbers of election-centered organizations are springing up, from the Tea Party to Swing Left. As people move from their private lives to the political realm, our democracy is enhanced. More engagement is a good thing. Three of the most prominent voices highlighting the potential dangers of our contemporary politics, E.J. Dionne, Jr., Norman Ornstein and Thomas Mann, teamed up to write an important book in 2017, dubbed *One Nation After Trump: A Guide for the Perplexed, the Disillusioned, the Desperate and the Not-Yet Deported*. They argue that Donald Trump may have actually helped save our democracy by jolting the nation into action: "The election of Donald Trump could be one of the best things that ever happened to American democracy ... [H]e has jolted much of the country to face problems that have been slowly eroding our democracy. And he has aroused a popular mobilization that may far outlast him." They continue, "If Trump has exacerbated the problem of media echo chambers ... he has also created a newly powerful constituency that cherishes a free press – witness the soaring digital circulation numbers of the *Washington Post*, the *New York Times* and many other media outlets devoted to hard-hitting reporting and analysis."[2]

We might also add that there is now greater candidate diversity, especially in the 2018 election with a record number of women and minority candidates. *Politico* reported that by the spring of 2018, nearly 600 women had declared their intention of running for the US House, governor or Senate.[3] Hundreds more were vying for state legislative and municipal posts. No doubt Trump's ascent to office has spurred many women and minority candidates to jump into the fray. Either way, this movement was long overdue.

Unfortunately, the list of regrettable shifts is long. As noted by David Brooks, "right now our politics is heading in a truly horrendous direction – with vicious, binary political divisions overlapping with and exacerbating historical racial divisions."[4]

A shrinking number of Americans trust the system, and turnout remains lackluster – especially compared to other democracies. We are paying attention, but often that intensity spills into demonizing the other side and spewing ugliness. Instead of seeing the other side as temporary opponents, they are cast as our mortal enemies. Civility in public life has bottomed out.

Americans are increasingly likely to insulate themselves from contrary information by their selection of news outlet, who they socialize with and where they live – leading to narrowed perspective and intolerance. The decline in trust in the media is cause for concern. If we no longer trust the media, where will we get the information so critical to making enlightened choices?

One of the most disturbing trends has been the concerted move to limit voting. Instead of broadening the opportunities for voting, as has been the trend for generations, many are seeking ways to block access to the ballot box. The purported rationale is to reduce election fraud, but that is a canard. These moves, which come in varied forms, are being undertaken to gain an electoral advantage. It is only honest to admit that.

Political parties, once seen as an important vehicle for socializing new citizens into the civic culture, have all but faded at the local level. In their place we have social media, ripe for vitriol and, as we now know, manipulation. What is more, for many Americans, particularly young citizens, time spent on social media too often becomes a placebo for real-world engagement. Given all that transpired during the 2016 election, it is telling that the creator of the World Wide Web, Tim Berners-Lee, a man named as one of the most important figures in the 20th century by *Time*, expressed profound regrets. He was, by one account, "devastated" by what has transpired and has dedicated the rest of his career to returning the web to its more democratic roots.[5]

All of this, and many other changes, has crippled governing institutions. There are so few moderates in either party that the very idea of bipartisan compromise, prevalent throughout much of American history, seems a relic of the past. Brooks continues, "The whole way of practicing politics has been transformed. Each party imagines that it is one wave election from destroying the other side and gaining total power."[6]

As mentioned in the early pages of the book, even during the turbulent, transformative period of the 1960s, the vast majority of Americans believed that positive change could come from politics. We certainly do not see that today. Some of this has to do with the complexity of big issues, especially the decline of the middle class and the vanishing American dream, but much blame should be placed at the door of elections. The process of allowing average citizens to select their leaders through an open and fair contest, through the lively exchange of ideas and candidate qualifications, has morphed into an unseemly, shady spectacle. Former US Attorney General Eric Holder called voting and elections the "lifeblood of our democracy."[7] If that's true, the patient is very sick.

But is change possible? Can Americans redeem their politics? If so, what would that shift look like? The aim of the book has been to chart several of these fundamental alterations. It is not a reform polemic, but rather a diagnosis. Unlike many other recent works, this volume does not offer a laundry list of reforms. We will, however, end with a few overarching themes – broad elements that might guide thinking about potential changes in the years ahead.

Greater Ideological Diversity

One of the most momentous problems with our politics springs from a failure to appreciate the legitimacy of the other side. Some of this sorting comes from lifestyle choices, which often parallel political ideology, but a growing number of Americans do not want to be around "those folks." One of the most disquieting bits of data discussed in this book is polling numbers that suggest partisans do not like or respect the other side, and would be loath to socialize with them. And heaven forbid someone in their family marries into the other party!

The easiest place to create a bubble is through the selection of news. As noted, we now gorge on consistent information and shun anything contradictory. Only watching Fox News or reading the editorial page of the *New York Times* does little to help us understand and appreciate the complexity of issues or the concerns of our fellow citizens. Americans are also less able to make accountability judgments about candidates or parties when they do not receive a broad range of information. Knowing more about the legitimate concerns, interests and perspectives of others also makes us better neighbors. We become more tolerant, thus more willing to make compromises.

Eleanor Roosevelt was an outspoken, passionate progressive and in many ways far ahead of her time when it came to civil rights and women's rights. At the age of 76 (in 1960), she wrote a widely read book, *You Learn By Living: Eleven Keys for a More Fulfilling Life*. Among many pearls of wisdom, she writes, "It is not only important but mentally invigorating to discuss political matters with people whose opinions differ radically from one's own ... Find out what people are saying, what they are thinking, what they believe. This is an invaluable check to your own ideas. Are you right in what you think or is there a different approach ...?"[8]

But calling upon Americans to consider the opinions of the other side and to see their positions as legitimate, deserving of respect, then as now, is easier said than done. Why would today's hard-core Democrats or dyed-in-the-wool Republicans listen to commentators on the other side, or read diverse information? One route might be to promote some sort of "diverse politics curriculum" in high school or college. Many states mandate the teaching of US government in high school, but how much time is spent on ideological diversity? Communities might also sponsor town hall discussion where folks can come, with an open mind, to hear their fellow neighbors.

An important institutional fix would be to move toward non-partisan redistricting commissions. Currently, about one-third of the states use them. Drawing district lines based on housing trends and population shifts, rather than political considerations, would go a long way toward diversifying congressional and state legislative districts. Much of the gridlock we see at all levels of government springs from legislators representing ideologically homogenous districts. But waiting for the courts to finally make a definitive decision regarding the constitutionality of gerrymandered districts will only lead to delays and frustration. As of the summer of 2018, the federal courts seem in no hurry to jump into this political quagmire. States can act immediately and they should.

We might also consider expanding the number of seats in the House of Representatives. For roughly half of our nation's history, the size of the House expanded as the population grew. In 1929, Congress froze the chamber at 435, and since then the number of constituents per district has exploded to about 750,000. A simple act of Congress could expand it by 150 seats or so, putting it in line with the legislator–constituent ratio found in most other democracies. More importantly for our concerns, coupled with non-partisan redistricting the net result would be a greater number of ideologically diverse districts – leading to much more electoral competition. As noted in one analysis, "Expanding the House would mean not just a government with more representatives, but one that is literally more representative – including more people from perennially underrepresented groups, like women and minorities, and making for a fuller and richer legislative debate."[9]

Broadening Electoral Engagement

Any move to limit the voting opportunities of citizens should be rejected. Backtracking on voting rights should be called out for what it is – in the starkest terms. One of the most illuminating books in years was penned by Carol Anderson in 2018. It is called, *One Person, One Vote: How Voter Suppression is Destroying our Democracy*. Anderson offers a deep-dive into the history of minority voter suppression, the inequity of voter ID laws, the inhumane and increasingly common practice of purging voter lists (moves that are not known until Election Day), and racial gerrymandering, among other issues. Relying on detailed accounts and empirical evidence, Anderson makes a convincing case that assaults on this fundamental right are serious and recurrent.

We also know that the formula and preclearance in the Voting Rights Act was found to be outdated in the 2013 Supreme Court case of *Shelby County v. Holder*. The court did not strike down Section 5 (the preclearance provision), but without a formula there could be no list of violators. Section 5 became unenforceable. Congress could reauthorize the act and revamp the formula, but partisan divisions have made reauthorization unlikely. Citizens on both sides of the partisan divide should demand action on this issue.

A growing number of states (13 in 2018) are moving toward an opt-out system of voter registration, rather than opt-in. Mechanisms to automatically enroll young citizens, such as when they seek a driver's license or even when they register for school, make sense. Turnout in these states tends to be higher. We might even consider some sort of compulsory voting mechanism, like a $10 tax break. At the very least, citizens should be allowed to vote until they tell the government that they do not want to be enrolled. They should have to opt-out.

Elements of the Constitution, the Comity and Full Faith and Credit clauses, prevent a state from treating citizens of another state in a discriminatory manner. They also stipulate that the public records of one state shall be accepted by the other states. You might live in Vermont, but you have the right to travel throughout Nevada. Your divorce in South Dakota will be recognized in Michigan. The Constitution also grants states the right to regulate some voter qualifications, such as residency requirements, but it is odd that voter registration does not carry from one state to the next. If you were registered to vote in Oregon, but you move to Washington, your registration does not transfer. The creation of a national voter registration bank, allowing citizens to vote where they reside on Election Day, is long overdue. Technologically, it would be a snap. There might be a minimal residency requirement, but voters should not have to worry about redoing the paperwork every time they move to a new state or community.

Beyond this, Congress could move Election Day to the weekend, or perhaps make it a national holiday. One can imagine parades, concerts, fireworks and special foods on these festive occasions – and certainly a day off from work and school. It would be a day to celebrate democracy, the opportunity to acknowledge that on this day factory workers and factory owners, carpenters and CEOs, nurses and surgeons, stand on an equal footing. We celebrate the signing of a document that set forth the idea of a government by the people, as we should, but relegate elections to a regular Tuesday in early November. The media likes to remind us that Election Day is sacred, and that the outcome could shape policies for a generation. But few get the day off work or school, leading to massive lines early and late in the day. Why should voters in the United States, in the 21st century, have to wait in line three hours to vote – as many did in the 2018 midterms? That makes no sense.

Reformers have made much out of the need to offer citizens greater opportunities to vote over a long period of time, rather than on a single day. Early voting, mail-in ballots and no-excuse absentee balloting have become common. But evidence that these moves actually increase turnout is mixed. Why would that be true? One argument against extending the voting period is that Election Day loses its intensity – its excitement. Voting becomes a chore, like paying a bill. Citizens should have numerous avenues for voting, to be sure, but Election Day should be a big deal.

In the 19th century, when turnout sometimes reached upwards of 80 percent, Election Day was an occasion for tremendous exhilaration and celebration. If Super Bowl Sunday or Black Friday can be a national holiday of sorts, certainly we can make a big deal out of voting. The first step is to make it a holiday. If Congress will not move on this, states can.

As a final note, there are some moves afoot to broaden voter engagement.[10] Enough signatures were gathered to put on the Florida ballot in 2018 a measure that would restore the voting rights of some 1.5 million convicted felons, for example. And when the voters had their say, the measure passed. Prior to the change, 10 percent of the state's overall population were denied the right to vote. In Nevada there is a move to automatically register voters when they get a driver's license, and legislators in New York are considering ways to make registration easier. Washington State will soon allow 16- and 17-year-olds to pre-register.[11] These moves and others are an encouraging sign that many understand the growing threats and are ready to do something about it.

Confronting the Nomination Quagmire

The goal of progressive reformers at the turn of the 20th century was the same as that of those who pushed changes to the presidential nomination process in the 1970s: elections would be more democratic if party bosses were stripped of their role in picking party nominees and the job was given to rank-and-file partisans. By opening the system, regular folks would have more of a say in the nomination process, thereby making the general election more egalitarian and the outcome more legitimate.

This is no longer true, if it ever was. It is illustrative that in the very first opportunity to use the binding primary model, in 1972, the Democrats selected a far-left candidate, Senator George McGovern, who won a single state (Massachusetts) and the District of Columbia. He did not even win his home state of South Dakota.

The problem with the current nomination system is that the most partisan voters turn out during primaries and select the most ideological candidates. General election voters are left with two extremists. This is particularly true when a plurality winner is allowed, meaning that in a multi-candidate primary the winner might get a fraction of the overall vote. Primaries are a powerful force in our politics today, due to the intensity of each party's base. Once in office, officials are ever-fearful of losing the next primary election. For their base, any sign of moderation is tantamount to treason – surely reason to vote them from office. It is little wonder that party unity scores are at record highs and that even the most pressing problems remain unsolved.

When the party elite played a prominent role, there was a screening mechanism. Some candidates were deemed too young or inexperienced, and others tainted by corruption. Many would-be candidates were filtered out because they were unwilling to toe the party line, but in any event the party elite had a clear rationale for picking nominees who would appeal to general election voters. They did not always act in a purely pragmatic way (as witnessed by Barry Goldwater's Republican nomination for the presidency in 1964), but usually ideological concerns took a back seat to moderation – electability. "About a dozen times in the twentieth century, parties nominated candidates who were not the top primary vote winners – including William Howard Taft, Woodrow Wilson, Dwight Eisenhower, Adlai Stevenson, and Hubert Humphrey – because they were deemed the best suited to lead the party's ticket to victory."[12]

Winners, chosen by an inclusive pool of voters, were able to reach across the aisle to find common ground. The story of policy development in the United States is one of incremental change and moderation – and a good bit of that came from the nomination process.

The current system is a free-for-all, with no filters. Well-funded or celebrity candidates, or those best able to stay in the public eye, can rise to the top. Thoughtful, experienced candidates are left in the dust. Would Abe Lincoln stand a chance in today's nomination system?

Many believe that if Republican Party elites had had more of a say in the 2016 nomination contest that Donald Trump would not have prevailed. Most states used either a winner-takes-all model, or a winner-takes-more approach. In a multi-candidate field, as was the case that year, netting just 30 percent of the vote meant larger and larger blocks of delegates. Through the early part of the nomination process (by March 9), Trump had netted 35 percent of the vote, but 43 percent of the delegates. It is also the case that many in the party thought Trump would be a weak general election candidate. Arguably, he was: no presidential candidate has had higher negative ratings than Trump and he lost the popular vote by 2.9 million. They also worried that if he would win, his commitment to traditional GOP policies would be tepid. Most also thought it almost impossible for the Democrats to retake the House in 2018 – which of course they did in large measure because of a backlash against the president.

To be fair, there is no doubt that Hillary Clinton *was* the darling of the Democratic elite and that she would have been selected by them for the general election. Bernie Sanders, so popular with the left wing of the party, would not have stood a chance with party elders. She was experienced, smart, skilled and connected. Her approval ratings were high as the nomination process began, but in the end she too was a deeply unpopular candidate.

So what are we to do about the nomination process? Two options come to mind. The first is to create some sort of mechanism to allow party elites a greater say in the process. This would not be a popular change. As noted in a previous chapter, in the summer of 2018, the Democratic National Committee moved to strip superdelegates of their powers. But surely the 2016 election demonstrated the need for screening mechanisms. Cannot parties use whatever nomination process they would like? To reiterate, elites would have a powerful, built-in reason for picking a candidate that would appeal to general election voters. Why would they pick someone who would likely lose and embarrass the party?

But what would this look like? A fundamental problem with the so-called smoke-filled rooms of the past was that they lacked diversity. What if the party figured out a mechanism to pull together an inclusive, diverse group of party followers and give it the opportunity to sort through a host of issues and endorse certain candidates? Several years ago, scholar James Fishkin introduced deliberative polls, also called "deliberative democracy."[13] Here a randomly selected group of citizens are brought together for a short period of time (such as a long weekend). After presentations by experts, and review of detailed information and conversations among participants, a vote on policy questions was held.

This process gave citizens the chance to really think through issues and to hear from others. These events are, essentially, old-style town hall meetings with a high-tech spin. As noted by Fishkin, "If people think their voice actually matters, they'll do the hard work, really study their briefing books, ask the experts smart questions and then make tough decisions."[14]

Perhaps the parties could recast their conventions along these lines. Instead of holding them at the end of the nomination process, when the winner is already known, why not hold them at the beginning of the calendar? Participants could be randomly selected from across the nation (like a poll) and they could come together for a week or so. A financial stipend might be used, but it might also be an honor to attend. They would listen to experts, watch a diverse set of presentations, and get the chance to chat with candidates in small settings. The candidates who rise to the top on a final vote might have a leg up on other candidates – but not a complete lock. In short, one way out of the nomination mess might be to create a democratic process whereby enlightened partisans have a greater say.

Another option would be to use a ranked-choice voting system. As discussed in a previous chapter, this is where primary voters rank the candidates on the ballot. If no candidate nets a majority of first-place votes, the candidate with the fewest first-place votes is eliminated. Voters who preferred that candidate would have their second-choice vote counted instead. The process would be repeated until there is a majority winner.

The idea behind ranked choice voting is to rid the system of plurality winners and, at the same time, yield nominees who have the most appeal. If a candidate is backed by, say, 30 percent of the primary electorate, but loathed by the other two-thirds, their path to victory would be narrow. Put a bit differently, rank-choice voting reduces the likelihood of extremist candidates winning the party's nomination. This model would make good sense at all levels, but especially for state and local contests.

We sometimes believe that elections give voters a chance to express their preferences. That's not true. Because of the hijacking of party nominations by extremists, general elections are often about the choice between the lesser of two evils.

Let Light Shine In!

The story of big money in elections is also complicated. Giving money to a candidate or cause, as the Supreme Court said over 40 years ago, is a form of free speech, protected by the 1st Amendment. That will not change. We might look to a constitutional amendment, but that is pie in the sky. It is reasonable to expect that a new court might backtrack on *Citizens United*, but such a change would only nip at the edges. The story of money in American politics is of loopholes and cracks. One way or another, money finds its way in.

Public financing of elections would help level the playing field and break the donor–candidate nexus. Regardless of whether it is "lead or follow," wealthy donors are not stupid. They give money for a reason and quite often it is about a policy payoff. Public financing could help curb this dynamic and add a dose of legitimacy to the system. Candidates also do not want to spend so much time fundraising. There seems to be growing interest at the state level for changes of this sort, but it is doubtful that Congress will make a similar move.

One of the most significant changes that can be made is to mandate disclosure for funds given to candidates and spent in a primary or general election. The courts have sanctioned disclosure laws, and there are currently myriad reporting requirements. But here again loopholes abound. Dark money has crept into our politics like a poison. Complete disclosure – sunlight, so to speak – would serve as an antidote.

And while we are at it, the same sort of disclosure should be used for the funding of political organizations. It is a fundamental right to participate in and fund political organizations. But huge sums of money are changing the essence of grassroots mobilization. Knowing who is funding these groups would add a layer of transparency, leading, among other things, to greater trust in our politics.

Developing a Critical Eye for "News"

One of the most sudden changes to the election process is also one of the most important. The merger of hyper-partisanship, social media and the growing number partisan media outlets has made the objective assessment of information scarce. If we add to this the creation and distribution of fake news through social media and automated bots, it would seem the ability to sort fact from fiction would be a growing threat to our system. As noted by one scholar, "Rather than using digital tools to inform people and elevate civic discussion, some individuals have taken advantage of social and digital platforms to deceive, mislead, or harm others through creating or disseminating fake news and disinformation."[15]

Beyond merely distorting "news," these fake stories can embolden discriminatory and incendiary ideas and degrade public discourse. "Once embedded," notes a team of scholars, "such ideas can in turn be used to create scapegoats, to normalize prejudices, to harden us-versus-them mentalities and even, in extreme cases, to catalyze and justify violence."[16]

But what can be done about the proliferation of fake news? One thought might be to tighten regulations, such as making sure we know the identities of the creators of websites, Facebook pages and Twitter accounts. This is the route suggested by many on both sides of the partisan aisle following the 2016 election. Major high-tech executives, including

Mark Zuckerberg of Facebook, have pledged to tighten controls and provide greater oversight. Several of these companies are exploring the use of algorithms to weed out obviously false stories, as well as highly offensive posts.

This is being confronted in other nations, and cracking down on fake posts seems to be one route. For example, in June 2017 Germany passed legislation that forces large social media companies to "delete illegal, racist or slanderous comments and posts within 24 hours."[17] But that would be difficult and probably unconstitutional in the American setting. A long line of court cases has affirmed that the 1st Amendment does not compel media outlets to publish accurate information. And how would one separate fake news from opinion? Government regulation of Facebook and Twitter is probably a bad idea; it would be a slippery slope if ever there was one.

Another route might be the creation of several non-partisan, non-profit fact-checking organizations. One of the more positive trends in investigative journalism in recent years, and there have not been many, has been the creation of autonomous non-profit units, usually supported by endowments. A good example would be ProPublica, which was founded in 2007. But instead of focusing on long-form investigative journalism, these new units, what we might call third-party fact checkers, would solely focus on verifying or debunking online news stories. They would do it quickly, of course. One might even imagine a pop up warning on computers alerting the reader to the likelihood of the story being fake.

A final approach, similar to an idea noted above, would be to double-down on media literacy. A growing number of colleges and universities are making this a core learning goal, but it remains a missing element in most secondary schools across the nation. The ability to sort through conflicting claims, to discern objective sources from clearly biased ones, and to understand the difference between fact and opinion has always been important – but they are essential skills of citizenship in the 21st century. We take great pains to help budding citizens understand why they should vote – why they should engage in the broader public realm. It is critical that we now help them navigate through the minefield of the internet and social media.

Reinvigorate the Local

Finally, one of the main limits of contemporary elections is that voters will too often assume these contests are their only vehicle to bring about change. Our passion for elections curbs other forms of engagement – many of which are more likely to bring about the changes we desire. It was, for example, local interest mobilization that helped secure the right to vote for many minority groups. One of the defining characteristics of contemporary politics is the breadth of political engagement. While levels of turnout have remained more or less constant, other indicators of engagement have shown remarkable growth – as noted above. According to the American National Election Study, the percentage of Americans who attended a political meeting has more than doubled since the late 1990s. A 2014 Pew Research study found that 40 percent of liberals and conservatives remain mobilized during non-election periods. Americans of all stripes stand ready to engage.

Beginning with huge demonstrations the day after Donald Trump's inaugural and continuing at numerous venues, particularly the town hall meetings of federal legislators, progressive groups have sprung to life. As with the Tea Party a decade earlier, it is likely that this mobilization comes from both professional organizers and the anxieties of average folks. In April of 2017, Massachusetts Senator Elizabeth Warren echoed the call for broad-scale activism:

> This is not about what happens every four years, or what happens four years from now. We have to be in this fight right this minute. This is what has changed in democracy in America. It's not the case that we can simply put this off and every four years we'll all kind of get interested in one big race – or maybe every two years for congressional races or Senate race ... We have to be engaged, and we have to be engaged right now. I mean, between now and the end of the day.[18]

How might local political mobilization be refined for the 21st century? From food and employment, to housing, recreation and culture, Americans are discovering the power and potential of the local. In some ways, the argument will parallel scholar Yuval Levin's conclusion in *The Fractured Republic* regarding the revival of the middle layers of society – families and communities, schools and churches, charities and associations, local governments and markets. Journalist Sebastian Junger's latest work, *Tribe*, strikes a similar note: "We have a strong instinct to belong to small groups defined by clear purpose and understanding – tribes." He suggests local connections will be the key to our psychological well-being, and the same can be said about our politics.

What is more, there is a growing understanding that deep cultural differences will continue to make inclusive, national policy solutions difficult. As Levin notes, "We are now a highly diverse and multifarious society defined by its profusion more than its solidity"[19] For decades, conservatives clamored for local control, but today many on both sides of the ideological divide understand that reaching a collective good is less likely for issues linked to rights and equality, especially given the ideological homogenization of communities. For conservatives and liberals, new federalism is an increasingly accepted response to the strains of the federal policy morass. As David Brooks noted on the PBS News Hour in July, 2018: "Sixty-six percent of Americans think their own locality is doing well. And only 18 percent trust the federal government. [So] it's not only local power, but it's a different kind of power. It's not abstract. It's not ideological. It's much more pragmatic. It's much more personal, and it's much more tangible." He added, "And it seems to me, in an age where nothing's getting done in Washington, it's a better kind of power being wielded at the local level. So it was just sort of saying, let's do that. Let's move down."

All this underscores a key change in the American landscape. Local party committees, once considered the key cogs in the electoral system, have withered. There is some evidence that these structures are hanging on and in some way adapting to the social media age, but they have little resonance for younger citizens and few candidates pay them even scant attention. Local structures encouraged some citizens to run for office (while filtering out others) and performed a host of social functions. One might hope that, along with the growing movement to resurrect the local, party structures might find new life and new meaning. Similarly, we might have aspirations that these revitalized organizations expand their efforts beyond elections to also include effective approaches to better shift public policy to reflect the interests of their local partisans.

* * *

Howard Fast was a mid-20th-century novelist. During World War II he worked as a government scriptwriter for the Voice of America, but in 1950 was pulled in front of the House Committee on Un-American Activities, and charged with being a communist. He refused to give the names of other contributors to a fund for a home for orphans of the Spanish Civil War, and was convicted of Contempt of Congress. Fast served three months in prison, where he continued to write. Upon his release, he was blacklisted, shunned by many of the large publishing houses in New York and forced to self-publish a number of his books. Before his death in 2003, Fast had written a dizzying number of books, articles and screenplays; he was one of the period's most prolific writers.

One of his novels, *Freedom Road*, was first published in 1944 and would eventually sell over 30 million copies. The book chronicles the life of Gideon Jackson in the post-Civil War South. Gideon is a strong, honest ex-slave, who had served with the Union during the war. He is chosen by his black neighbors to represent them in the new state government. The first chapter is titled, "How Gideon Jackson Came Home from Voting."

He was bombarded with questions from his neighbors and family about this voting: "They came fast and furious as rain."

"What's this voting?"
"How come you didn't bring nothing back? Where this voting is?"
"You done bought this voting?"

"How many them voting you find along down by the white folks?"

"How big them are?"

"How many?"

"Brethren" said Gideon's brother Peter, "a little peace, a little quiet and we all will give out them answers."

"This here voting's like a wedding or Christmas sermon, matter for all. Government put out a strong right arm, like the angel Gabriel, and says, declare yourself. We done that. Along with five hundred other[s].

"We gone and voted," said Gideon.

It turns out that the delegation picked Gideon to go to the South Carolina Constitutional Convention assembled in Charleston in 1868, along with 74 others blacks and about the same number of whites. "Gideon shakes off the despair bred of ignorance and illiteracy and matures intellectually in a short time," noted one reviewer of the book. "The sulking white gentry and mocking press soon realize the capabilities of determined blacks."[20] Several chapters detail how the newly freed slaves built a vibrant community, as well as Gideon's rise in politics and eventual election to the US House of Representatives. It seems, at first, a story of the promise of a vibrant democracy.

Indeed, Americans have long pinned the character of their democracy on voting – the idea that government will grant each an equal say in its conduct and that the fruits of this act will reflect a collective judgment. We hold that elections are the best avenues to express grievances and that, by granting new groups the franchise, our nation will move closer to the ideal of a government by the people.

But there are risks. For one, placing too much faith in voting and elections may limit other, potentially more vibrant, acts. Elections have the potential to radically change public policy, but it is also possible that these events can limit the voice of the people. Are not the prospects of mass movements, maybe even radical changes, minimized when the next election is always around the corner? Are these events structured to reflect the public's concerns – or buttress the interests of a few? Do candidates compete on a level playing field?

Across the globe, the corruption of the election process has become a harbinger of the decline of popular governance. That is to say, authoritarians will often come to power under the guise of democratic methods – through elections – and from that position corrupt the system under a veneer of legitimacy. In the early pages of their important book, Levitsky and Ziblatt warn that "most democratic breakdowns have been caused not by generals and soldiers but by elected governments themselves ... The electoral road to breakdown is dangerously deceptive."[21]

Another risk is that we take for granted that the strides made to enhance the system will remain – that once the electoral system becomes more democratic, it never retracts. As this book attempts to explain, this is not true. Each generation must make a frank assessment of the process, scrutinize the conduct of elections and demand needed changes. The election process inevitably shifts as our society changes. But have the changes made the system better, or have they caused a retraction?

Which is where we will leave things. *Freedom Road* is a novel about the potential of vibrant citizenship, the promise of voting. Why vote? As Gideon walked off to the state convention to cast his lot as a full citizen, he sang aloud: "There ain't no grass grows under my feet on freedom road!" We should celebrate elections and our opportunity to vote. We cannot be a democracy without a vibrant electoral process. But *Freedom Road* is also tale of oppression, of America's darker side. Gideon, and the thriving community that he helped create, was crushed when Rutherford Hays was made President in 1876 in a deal that ended the Federal occupation of the South. Millions of former slaves – having been given a taste of political equality, a seat at America's democratic feast – were once again ravaged by state-sanctioned discrimination. The curtain of Jim Crow was drawn. Gideon Jackson was stripped of his vote, his dignity. The promise of equality, the strong arm of the angel Gabriel, was broken.

But certainly nothing like that can happen in this day and age! Perhaps not. But voting and elections belong to the citizens of a democracy, and they must bear in mind that important transformations, often below the surface, can corrupt the process. They must remain vigilant. It is theirs to use and to protect.

Notes

1 E.J. Dionne, Thomas Mann, and Norman Orenstein, "How Trump Is Helping to Save our Democracy," *Washington Post*, September 22, 2017.
2 As noted in E.J. Dionne, Jr., Norman Ornstein, and Thomas Mann, "How Trump is Helping to Save our Democracy," *Washington Post*, September 22, 2017 (www.washingtonpost.com/outlook/how-trump-is-helping-to-save-our-democracy/2017/09/22/539b795e-9a1f-11e7-82e4-f1076f6d6152_story.html?utm_term=.2f91531771d2).
3 Heather Caygle, "Record Breaking Number of Women Run for Office," *Politico*, March 8, 2018.
4 David Brooks, "One Idea to Save America," *New York Times*, May 31, 2018.
5 As cited in Katrina Booker, "I Was Devastated: Tim Berners-Lee: The Man Who Created the World Wide Web Has Some Regrets," *Vanity Fair*, July 1, 2018.
6 Brooks, "One Idea to Save Democracy," May 31, 2018.
7 As reported in Kapor Center, "Protecting 'The Lifeblood of Our Democracy,'" December 13, 2011 (www.kaporcenter.org/protecting-the-lifeblood-of-our-democracy/).
8 Eleanor Roosevelt, *You Learn By Living: Eleven Keys for a More Fulfilling Life* (New York: Harper, 1960).
9 Editorial Board, "America Needs A Bigger House," *New York Times*, November 13, 2018.

10 David Leonhardt, "One Person, One Vote," *New York Times*, January 25, 2018.
11 Ibid.
12 John Fredrick Martin, "Our Broken Presidential Nomination System," *The New Republic*, February 24, 2016.
13 James Fishkin, *Democracy and Deliberation* (New Haven, CT: Yale University Press, 1993).
14 As noted in Joe Klein, "How Can a Democracy Solve Tough Problems?," *Time*, September 2, 2010.
15 Darrell West, "How to Combat Fake News and Disinformation," Brookings Institution Report, December 18, 2017.
16 David Lazer, Matthew Baum, Nir Grinberg, Lisa Friedland, Kenneth Joseph, Will Hobbs, and Carolina Mattsson, "Combating Fake News: An Agenda for Research and Action," Harvard Shorenstein Center on Media, Politics and Public Policy and Harvard Ash Center for Democratic Governance and Innovation, May, 2017, 5.
17 Darrell West, "How to Combat Fake News and Disinformation," Brookings Institution Report, December 18, 2017.
18 Interview on National Public Radio, April 6, 2017.
19 Yuval Levin, *The Fractured Republic: Renewing America's Social Contract in an Age of Individualism* (New York: Basic Books, 2016), 186.
20 Gerald Sorin, "The Long Unfinished Journey of Howard Fast's *Freedom Road*," Indiana University Blog, November 11, 2014 (http://iupress.typepad.com/blog/2014/11/guest-post-the-long-unfinished-journey-of-howard-fasts-freedom-road.html).
21 Levitsky and Ziblatt, *How Democracies Die*, 5.

Index

FEB 2 7 2020

9 781138 617926